THE CONNING, THE CUNNING OF BEING

BY THE SAME AUTHOR—

Kierkegaard and the Problem of Writing

(The Florida State University Press, 1987)

THE CONNING, THE CUNNING *of* BEING

Being a Kierkegaardian Demonstration
of the Postmodern Implosion
of Metaphysical Sense
in Aristotle and the Early Heidegger

Pat Bigelow

The Florida State University Press
Tallahassee

The Florida State University Press
© 1990 by the Board of Regents of the State of Florida
♾ Printed in the U.S.A. on acid-free paper.

The Florida State University Press is a member of University Presses of Florida, the scholarly publishing agency of the State University System of Florida. Books are selected for publication by faculty editorial committees at each of Florida's nine public universities: Florida A&M University (Tallahassee), Florida Atlantic University (Boca Raton), Florida International University (Miami), Florida State University (Tallahassee), University of Central Florida (Orlando), University of Florida (Gainesville), University of North Florida (Jacksonville), University of South Florida (Tampa), University of West Florida (Pensacola).

Orders for books published by all member presses should be addressed to University Presses of Florida, 15 NW 15th St., Gainesville, FL 32611.

Library of Congress Cataloging-in-Publication Data

Bigelow, Pat.
    The conning, the cunning of being; being a Kierkegaardian demonstration of the postmodern implosion of metaphysical sense in Aristotle and the early Heidegger / Pat Bigelow.
       p. cm.
  Includes bibliographical references.
  ISBN 0-8130-0952-9 (alk. paper)
    1. Ontology. 2. Aristotle—Contributions in ontology. 3. Heidegger, Martin, 1889–1976—Contributions in ontology. I. Title.
BD311.B49 1990   89–36676
111'.092'2—dc20   CIP

Would that we could all become unpublished authors

Things are more like they are now than they ever have been before.
              Dwight D. Eisenhower

Philosophy, then, is that thinking with which one can start nothing and about which housemaids necessarily laugh.
            Martin Heidegger, *What Is a Thing?*

. . . there is a serious explanation and also a facetious explanation for both these names; the serious explanation is not to be had from me, but there is no objection to your hearing the facetious one; for the gods too love a joke.
                 Plato, *Cratylus*

Concerning a Preface as the Occasion Might Have Elicited from an Other

> . . . if the whole stole stale mis betold.
> James Joyce, *Finnegans Wake*

In response to an unpublished author who had asked him to write an introduction or prefatory note to his work Mallarmé wrote, "I abhor prefaces that come from the author himself, but those that come from someone else I find even more distasteful. My friend, a real book needs no introduction; it's a bolt from the blue and it behaves like a woman with her lover, needing no help from a third party, the husband."

But even Mallarmé, a truly secretive and discreet poet, gives some hints as to the manner in which *Un coup de dés* should be read, opening with the disclaimer, "I should like this Note to be left unread or, if glanced through, even to be forgotten." He could not resist. Yet his hints amount to noting, in writing, that though he is the author, he cannot know what he has written, even if all he has written he has written only to find this out. Nonetheless, in his self-defection and auto-evanescence brought about by his writing, in the writing's dismissal of the author, Mallarmé claims a kind of proprietary right upon the readership: *Noli me legere*—no one will read me for no one comes to my writing except through me.

So what of the preface? Whereof Mallarmé's self-proclaimed abhorrence? A book becomes "real," as I understand it, to the extent that it keeps itself ensconced within a frame of silence, the silence of the author who refuses to explain himself and who disappears entirely in the face of the question of what the book is about, if only because the book is about eliminating the author. If the book is the torsion and torquing of a secret, a secret twisting to elaborate itself while turning away from itself toward the promise of its other, the absence of the book—nonetheless the book, the "real book" as Mallarmé says, the book that remains unmolested by an author constantly tripping over himself to show his sleeve full of hidden aces, remains light, untroubled, buoyant with an innocent and playful mischievousness, winsome with whimsy, facile with a soft and easy insouciance. Such a book flows overfull with a limpidity that puts an end to the ponderous and lumbering excavations of seriousness. For such excavatory maneuvers can only protest with pride the extent of profundity at stake, while the book of which Mallarmé writes is obscure and profound only because of the completeness of its limpidity. The real book has the transparency of a cipher left unread.

But of all this the author must remain silent. Yet upon all this, the author cannot refrain from commenting. If the book is framed by the silence of its authorship, this silence enunciates itself by reducing the book to being an oblique and indirect commentary upon it, making the book a commentary that is, then, a covert and unavowed corroboration of said silence, but one that nevertheless demonstrates programmatically that the book retires from addressing the book. Both necessary and impossible is it, then, for the author to remain silent about his authorship. But, then, both necessary and impossible is it for the author to breach this silence and address his authorship. Kierkegaard, whose relationship to his authorship is as complicated and self-conscious as any that we know of, says it beautifully in *Of the Difference between a Genius and an Apostle.*

> It is modest of the nightingale not to require anyone to listen to it; but it is also proud of the nightingale not to care whether anyone listens to it or not.

> Like the nightingale the genius has his work solely within himself; and in fact it is he who defines what is to be his work

and so defines himself in accordance with his work and thus, just as the nightingale is really its song and projects itself as its song, the genius has as his work the project of defining his work. And this without regard for his personal fortunes and misfortunes. They are merely accidental with respect to his genius and as such they cannot except in a most farcical fashion become its basis. The genius lives, perhaps withdrawn into self-delight and merriment over his genius, perhaps regaling others with talks told with a deliciously wicked wit, perhaps with a self-satisfied smile, perhaps as a taxman; but the genius lives in earnest with respect to his genius and *only* with respect to his genius, regardless of whether anyone profits by it or not, himself included. And that, notes Kierkegaard, is at once the pride and the humility of the genius: the genius understands quite well that no one needs his genius; yet he knows just as well that it is a most precious gift both to himself and to the world. The genius understands well enough the polemical relationship of his genius to the world, that the world reproves the reckless way he squanders his gift while he is himself so humbled by the overwhelming gratuity of his existence that he must give back to the world the gift of this squandering. The genius knows himself to be both an unnecessary superfluity and a precious ornament.

But the apostle speaks from elsewhere than where he and we are and by the authority of something otherwise than what is and otherwise than what is not, and so cannot justify or even question what he says, nor can anyone say of it whether it is profound or even valid. The apostle speaks not of a problem he has pondered. For he does not speak on his own behalf and he does not speak for his own sake. He proclaims; that is his task. He is under "divine authority" and for that reason cannot author an authorship.

In "comparing and contrasting" the apostle and the genius Kierkegaard shows acute insight into the *problématique* of his own authorship. But I think he is also marking out the paradox involved in writing philosophy. For philosophy is a calling; like the apostle, we who practice philosophy obey a call to offer and communicate; we are under the obligation and the authority of that call. But like the apostle, we cannot justify being called, we can say nothing about our calling and our obligation to come under its authority; it cannot even occur to us that we can say nothing about it. We are examples, each of his or her own life, examples of what it is like being called into the practice of philosophy. As with the apostle, such is the nature of the authority by which our calling claims us that this authority cannot become the object of our calling—in fact, it cannot become an object at all. Our calling claims us by calling up from behind us "thoughts that wound from behind."

Yet we who practice philosophy are like the genius, finding ourselves to be our work and in such work our end and so the working out of our end. As with genius, we who practice philosophy take ourselves up and make of ourselves the project of working ourselves out. If we are called that is because we are ourselves the calling, for the philosophic calling summons us to interrogate the calling until we find that the calling is *us, ourselves*, until, that is, that we are called to call the calling *us, ourselves*. This is its genius. This is our genius: to hearken to the summonings of our call, to call after it and back to it, to call it, so that the call becomes our secret delight, our desires, ourselves, our calling forth ourselves and our calling ourselves back to ourselves. Philosophy is the coincidence of the calling with what calls as well as with we who are called.

But if philosophy enjoys a genius, it is only to deliver adequately apostolic instruction; yet if philosophy bears an apostolic mission, this mission is enacted through a struggle to appropriate that authority by which it is summoned, a struggle that is more of a seduction, clever, charming, coy, devious, insincere. This is the dilemma that goes by the name of philosophy: to the extent that philosophy is genius, just to that extent then is its authority undermined. But to the extent that philosophy is apostolic, just to that extent does it forfeit its insightfulness.

Now, this paradox inherent in philosophy becomes particularly painful in writing philosophy, for if one is to write philosophy it is necessary to disguise the apostolic intentions with the cleverness and trappings of genius yet subdue the tendency of genius to delight in its own extravagances of decoy, decoration, subterfuge, literary inventions and masks, the desire for polish and facile wordplay, etc., so that the apostolic instruction might be communicated with the appropriate authority. The practice consists in one's genius trying to become clever enough to become apostolic even while the apostolic in one wants to embellish a bit as to what its authority is, smugly assuming ascendancy over that wherefrom it is authorized.

Philosophy is this endless polemical contesting between the intoxication and seduction of genius and the authority of the apostle. It is not a happy drama, at least as it is played out in the individual. Some see this contesting as the comical per se, so that the *Phenomenology of Spirit* shows us to be the cosmic comedy of errors; others see it as the essence of the tragic; while others find it preposterous, arguing as a philosopher that philosophy presumes to be the cure for which it is itself the only illness. But most cannot see this contestation at all: the genius is off secretly delighting in the nudge-and-wink joke of his literary ornaments; the apostle has no time for such foolishness; and everyone else is just plain too busy.

In any event one does write; writing philosophy is the enacting of just this *agon* between the genius and the apostle. So I suppose I enact it here in this little book. Which would mean, I suppose, that it is necessary to give a sort of authorial disclaimer even while I indicate what the author intended to get shown. But before that, let me state, for the record, as it were, the only solution I know of to the dilemma of finding oneself writing philosophy: writing philosophy is at one and the same time both the art of writing stillborn books and the art of writing posthumous papers. Philosophy is written correctly when it comes out both stillborn and posthumous: it is finished before the author has yet to begin, and it is begun after the author has come to an end. As stillborn, the philosophic work leaves uncontested its apostolic authority and ministry, for the authority commanding a stillborn book commands it to be stillborn, unauthorized, without authority, without author.

The stillborn book attests to an authority that has always already and henceforth renounced authorizing the book. As a desultory collection of posthumous papers, the philosophic work passes itself off as the fragmentary and unfinished collection of papers of a genius, inviting the reader to sort through them, to assemble them in a way that won't betray the reader's own whimsy, in order to expose the presumed profundity beneath the papers' random ramblings.

In between the stillborn book and the posthumous papers, a life is lived, but a life, because of the work of writing, that goes unlived, haunted by being stillborn yet already interred. "Life," as Rimbaud says, "is elsewhere."

Yet philosophy is about this stillborn yet already posthumous life in the sense that philosophy lives from life, and thus away from life, yet occasionally comes up against life and, in a kind of terrible astonishment, finds that life has become both stillborn and posthumous, never yet alive but already dead. Philosophy turns that which it lives from into an elsewhere and an otherwise than which it can never get back to. Life is an ellipsis within a parenthesis.

Stillborn yet posthumously, then, appears a book, this book that is, then, because of its arriving stillborn, nothing more than a completely inadequate excursus on the principle of inadequation that betrays every book, yet, due to its posthumous character, appears to be an accidentally assembled fragment intimating what would otherwise carry us away beyond all books and so appears as an incompletable cipher that draws us toward this absence of the book. If this book contains anything that is precious or precocious, this is due entirely to the serendipity of appearing merely quixotic in the way in which the seemingly fortuitous unfolding of its logic comes to take on the force and weight of necessity itself. In this regard, perhaps it would be best to make an analogy with mathematical truths, which appear to be simultaneously neither necessary nor merely conventional and yet nonetheless both. What appears apostolic about this book is only the *presumption* of having proceeded from something—classical philosophy—the authority of which it presupposes in order to show that such authority ultimately disavows itself; by proceeding resolutely and rigorously according to canonical principles, the authority of these principles is undermined by just such a procedure.

* *

All this being said, and, *nota bene*, being said by the putative author of this book and thus being put forth strictly as an authorial disclaimer, the author retires—or rather confirms our suspicions that he was already well into retirement before the occasion of this preface—with but a muffled murmur, "I have to tell you else none of it is true, all I've said is just instead of having to live it through." So all this being said, it still devolves upon the author not to appear an utter superfluity for being tempted to describe the activities of his wife with her lover. To rise, as it were, to this occasion the author can neither turn away in a pretense of ignorance nor find the comings and goings objectionable without himself looking like an unemployed extra. Rather, I suppose such an occasion merits being left alone, left to become the occasion for others to poke about in, for it is left to these others to adduce what is, as it were, the occasion in this occasion, to make of this occasion—an occasion. The author knows this well and cannot help but wonder nervously, as if in complicity with his own being baited for a pratfall—what the occasion occasions. Certainly one would hope for something most occasional. Yet here's the fear: if the punchline needs explaining, the joke is lost; yet if it is not at all certain whether there is any leg-pulling being done, and whose leg is being pulled, if we cannot tell if the stand-up comic is in his or her bit or if he or she is playing it straight, and if that is itself the joke, well then, some misunderstanding might arise. One could, of course, as Constantin Constantius remarks in *Repetition*, write, like Clement of Alexandria, in such a way that "the heretics cannot understand" one. Still, one would want that such deliberated misunderstanding be enjoyable, gleeful, delicious and delightful, as when on an unexpected holiday that we just now found out we have off we feel time's sheer freedom for having nothing to do.

The fear that such misunderstanding will itself be misunderstood rather than enjoyed needs a preface both to warn of it and to ward it off. But without thereby giving it away. This, however, can only be said in an unstoppable and infinitely unstable series of buck-passings, where each buck passer disclaims what the next buck passer will say of his own paltry attempt to say what this book is about. Terms like "deconstruction," "postmodern anxiety over the nature and possibility of philosophy," "performative writing" are the currency here, the sparks and the conduits, and the spare change as well. These terms, although no longer causing us (or the buck) to pause, do indicate a problem: the problem of *not* just noting parenthetically and in a footnote that philosophy has come to an end while nonetheless taking it upon oneself to set everyone straight about what's what, philosophically speaking and by, of course, speaking philosophically.

The problem is that philosophic problems do not go away simply by preparing an obit about them: they are still being lived through. And with somewhat more difficulty these days, it seems. What Heidegger calls the *Unumgänglichkeit* of science, that from which it arises and to which it is blind and around which it cannot get, this is the general structure of life's problematic: that life does on occasion press in upon itself as its own *Unumgänglichkeit*. Life is its own blind spot, the blind spot that opens up the field of vision as well as enabling our vision in the first place. And just as Heidegger came to renounce all *logos* activity in search of the astonishing obduracy, evanescence, and lubricity of the word, so too does a philosophic problem arise only with our complete inability to formulate it, to express it as anything other than our bewilderment in and of language, our utter bereftness, and yet so too does a philosophic problem disappear as soon as we are able at last to see it, to articulate what was problematic about it, which is to say, as soon as we can no longer even suspect how to articulate it, being bereft and abandoned by its dissolution. The problem is enacting this whole dynamic of the glance askance into what arises as its own emptying out of itself and the resistance of all this to being reduced to a set of propositions. The problem is, then, to show this completely indirectly, in a kind of sidestepping of argumentation in favor of an instantiation and performance of this problematic. The indirection would be here the assumption that this book reads like a series of propositions advancing a line of argument, rather than showing itself to be in fact an instance of performance of the inability to reduce anything to propositional argumentation. Such indirection would be at one and the same time performative as well as informative, in that the style would need to demonstrate the content but could only do so by being in contradiction to it.

That language might seem to consist essentially and normatively of propositional sentences is, I suppose, unavoidable. That it has in fact the structure of a pun, uncontainable dissemination without any fixable conceptual determination, "quashed quotatoes, messes of mottage" (*Finnegans Wake*, 183), resounding not with meaning but with the soundings of every word, infelicities and impertinences echoing and re-echoing infinitely in and throughout all attempts to stabilize meaning in the proposition, reducing us to not being able to say what the word says or doesn't say, not being able to put the word into words but drawing us into it as into a gamble in which we are both the game and the stake—that language, when left alone, is a funning punning—that insight itself unavoidably takes on the form of a proposition. And inside all these propositions, by which, apparently, we try to harness the happening of language but end up by trying to prevent language (whatever that is) from happening, there is still inextricably embedded within—the pun, the pun turning against the proposition and turning the proposition against itself, calling it into question without there being any question and without there being any question at all of anything being called into question; the pun, whose fun is to lead words back to us from their exile and truancy in the proposition.

It is about this funning punning that I write. But, of course, nothing really can be said *about* it. Its irony is that it is completely extratextual: what "truth" might emerge from this text is in this extratextual irony, that it is not about that whereof it speaks but rather about that ineffable "book of rumors" enframing this 'whereof' and that meets discourse with refusal and reserve and resistance, standing still within its own impermeabiltiy and uncontainability. This funning punning is, for me and for right now anyway, situated within normative philosophic discourse where the elaboration of a grammar of being is at issue. I say, for me and for right now, because the entire "Western" tradition of discourse is currently enjoying a very lively crisis as to its very possibility. (Which most of us really don't take very seriously, do we?) Even for those of us who can only dabble and tarry, this crisis seems, oddly, clear enough. It is the discomfabulating phenomenon of theory becoming its own literature while literature becomes its own theory, leaving no room for the one or the other. So I share this meditation on the possibility of the venture and vocation of discourse, discourse proper.

This possibility is language: language is the condition for the possibility of the discursive constitution of the human world. This is a given—but only insofar as language consists essentially and normatively in the proposition. As soon as we begin to catch on to the hint language gives itself of itself—that it has no essence, no form—just as soon do we suspect that it, like death, is the limit of the human, uncanny and overwhelming as that which gets away from us, "A breath of nothing, a wafting of the God," elemental overexposure to that which we cannot bear to be near, a tether to our nether where lies density and impermeability, an intractable reserve of pure refractoriness.

At issue is, I suppose, that philosophy, in "its eve and aftermath," needs to find its own expert knowledge disposed to contesting itself. Philosophy finds it needful that expert knowledge demonstrate ultimately that this expertise is the means for undermining the very principles that enable and empower expert knowledge. Why would this be needful? And how can anything be said about this at all that is not subject at once to the claims of expertise? As if we could even tell if such were said. Would not such a demonstration be founded on and so participate in the very principles it is intending to subvert? Just as Aristotle noted that it is impossible to hold a false view of the law of contradiction (*Meta.* K6. 1062b12–13), so it is impossible to use the principles of expert demonstration to subvert these principles. But there is something like a self-contestation in expertise, something like becoming dissatisfied with having achieved total satisfaction. Like desire, expertise does not so much want mastery as it does the obstruction of the very possibility of mastery. And like desire, expertise, in the face of such obstruction, finds that its own expertise is precisely what obstructs—impedes and defers—the possibility of complete mastery, i.e., of the mastery of its own expertise. (Note that a science cannot give an account of how it is done; expertise cannot explain itself.) What is needful, following the path expertise pursues, is to loosen and set into free play a kind of Socratic ignorance that would desire to be ignorant even of itself, that would work its way out of its own way of working into a way of unworking, into a way of unworking at unworking. Of course, this can never happen—which is, I suppose, one of the points of this book: does a deliberate and elaborately executed strategy of unknowing really enable the overturning or overthrowing of the expertise in knowing that is its condition of possibility? Or does such a strategy show itself to be, in the course of its elaboration, expert, expertly demonstrating its expertise in unknowing and so in knowing, in knowing that although the expertise of knowing cannot be resisted or subverted, this strategy nonetheless ignores this expertise, which is to say, again, ignores thus its own expertise, enjoying this ignorance by ignoring even it? One cannot enter into the dialectics such questions entail, for this dialectic is either unfathomably complicated or else evanesces absolutely just as soon as one begins to look at it. Or rather, of course: it is both.

Now this is the problem of expertise as it is posed by expertise. Expertise, in seeking to develop an expert theory of the anexpert, finds itself in a self-contradictory position, for it must be both the avowal of itself and the avowal of what resists and eludes and ultimately rebukes it. But the avowal of this latter (the anexpert) is the disavowal of avowing, since the anexpert disavows the very possibility of avowing. But the expert is itself avowing or is avowing itself. So the avowal of the anexpert turns into the disavowal of the very avowing that avows it. This does not eliminate the expert nor does it put it in question. Rather, the expert confounds itself in trying to avow what disavows expert avowal. As the avowal of what disavows it is also its own disavowal. Since it is nonetheless the avowal of this, it is also the disavowal of what disavows it. Which is not the same thing as the expert, the avowing that is the expertise of the expert. But this the expert disavows; the expert becomes the disavowal of itself as well as the disavowal of this disavowing. But without renouncing the avowing that it still maintains itself as.

The problem is much more radically posed when posed from out of Socratic ignorance. But it is precisely here that I myself must break off, noting only that Socratic ignorance does not invalidate expertise but leaves it alone, intact. Its strategy is one of unworking, of renouncing creating a work or a strategy and of announcing not that the problem has been worked out but rather of the always yet to come of the unworking.

Thus this little book leaves alone intact the pursuit of significance, the quest for sense—precisely by engaging in that pursuit and that quest. But to engage in these is ultimately to investigate the origin of sense. The pursuit of significance presses relentlessly toward collapsing into an utterly unremarkable and unintentional insignificance at the bottom of things. And the quest for sense is a quest for the complete and final sense to things, the completion of their sense. But this drives ineluctably to disappearing in the incompletability of things, their accidental and anecdotal and aleatoric character. The search for the origin of sense discloses, behind its own back, that the origin is the loss of sense, the breakup and breakdown of sense and the breakthrough of a certain indescribable nonsense. Now, the question is, can we make sense of this? We could not, for example, speak directly about this loss of sense—obviously; nor could we hope to speak about what renders significance insignificant or make sense out of nonsense. But we could somehow play with the play, the dissemination, and the ultimate undecidability of sense that sense makes when making sense of its origin. We could assume, as we cannot but do, that sense makes sense, but in trying to make sense we end up finding that the sense sense makes is the loss of sense. Or more precisely, if we were to try to make sense, the sense of this would lead us to the running out of sense: the sense sense makes is ultimately to run out of sense. But of course, no one can write the loss of sense nor does anyone run out of sense. What we have come to think is needed is that by making sense of sense, we could make sense of, not the loss of sense, but the sense of this loss, not what is there when sense has run out, but rather performatively to show the running out of sense by giving the sense that sense is running out. It is a matter of pressing to the threshold of sense, where unsense is simply the nascent becoming-sense of sense but where sense is just on the verge of lapsing into an unsense. Sense is the fulfilling of unsense and yet sense is the most realized when it disappears into unsense—without the question of this disappearance even being possible.

(It is the fortuitous, contingent, conditional, and incomplete character of things that must be kept in view. But these are the very things that thinking cannot track. The sheer gratuity and contingency of being are *themselves* completely intractable in their gratuitous and contingent bestowal of being. In this sense, sense arises as replacing that about which it can know nothing, yet, since sense implicates that about which it can know nothing, it relentlessly strives to reduce itself to it, to disappear into it.)

Now, all of this is about something that can only take place in a different time than when we reflect on it, being not yet there but already no longer there. As is the author; and to the author, the reader; and in between, the book.

And myself? Myself, I no longer know my way about at all, and that finally seems as it should be.

Abbreviations and Editions

References to Aristotle's and some of early Heidegger's works are cited in the text. I use the Loeb Classical Library texts for Aristotle; the translations are generally mine, although I routinely consult Loeb translations.

Aristotle

Categ.	*The Categories.* Translated by Harold P. Cooke. Cambridge: Harvard University Press, 1967.
De An.	*De Anima.* Translated by W. S. Hett. Cambridge: Harvard University Press, 1975.
De Int.	*On Interpretation.* Translated by Harold P. Cooke. Cambridge: Harvard University Press, 1967.
EE	*Eudemian Ethics.* In *The Athenian Constitution. The Eudemian Ethics. On Virtues and Vices.* Translated by Harris Rackham. Cambridge: Harvard University Press, 1952.
MM	*Magna Moralia.* Translated by G. Cyril Armstrong. Cambridge: Harvard University Press, 1969.
Meta.	*The Metaphysics.* Translated by Hugh Tredennick. Cambridge: Harvard University Press, 1969.
Nico. Eth.	*Nicomachean Ethics.* Translated by H. Rackham. Cambridge: Harvard University Press, 1975.
PA	*De Partibus Animalium.* Translated by A. L. Peck. Cambridge: Harvard University Press, 1937.
Physics	*The Physics.* Translated by Philip H. Wicksteed. Cambridge: Harvard University Press, 1970.

Poetics   *The Poetics.* Translated by W. Hamilton Fyfe. Cambridge University Press, 1973.
Post. Analyt.   *Posterior Analytics.* Translated by Hugh Tredennick. Cambridge: Harvard University Press, 1976.
Rhet.   *The "Art" of Rhetoric.* Translated by John Henry Freese. Cambridge: Harvard University Press, 1975.
Soph. Refut.   *On Sophistical Refutations.* Translated by E. S. Forster. Cambridge: Harvard University Press, 1965.
Topica   *Topica.* Translated by Hugh Tredennick. Cambridge: Harvard University Press, 1976.

HEIDEGGER

The Basic Problems of Phenomenology. Translated by Albert Hofstadter. Bloomington: Indiana University Press, 1985.

Being and Time. Translated by John Macquarrie and Edward Robinson. New York: Harper and Row, 1962. (*Sein und Zeit.* Tübingen: Max Niemeyer Verlag, 1977.)

"On the Essence of Truth." I use two translations: (1) in Martin Heidegger, *Basic Writings*, edited by David Farrell Krell (New York: Harper and Row, 1977), translated by John Sallis, 117–41; and (2) in *Existence and Being*, edited by Werner Brock (Chicago: Henry Regnery, 1949), translated by R. F. C. Hull and Alan Crick, 292–324. The source text is "Vom Wesen der Wahrheit," in *Wegmarken* (Frankfurt am Main: Vittorio Klostermann Verlag, 1967), 73–97. In using two different translations I seek only to preserve what I consider to be the flavor of the original text without departing from accepted translations. (E.g., much of this article hinges on Heidegger's words, such as *"Unwesen,"* which is translated in *Existence and Being* as "disessence" and in *Basic Writings* as "non-essence," and *"irren,"* or "errancy" / "error.")

"What Is Metaphysics?" Again, I use two translations: (1) in Martin Heidegger, *Basic Writings*, translated by David Farrell Krell, 95–116; and (2) in *Existence and Being*, translated by R. F. C. Hull and Alan Crick, 325–49. The source is *"Was ist Metaphysik?"* in *Wegmarken*, 1–19.

Preface

> . . . all that is needed to ensure that the beginning remains immanent in its scientific development is to consider, or rather, ridding oneself of all other reflections and opinions whatever, simply to take up, *what is there before us.*
>
> G. W. F. Hegel, *The Science of Logic*

> Indeed, the question which was raised long ago, is still and always will be, and which always baffles us—'What is Being?' [καὶ δὴ καὶ τὸ πάλαι τε καὶ νῦν καὶ ἀεὶ ζητούμενον καὶ ἀεὶ ἀπορούμενον, τί τὸ ὄν, τοῦτό ἐστι].
>
> Aristotle, *Metaphysics* 7.1.1028b2–4

> The relation of the philosopher to being is not the frontal relation of the spectator to the spectacle; it is a kind of complicity, an oblique and clandestine relationship.
>
> Maurice Merleau-Ponty, *In Praise of Philosophy*

> That which one calls a presupposition of philosophy is nothing but the expressed need for it. . . . However, it is awkward to express the need for philosophy as a presupposition of philosophy, since the need thereby receives a form of reflection. This form of reflection appears as contradictory propositions. . . . It can be demanded of these propositions that they justify themselves. The justification of these propositions as presuppositions is not yet supposed to be philosophy itself, and so the presenting of reasons and the accounting for grounds [*das Ergründen und Begründen*] begin prior to and outside of philosophy.
>
> G. W. F. Hegel, *The Difference between the Fichtean and Schellingian Systems of Philosophy*

Somewhere in *What Is Called Thinking?* Heidegger cautions his students to read Aristotle for ten to fifteen years before studying Nietzsche. This is no simple advice being offered, no simple task to carry through. For now Aristotle may be approached by sensibilities cultivated from Heidegger's metahistorical studies of the "truth of being," of the dispatches and envoys of epochs; by sensibilities cultivated from Heidegger's delimitation of metaphysics, from his stepping back away from its closure; by sensibilities cultivated from the primitivism of postmodernism, a primitivism elaborated with highly complicated textual machinery, with the urgency of the postmodern task and with its suspicions as to the meanings and intentions of history; by sensibilities cultivated from Nietzsche's analysis of nihilism offering an apprehensive glimpse into the possibility of absolute yea-saying and suggesting a delirious celebration of the worldplay; by sensibilities cultivated from suspicions about the ending of metaphysics, its foreclosure.

Above all, from these last suspicions. Philosophy has become apocalyptic in its discourse on itself. Today it is customary to document the foreclosure of metaphysics, to contribute to this foreclosure, to allege its end, to corroborate the exhaustion of its prefigured possibilities, to expose what comes to philosophy as its death, to expose this with a kind of eschatological mystagogy and to expose this mystagogy eschatologically. Philosophy today promotes itself eschatologically, as eschatological studies of eschatology, eloquent, vigilant, profligate and prodigal about the imminence of the last, the last last, the last lasting to the end, the last at last. Its eschatological exposition is a response to the ἔσχατον; but as a response it renders itself impossible, for the response can never be expected, never mind directed and developed, since it precedes that to which it is a response.

In the face, or perhaps I should say jaws, of an "apocalyptic tone recently adopted in philosophy," this book is my response, this book is a study of my response.

I am beginning to suspect that books are, to the degree that they are successful, failed projects, each wanting to bring itself to its own proper impossibility, to turn itself into the proof of its own impossibility. But then, forearmed with this suspicion, I would like to celebrate this failure, not deliriously, not exultantly, with neither rancor nor regret, with neither nostalgia nor *res-*

sentiment, but rather, as far as I can, soberly and cleanly, with rigor and temperance, attentive and patient.

This book is in two parts: the first part is on Aristotle; the second on Heidegger's *Being and Time*, that "magnificent torso." The second part proceeds from the insight gained in the first part into the "paronymous" nomination of being, that "being is said in many ways"—τὸ ὂν λέγεται πολλαχῶς—and from that insight looks at the amphibolous figuration of being enunciated in the breach between being and beings.

Part 1 is the attempt to elaborate a speculative grammar of being, given that being is not only "said in many ways" (λέγεται πολλαχῶς) but in every which way yet apparently being cannot be said at all if it is indeed a matter of finding the originary name of what is deployed in the dispatching of being. My motivation for turning to Aristotle's attempt to enunciate a πρώτη φιλοσοφία is complex, and I am not sure I could parlay it out without sounding trite and platitudinous. I will mention here only a few indicial words: Aristotle's first philosophy proceeds aporematically, entering into its study from irresolvable perplexities and coming each time to an impasse or dead end; also, according to him, there is a science of being *qua* being—however, each science concerns a determinate genus, yet being is not a genus; and finally substance, οὐσία, is always a particular, but we can know only universals, so not only can we not know particulars but we cannot even know that we cannot know them. These indices no longer direct us to a catalogue of classical problems. Rather, these indices are invested from the start with our postmodern concerns and sensibilities; they arise from such concerns and sensibilities, seeking to validate them, seeking, indeed, to be answerable to them. However, I do not try to put an end to the classical inquiry into the meaning of being. I neither conclude nor contest such inquiry; I am not particularly interested in starting fashionably by having been done with it. I should like, rather, to choreograph the mating dance of postmodernism as it tries to seduce its classical counterpart. Of course this is my own choreography; but that we are in fact in the middle of the mating season will elicit few protests, save for questions of eugenics. Having no nuptial plumage myself, wishing to be neither contentious nor sententious, I should just like to share with you how I would choreograph this dance.

If I begin, classically, by attempting to elaborate a speculative grammar of being, by virtue of our postmodern sensibilities and suspicions, this grammatization nonetheless gets immediately rhetorized. For, as we shall see, elaborating the grammar of being allows us to inquire into being, but the language by means of which we inquire denies the very possibility of such inquiry. As I hope to demonstrate, in the course of elaborating on its own *intrinsic* possibility the "science of being qua being" eliminates itself. Thus a speculative grammar delineates a paradigm that both asserts and denies the possibility of speculative grammars. This paradigm is itself the demonstration of the impossibility of articulating such a paradigm. In being the demonstration of this impossibility, the speculative grammar I advance proves that this impossibility is, impossibly, possible. That is to say, the science I attempt to articulate affirms the impossibility of such a science by venturing to realize this impossibility by the very discourse on this impossibility.

Furthermore, the grammatical exposition of being becomes rhetorical precisely because there is a contradiction between the grammar of being and the machinery necessary for its elaboration, between what gets said and how it gets said. Because of this, it is ultimately undecidable as to whether we are articulating the meaning of being or just the meaning of 'being'.

It is from within this undecidability that part 2 is ventured. If there is an essential ambiguity in the ontological enterprise, if we cannot clearly determine whether we are articulating the meaning of being or just the meaning of 'being', then this can be only because being, in its complicity in our pursuit of its grammar, gives itself duplicitously. In elaborating its grammar all we succeed in doing is to open up a breach between its grammar and the elaboration of its grammar, between, that is, logic and rhetoric. And in this breach being is found as the duplicitous figuration of itself.

From within this breach we fall into part 2, where this duplicity of being, in our attempt to delineate it, throws us into indetermination, a radical suspension of its grammar; we fall through the breach opened up between being and beings. It is not a question of mending the breach, or repairing it, nor is it a question of subtending it or even of holding it open, but rather of, precisely, falling *through* it.

This book, finally, is an attempt to explain its title, that the inquiry into the meaning of being involves a certain oblique complicity of being in the pursuit of its philosophic exposition, subsidizing the philosophic scam to get it to disclose itself fully while nevertheless confronting it with refusal and resistance and self-secluding reserve, with almost artful ruse and subterfuge, with a kind of obstructiveness and refractoriness, with a surprisingly rigorous obtuseness, revealing itself as the contrivance of traps, pitfalls, and swindles waylaying us even in our waywardness. The 'of' in the title, in its equivocation, explodes whatever sense we might make of 'the conning of being' or of 'the cunning of being'. This *of* makes of the scam a sham, of the cunning a shunning of cunning. This *of* marks a catastrophe involved in the enunciation *of* being, a catastrophe irreducible to a con perpetrated by or against being yet also irreducible to being being refractory, intractable, or simply enigmatic. This *of* would seem to be neither a subjective genitive nor an objective genitive. Rather, it marks the impossibility of its being disambiguated; it designates the indeterminability of the philosophic exposition of being, that there is a factor of systematic undecidability as to what gets said in saying being—being, its being said, or that being and its being said are the same. And the ',' in the title—we cannot catch our breath; we lose it over and over again, even before we have begun. The ',' marks a rift, a *Riss*, in being, that is, one might suspect, its nomination.

The first part is an exercise in the exposition of being. Here we have a nautilus growing in reverse, where each word cancels out the previous one, where each sentence erases the sentence before it, where each paragraph proves the next to be impossible, where each page repudiates the previous page while urging that the next be torn out and thrown away, where the whole project disappears into itself.

The second part, chastened by the lessons of the first, if not enlightened by them, looks for the words that say being, words that come only when they cannot be found anymore, where between each word untold words escape and vanish, never to be found again.

On "the eve and aftermath of philosophy," there is, subtending and sustaining discourse, motivating it, a secret yearning that we finally be granted our three wishes, having so painstakingly exhausted our powers in preparation, having become prudent, modest, chastened by our lust for comprehending the all. We would give it careful thought: the first two of the three wishes would be practical, would be, say, for creaturely comforts, a kind of lifelong and longlived easement, for, as it were, a natural overallotment of goods, an overabundance of goods that, by virtue of supersaturation, would distract us from wondering whether they would ever be depleted.

But the third wish, the odd one, the rogue wish, the final wish, the last wish, this would be the wish we would want to last, the wish that we might wish right at last. Here there is pure yearning, without object, without compensation, without satisfaction, a pure yearning that we do not misspeak ourselves, that we have learned prudence, that we wish the right wish, the wish that makes the world aright, the wish that we make the world aright just as it is. Here we would wish that we need wish no more. The final wish could only be a wish that we dare not wish more, for fear of not wishing aright; it could only be a wish that we no longer *need* to wish. Here we might wish that we might not have ever wished, might not have ever wished to compel the world to accede to our wishes. For here we would no doubt wish that we might have known the dangers in wishing, the terror of having our wishes granted, the terrible powers we unleash by simply wishing, the fearfulness in yearning, the consequences, the sheer consequentiality involved in wishing even while we wish that things be inconsequential. Here we might come to suspect that the best thing would simply be to refuse to wish any further, having perhaps learned that there is something corrosive in having our wishes granted, that there is a general corruption and decay that wishing infects everything with.

But who could refuse the third wish, the final wish, which would be of course the wish for the last wish, the wish that the last wish would last? Yet perhaps—I don't know—perhaps we might be wise enough to wish that, the first two practical wishes for health and wealth having been asked and granted, to use our third wish simply to wish that we might forget the whole thing ever happened; our comfort and ease magically assured and taken for granted, to forget we had ever known wishes could be granted, wishing rather to be returned to, if not innocence, at least to a more natural state of ignorance about those irruptions of power into the world that place such power at our disposal that wishing could only be a form of folly. Perhaps we would come to suspect such folly and so wish that our last wish would be to remain ignorant of the fact that these irruptions of power are really and truly, actually possible at all.

And of course it could be that just such a thing had already happened. That third wish might right now be already granted, we ignorant now of our good fortune and still playing with the possibility of wishing that we be granted our wishes, still wanting to place the world at the disposal of the power of such wishing. Perhaps—I don't know—there would be no way to tell—we could have been visited this very morning; this moment might be the first moment of our fortune, this writing the first writing written as the forgetting of the desire to have our wishes granted, that is, the forgetting that we got our wishes.

But, of course, we could never know this. And so this writing would then be the attempt to retrieve the possibility of this forgetting, the attempt to retrieve the knowledge that we might have forgotten that we were granted our wishes, and so would be the attempt to recover this the last wish, the wish that puts an end to wishing, to recover the possibility of this last wish, the one wish that would then be still outstanding, thus making all wishes, wishing itself, still outstanding, making wishing possible in the first place, thus generating again this very inquiry into wishing, promoting again the suspicion that perhaps we might wish to forget this whole thing of wishing. This book would then be the attempt to be, again, this last wish, this wish that we no longer and dare not wish and so again and again would celebrate that we forget that we got our wishes, and so would suspect that we might have already been granted the last wish, the wish that we forget we got our wishes. This writing would, then, attempt to recuperate, over and over again, the possibility of such forgetting and so would be the attempt to recuperate the wish that would wish such forgetting. But then this writing would be the interminable repetition of coming to know the impossibility of knowing that we got our last wish, the wish that we forget we got our wishes. This writing would, then, come to know itself as the impossibility of knowing *this*, and so would come, finally to know that it, this book, is neither the first book after having gotten our wishes nor the last book to announce that we wish to forget that we got our wishes. This book, in the end, would be neither the first nor the last, neither the first of the last nor the last of the first, but rather simply and immediately just another book, a book that could be just another book only by, having been written, being unwritten, that is, only by being just another unwriting of the book.

Just another unwriting of the book. But then we all have all along been unwriting the book. It is as if we all—unbeknownst to ourselves—have been elected president of a great secret society, the great secret book-unwriting society. It is not, as some of us might be of a mind to think, that we have been excluded membership in this secret society, being condemned instead to the preterition of knowing books, books, books, only books. Rather, we have each of us been elected president to this great secret society. However, the very existence of this secret book-unwriting society, our membership, our presidency, all have been kept secret from us. But even so, haven't we all secretly suspected the existence of such a secret society? Are not we constantly coming upon each other in surprise—You! not *you* too!—wanting to tell the secret but finding that not only can the secret not be told, but all telling, every tale, simply proves only that there could never have been such a secret, that what is secret about the secret book-unwriting society is that there never was and there can never be one, yet in coming to see *this*, realizing that it *is*, this very realization keeping it secret. Perhaps this is how we finally catch up with our third wish.

PART I
THE CONNING OF BEING

ARISTOTLE'S PARONYMOUS ONTOLOGY

> Since these concepts are indispensable for unsettling the heritage to which they belong, we should be even less prone to renounce them. Within the closure, by an oblique and perilous movement, constantly risking falling back within what is being deconstructed, it is necessary to surround the critical concepts with a careful and thorough discourse—to mark the conditions, the medium, and the limits of their effectiveness and to designate rigorously their intimate relationship to the machine whose deconstruction they permit; and, in the same process, designate the crevice through which the yet unnameable glimmer beyond the closure can be glimpsed.
>
> Jacques Derrida, *Of Grammatology*

> A literary text simultaneously asserts and denies the authority of its own rhetorical modes. . . .
>
> Paul de Man, *Allegories of Reading*

> The sibspeeches of all mankind have foliated (earth seizing them!) from the root of some funner's stotter.
>
> James Joyce, *Finnegans Wake*

Irrespective of our particular bents, training, and talents, today we can no longer glibly dismiss the charge issued by—to name the most prominent—Heidegger, Wittgenstein, and Derrida that metaphysics has in some sense exhausted itself, that it has not delivered on its promise, that it has defrauded itself—and us—as to the force of that promise, namely, that a comprehensive account of the whole is both possible and necessary, that the originary presence of things can be recuperated.

For Wittgenstein metaphysics has systematically corrupted our linguistic sensibilities by imprisoning sense exclusively and exhaustively inside representational tropes. He patiently plays with our misprisons until he pries open a sense that enjoys an immediacy with that of which it is the sense. In fact, his overriding concern is to show that the sense of something is just this, its immediate presence in the world, and not anything like a representation of it. Instead of isolating sense on the side of the subjective while casting that of which it is the sense out into the intractable objective, as philosophy has always purportedly done, Wittgenstein demonstrates that all there is is the enacting of the enownment of word and world to one another, the twinning kinning of word and world, with nothing coming in between them.

For Heidegger, on the other hand, the reason for our misimprisonment in representational tropisms is that the history of metaphysics has been the progressive and systematic oblivion of the meaning of being, the sense of which, he repeatedly insists, cannot be reduced to either the meaning of the word or the concept 'being'. Rather, being has something to do with a heightened sensitivity to the *appearing* of the entitative order to the world, to the ontological fact that entities are present in the world, that they present themselves in the world. For Heidegger, *that* the entitative order presents itself is itself nothing entitative; and he insists that metaphysics is precisely that way of the world in which everything—including that the entitative order presents itself as such—is reduced to the entitative. It is only by stepping back behind this entitative reduction that we can retrieve the nonentitative evanescence of being as it recovers itself from out of its own obfuscation. Being, Heidegger constantly reiterates, conceals itself in unconcealing entities. That is to say, the entitative reduction conceals within itself the fact that the condition for its possibility is necessarily nothing entitative.

And Derrida finds in the Heideggerian dictum that being conceals itself in being the unconcealing of beings the siting of metaphysics into its closure. He repeatedly, and with a sense of great and anxious urgency, contends that this closure is no linear circumspection of presence. Rather, the force of his deconstruction has been to show that the text of metaphysics—that is, any text in the tradition, any text—harbors within itself both the necessary imposition of closure, of the self-enclosure of presence, one that is rigorously and inviolably enforced, as well as a slippage and seepage of sense, a faltering faulting fissuring, a breaching of this self-enclosure, and a broaching by this breaching of an unnameable something *other* that is unenclosable, the inbreaking of near absolute nonsense, the insinuation of radical alterity, and the threat of the almost complete loss of meaning.

Yet for all these contestations of the legitimacy of metaphysics, a legitimacy that could only be self-adjudicating, there is still the properly philosophic desire to give a comprehensive account of the whole, to recuperate the originary presence of the whole, to attain to a transcendental attunement with this originary presence.

I

Knowledge of the impossibility of knowing precedes the act of consciousness that tries to reach it.
         Paul de Man, *Blindness and Insight*

It is in this way that an *aporetic* reading of Aristotle highlights by contrast the doctrine of analogy, to the very extent that this reading began by bracketing it. Even if one finds this notion to be nothing but a problem hypostatized into a reply, it nevertheless designates the conceptual labour by which the human, the too human, discourse of ontology attempts to respond to the entreaty of *another* discourse, which is itself perhaps only a non-discourse.
         Paul Ricoeur, *The Rule of Metaphor*

The problem, then, is well known: how to conceive and enact metaphysics in light of the exhaustion of its prefigured possibilities.

The problem is more than well known. It is a bit tiring today, a trifle tedious to repeat the litany that every modern philosopher has exacted against the metaphysical vocation. The problem, despite its urgent overtones and overtures today, is, we might be led to suspect, at least as old as the history of metaphysics. In any event, it does seem that the tone and tenor of "postmetaphysical" thought draws its force from maintaining that metaphysics has always been imperiled from within, that metaphysics has always defrauded itself, undermining itself by the very force of its promise. From Kierkegaard and Nietzsche on, the philosophic scenario has been developed from a struggle to overcome the traps, pitfalls, and swindles hidden in the traditional matrix of problems.

For Kierkegaard, it was necessary to leap with a warrior's sobriety through "the secret trap door of language" (*The Concept of Irony*) of the irony inherent in language, that there is a radical incommensurability between the form of language and the inwardness which it addresses, between the linguistically enhorizoned world and those tremulous, squinting and straining glimpses into the antipredicative that we have no choice but to hearken to as we would a summonings enjoining us to achieve a sort of escape velocity out of our linguistic atmosphere.

For Nietzsche, perched precariously as he was on the brink of a thinksink, the history of philosophy is the inward rotting of all valuation, that the highest values irresistibly devalue themselves, inverting the world, being the agents for the valorization of their false and inverted images.

For Heidegger, the history of metaphysics has been nothing but the history of nihilism. Etc.

But if I were to argue against what some may construe as the excesses of the postmodern sensibility, I would perhaps begin a discourse on how philosophy has always fascinated itself with its false images. Even a casual reading of Plato would be sufficient to document my case: the sophist and false philosopher are never far from the central issue of a Socratic dialogue. I would then perhaps try to show that philosophy has always been preoccupied with its final end as much as it is with a radical beginning anew. This,

I might try to say, is because philosophy always and everywhere demands that it give itself an account of its own self-adjudicating legitimacy, that it validates itself as that which gives itself its own name.

By reflecting upon its own legitimacy, however, philosophy cleaves itself in two: the immediate descriptions of the phenomena and the reflective validation of these descriptions, where both of these movements go under the name of philosophy. Moreover, neither one can be given priority over the other; for if either were, philosophy would be reduced to being either poetry or logic, and these would become, in turn, the same. Let me try to explain what I am getting at.

Philosophy consists in the first place in learning to describe the world in a pure and simple fashion. That is to say, doing philosophy consists in attempting to retrieve the originary sense to the phenomena from out of the layers of sedimented sense from which experience abstracts its constitutive objects. Philosophy is the attempt to give a description of the world shining forth in its immediacy. But the sense of the world has always already been constituted in a thoroughly passive way, such that the attempt to describe the world as it shines forth in its immediacy is ineluctably driven back to secure the appropriateness of this description, to guarantee that the originary constituting of the sense to the world is in fact and in act retrievable just as it is. But this originary sense-constituting activity is an activity that can be seen only as being more passive than the most passive passivity: it necessarily precedes the event of each phenomenon giving itself to be constituted into a sense. Since it precedes the activity of constituting, it is prior to any act of reflection; in this way philosophy must learn to appeal to a rigor that is not demonstrable by reflection; it must learn to rejoice in the passivity of inspiration and give voice to the intoxication it enjoys in bearing an immediate relation to immediacy. In a word, philosophy becomes a poetic enterprise.

However, if philosophy were to insist upon the demonstration of the rigor it knows in proceeding from its primitive insight—and philosophy, to be called philosophy, can scarcely refrain from insisting upon just such a demonstration—if philosophy were to demand that it validate itself, it would lose itself in the process of reflecting upon its own legitimacy, for it would be able to carry out its descriptions of the world shining forth in its immediacy only after it had completely secured the method appropriate to recovering the originary sense of the world. But this is to say that it would never be able to carry through with its descriptions, for it could never get past the beginning series of reflections upon the method of conduct appropriate to it. The most it could hope to discover in this event would be what Kierkegaard knew to be the case, namely, that the process of reflection cannot be gainsaid by reflection, and what Husserl had amply demonstrated, namely, that reflection is a *"Nachgewähren,"* a perceiving something after the fact of its immediate presence and in its departure from immediate experience. It would also learn what Freud was continually cautioning us about, namely, that experience, inasmuch as it can be reflective, that is, conscious, is only *"nachträglich,"* only an aftereffect or afterthought, supplementing the originary process, a process that can never show itself directly.

If philosophy were to reflect upon its immediate descriptive relation to immediacy, the process of reflection would transform its necessary condition into what it is not, into an apprehended object, an object of reflection, rather than respecting it as the generative process making possible all acts of apprehension. That is to say, to the extent that we have an immediate awareness of the ego in the world, of, that is, the world shining forth through the ego, it is not produced through reflection; but to the extent that we reflect upon the ego in order to recover the originary activity of the world shining forth through it, to that extent neither the ego nor the world can be known either immediately or concretely.

Philosophy, then, would be a sort of inverted infinite regress of reflectings upon its own legitimacy: at each stage in its reflections, that stage is secured by closing off on the immediate awareness of the object upon which it reflects. But this immediate awareness that the current stage of reflection is investigating can only be viewed as being itself a previous stage of reflection, for since its essential possibility has been closed off by reflection—and since it is the nature of reflection to understand this—this being-closed-off must be assumed to be the closing off of a previous stage of awareness, a closing off that one presumes made possible that first awareness. Moreover, since reflection comes to understand itself at each station along its way as having closed off upon those possibilities of experience that have made it itself possible, each stage generates the need to take itself up and reflect upon itself as to its own legitimacy, suspecting that, since what has made it possible is precisely the thing that it has closed off upon, it is at best specious and spurious. This suspicion would then generate a higher order of reflection which, as soon as it is reached, comes to understand that its essence consists in having already closed off on the awareness that is its necessary condition. So at each stage of reflection, that stage is made possible by the closing off of the condition necessary for its realization and itself gives rise to that level or order of reflection for which it will be closed off. In this way philosophy learns to look for those possibilities of itself that it has closed off upon—and tries to recover them. Philosophy becomes a purely formal affair, an exercise in the purely formal logistics of recursability.

But none of this can be believed. It is controverted by fact, the fact of language, the fact that, although language is of a different ontological order from that of being, it suppresses its difference from being and in a presumed immediacy with being gives us the enunciation of being. But as soon as language is thought as such, what gets thought is not so much this presumed immediacy with being as it is the failure of language to name being pure and simple, in an immediate relationship to the immediacy of being. Although it is language that first opens up the ontological dimension to the world, it does this only by suppressing the real difference of meaning from being. But as soon as this is noted, language achieves self-consciousness. And with this achievement language identifies itself with a strange and alien suspicion, a suspicion so alien that language can scarcely give it voice, the suspicion that it is the exceeding of being with respect to language and the deficiency of language to capture what exceeds it that indicate a yonder tucked into language, a linguistic yonder, a yonder of language, a nameless faceless something *other* lodging deep inside language like little black hole eddies of the antipredicative.

Yet this suspicion dispels itself as soon as it arises, for it forces language to search within itself for a purer but also more unobtrusive language, capable of calling into question—in order to disappear in it—the very Other of all language, this Other, which, however, is nothing more than a language that also has the essential task of searching within itself for its Other in order to disappear in it. Our trust in language, in its appropriateness, in its twinning kinning of meaning and being, becomes distrustful of itself, becomes *défiance*: defiance *of* language, situated *in* language, which finds within language the terms of its critique, its repudiation. As soon as we suspect that language is not completely appropriate or adequate in its designating of being, we recognize this inappropriateness and inadequacy as the essence of all saying so that it runs the risk of never being inappropriate or inadequate enough.

It is in this way that philosophy becomes a poetics; but philosophy also becomes a purely formal logistics. And these two, seemingly opposing movements, nonetheless carry us to the same impasse, namely that language and the limits of language always and everywhere coincide. By naming being the philosopher names the identification of the meaning of presence with the presence of meaning. This is its poetic movement. But this name names, we now suspect, the impossibility of naming anything but an order that in its essence forfeits an immediate relationship to the immediacy of being in favor of a commentary on the meaning of being, a commentary that is itself the being of meaning. As soon as the philosopher identifies the meaning of presence with the presence of meaning, entities disappear into their meaning, and meaning emerges as the entity proper. For this reason the entity becomes the distancing of itself into its meaning; it turns into its own obfuscation. And for this reason being becomes the entity that is its own meaning.

These two movements—toward a pure poetics and toward a purely formal logistics—refer to the same activity that goes under the name of philosophy. And each is indispensable; it is necessary to establish both. Yet it is seemingly impossible to establish either, for each is the undoing of the other. What is needful, I would like to argue, is for each to forget itself, so that reflection loses itself in the descriptions of the phenomena upon which it began reflecting, and immediacy, with its ceaseless and unreflective describing of the world and its total fascination with these descriptions, its being carried off by them, forgets that it is immediacy and thereby is forced to try to recover its sense of immediacy, is forced to re-attune its way of describing, becomes reflective.

This, then, is something like what would be at stake in carrying out first philosophy, and, no doubt, were I to carry through with my discourse, we both would come to learn of the aporia at the heart of instituting first philosophy.

But here I might pause, and not just out of breath but out of passage, for I would not even have begun my little discourse before it would have come to an end. So I might retrace my steps, step back, not behind the tradition, but back to the place where we find the conception of πρώτη φιλοσοφία, first philosophy: in Aristotle. For with this *terminus technicus* we are given the name for the first great attempt to give a properly metaphysical account of the world. In fact, metaphysics, whatever this term conjures up for us, receives its name from a more or less fortuitous classification of select volumes by Aristotle in the catalog of ancient works. Of this placement Heidegger notes:

> It is well known that the meaning of the expression τὰ μετὰ τὰ φυσικά (as the collective name for those treatises of Aristotle which were classified as following those belonging to the "Physics"), which was first purely descriptive, later came to express a philosophical judgment concerning the content of those works. This change in meaning does not have the harmlessness attributed to it. Rather, it has forced the

interpretation of these treatises in a particular direction and thereby has determined that what Aristotle discusses therein is to be understood as "metaphysics."[1]

The classificatory expression that occasioned this interpretation of Aristotle's writing itself arose from a difficulty concerning the overall structure of the *corpus aristotelicum*. According to Andronikos of Rhodes, upon whom it devolved to classify the works of Aristotle, although the works dealing with logic, physics, and ethics clearly had their assigned places, no discipline or framework could be found into which could be fitted what Aristotle pursued as πρώτη φιλοσοφία. This basic philosophical difficulty is preeminently a question concerning the unity of the collection of writings, which only acquired their title τὰ μετὰ τὰ φυσικά in about 60 B.C., when Andronikos of Rhodes prepared his edition of the collected works of Aristotle. The question is why *did* Aristotle leave this, alone of all his treatises, without a title? Τὰ μετὰ τὰ φυσικά is thus the title of a basic philosophical difficulty. Heidegger writes:

> This difficulty has its origin in the obscurity which envelops the essentials of the problems and ideas discussed in the treatises. Insofar as Aristotle expresses himself on the subject, it is evident that there is a curious ambiguity in the definition of "first philosophy." It is knowledge of the entity *as* entity (ὂν ᾗ ὄν) as well as knowledge of the highest sphere of entities (τιμιοτάτον γένος) through which the entity in totality is defined.[2]

It is a question, then, of the unity of that collection of works that go under the title τὰ μετὰ τὰ φυσικά. And unlike Aristotle's other treatises, the τὰ μετὰ τὰ φυσικά takes a leisurely approach

---

1. Martin Heidegger, *Kant and the Problem of Metaphysics*, 10–11.
2. Ibid., 11–12.

to its objective and a more or less rhapsodic investigation into various problems. Of its fourteen books, six—or, if we disregard books 2 and 5 as not strictly parts of the collection, four—only touch on these problems and offer a preliminary and positive discussion. In the course of these books (1, 3, 4, 6) Aristotle examines, from diverse standpoints, the fundamental philosophical science which he calls first "the sought-for science" (ἡ ζητουμένη ἐπιστήμη) and the "first philosophy" (πρώτη φιλοσοφία).

One of the most difficult problems this title, τὰ μετὰ τὰ φυσικά, causes us is the fact that in book 4 the "sought-for science" is characterized very precisely as the science of "being qua being" (ὂν ᾗ ὄν) (*Meta*. 4.1.1003a21, 24, 31). But on the other hand—and astonishingly—we *also* discover that in *Metaphysics* 6.1—only a few pages further on, if we exclude book 5, since it is but a collection of definitions, a glossary, as it were—Aristotle seems first to accept this thesis and then, immediately afterwards, to embrace its exact opposite. For in 6.1 we again find an analysis of the sciences designed to establish the proper place of πρώτη φιλοσοφία. Here, however, Aristotle does not, as he did in book 4, distinguish the "sought-for science" from all other sciences by its greater generality. First he divides philosophy into three parts: speculative (θεωρητικῆς), practical, and productive; and then he splits speculative philosophy into three disciplines. To each of these disciplines correspond rigorously defined objects. The "sought-for science," referred to in book 4 as the "science of being qua being," he now calls "first philosophy" and defines it—in contradistinction to the other two, physics and mathematics—as the science of what is "eternal and immutable" (ἀκίνητον καὶ χωριστόν = changeless and separable). He then expressly gives it the name of "theology," and it is "the most honorable science" (τὴν τιμιωτάτην) (*Meta*. 6.1.1026a10–12, 17–18, 21).

That Aristotle should attempt to elaborate *both* enterprises in terms of a *single* science is astonishing. Moreover, the name πρώτη φιλοσοφία for the study of "being qua being" lost its point and became unacceptable once the connection between theology and ontology was abandoned. In fact, it appears that Aristotle made a conscious effort to *avoid* the phrase πρώτη φιλοσοφία in the period when books 7–9 were already written. This is indicated by the fact, which is otherwise not easily explained, that in all the places listed in Bonitz's *Index* where Aristotle refers to the *Metaphysics* by the phrase πρώτη φιλοσοφία, his reference is to book 12. Books 7–9, on the other hand, are referred to by such phrases as "it has been said elsewhere" or "it is the subject of another type of investigation" (*De Int.* 17a14; *Physics* 18.191b29; cf. *Nico. Eth.* 1.6.1096a30).

It is a question, then, of establishing and securing the properly philosophical science of "being qua being"; and this in turn would be a question of securing philosophical discourse in its autonomy and intrinsic possibility, for this science which Aristotle wants to establish is "without antecedents of immediate posterity,"[3] and its object, necessarily not derived from anything else, determines an autonomous science. There are a number of problems to consider here.

As has already been intimated, the *Metaphysics* introduces an astonishing and seemingly irresolvable tension between ontology and theology. But given even the most cursory reading of the *Metaphysics*, we also find three distinct but apparently interrelated notions: (1) the science of being qua being; (2) first philosophy; and (3) metaphysics. It is precisely the relationship among these three that spans the tension between ontology proper and theology proper.

It is the duality of ontology and theology that expresses a basic ambiguity in the definition of first philosophy: metaphysics is, to cite Heidegger's dictum, "onto-theo-logy," the science of the first *and* highest being.

That Aristotle is here contradicting himself has been the prevailing view in textbooks and commentaries since the middle of the last century. Thus we find a kind of therapeutic surgery at the

---

3. Pierre Aubenque, *Le Problème de l'être chez Aristote: essai sur la problématique aristotéliciene*, 59–63.

hands first of Paul Natorp,[4] and then, more recently, of Werner Jaeger.[5] Natorp resorted to the classical remedy of the last century, the obelus; while Jaeger replaced this by its modern and more lenient counterpart, stratification. These attempts to solve the fundamental riddle of one science standing for both ontology and theology may be seen as the end points of a whole spectrum of related solutions.

That we are dealing with a single text is generally conceded. But that the elaboration of an ontology is in direct conflict with the enterprise of developing a theology would make, if this is in fact the case, some sort of patchwork out of the text. However, as early as the first book of the *Metaphysics* we find support that there might not be a direct conflict or contradiction between the ontological aim of the text and its theological conclusion. The passage in question reads:

> For the most divine science is also the most honorable; and this science alone must be, in two ways, most divine; for the science which would be the peculiar possession of God is a divine science, and so is any science that deals with divine objects. And this science alone fulfills both these conditions; for (a) all believe that God is one of the causes and a kind of principle, and (b) God is the sole or chief possessor of this sort of knowledge. Accordingly, although all other sciences are more necessary than this, none is more excellent [ἀμείνων]. (*Meta.* 1.2.983a5–11. Cf. *Physics* 2.2.194b14–15: "The mode of existence and the essence of the separable it is the business of first philosophy to determine.")

And if we continue our reading of book 6 we find, immediately after the controversial identification of theology with "first philosophy," a remarkable passage. It reads:

---

4. Paul Natorp, "Thema und Disposition der aristotelischen Metaphysik."
5. W. Jaeger, *Aristoteles: Grundlegung einer Geschichte seiner Entwicklung.*

One might indeed raise the question [ἀπορήσειε γὰρ] whether first philosophy is universal [καθόλου] or deals with some one kind of genus of nature [ἢ περί τι γένος καὶ φύσιν τινὰ μίαν]; for not even the mathematical sciences are all alike in this respect—geometry and astronomy deal with a certain kind of nature [τινα φύσιν], while universal mathematics applies alike to all. We answer that if there is no substance [οὐσία] other than those which are formed by nature, natural science will be the first science; but if there is a changeless substance, the science of this must be prior and must be first philosophy, and universal in this way, because it is first. And it will be the province of this science to study being qua being—both what it is and what the attributes are which belong to it qua being. (*Meta.* 6.1.1026a23–32)

Two problems are at issue here. The first is the problem of relating a science that the divine possesses to a science within the comprehension of human knowledge. This is, speaking strictly, a matter of how what is intelligible *in itself* is intelligible *for us.* And this has to do with the problem of beginning first philosophy.

The first philosophy would be "prior" to the physical sciences, even though it is necessarily postphysical. In book 6, as we have seen, we find Aristotle insisting upon the anteriority of first philosophy with respect to the "secondary" sciences, mathematics and, above all, physics:

Obviously it is the province of a speculative science to discover whether a thing is eternal and immutable and separable from matter; not, however, of physics (since physics deals with mutable objects) nor of mathematics, but of a science prior to both [ἀλλὰ προτέρας ἀμφοῖν]. (*Meta.* 6.1.1026a10–13)

In what sense does the priority of first philosophy consist? The expressions πρότερος (earlier) and ὕστερος (later) are studied in book 5 of the *Metaphysics.* Aristotle distinguishes three senses

(*Meta.* 5.11.1018b19ff.). Priority, or, we might say, anteriority, designates at first a position defined by relation to a point called *first* (πρῶτον) or *starting point* or *principle* (ἀρχή); in general, what is nearer to the starting point is said to be prior in character or anterior, and what is further away, posterior. The relation of anteriority supposes, then, in this case, the preliminary choice of an archē, a choice that can be suggested by nature (φύσει) or arbitrarily (πρὸς τὸ τυχόν). The second type of anteriority is the anteriority according to knowledge (τὸ τῇ γνώσει πρότερον), which is thus designated as anteriority *taken absolutely*. It is subdivided according to whether one takes for its criterion discourse (κατὰ τὸν λόγον) or sensation (κατὰ τὴν αἴσθησιν): in the first case, it is the universal which is prior; in the second, the individual. Finally, the third type of anteriority is the anteriority according to nature and substance (κατὰ φύσιν καὶ οὐσίαν): in this sense are "all things which can exist apart from other things, whereas other things cannot exist without them" (*Meta.* 5.11.1019a1 f.). This is, Aristotle adds, the fundamental sense of anteriority, for all the others can be related to it (*Meta.* 5.11.1019a12). The exposition of book 5 omits, it should be added, a fourth sense, which was given in the *Categories*: there *anterior* designates "the better and more estimable." This is, however, "the most out of the way of all the senses of anteriority" (*Categ.* 12.14b7). The chronological anteriority, which was presented in the *Categories* as "the first and fundamental sense," is not found in book 5 of the *Metaphysics*.

It is, we could argue, in all these senses that anteriority is applied to first philosophy.

Moreover, if first philosophy is prior, then it has to be because Aristotle recognized that the principle or ἀρχή, by which everything else is known, could not itself be known confusedly or haphazardly. Nor could it be obscure. Here we find the idea of an intelligibility *in itself* bound to the essence of that principle, and that seems posed a priori outside of all reference to human knowledge. For Aristotle, true knowledge unfolds itself for itself according to an order that is not solely logical but also chronological: no demonstration is possible if it does not *pre*suppose the truth of its *pre*mises. But for this reason there will be no possible demonstration of beginning: the premises of the first syllogism will be "first and indemonstrable" (*Post. Analyt.* 1.2.71b26). Aristotle insists that there is an inevitable paradox within this double exigency: the premises are first, *although* indemonstrable; but they are also first, *because* indemonstrable, "for otherwise one could know them for want of having the demonstration" (*Post. Analyt.* 1.2.71b27).

Aristotle says precisely in what sense it is necessary to understand this primacy of the premises:

> They must be causes of the conclusion, be more known than it and prior to it: causes, since we have a science of a thing only at the moment when we have known the cause; prior since they are causes; prior, that is, for the point of view of knowledge. (*Post. Analyt.* 1.2.71b29)

The priority of the premises will be at one and the same time logical, chronological, and epistemological: at least it is necessary that these three orders coincide if the demonstration, hence the science, is to be possible. All this is to say that the *idea* of knowledge implies that its order would be the same as that of being; that the ontologically first would be the epistemologically prior.

And, as Aristotle says, "Indeed, the question which was raised long ago, is still and always will be, and which always baffles us—What is being? [τί τὸ ὄν, τοῦτό ἐστι;]" (*Meta.* 7.1.1028b2–4). But this requires that we "render intelligible for us that which is intelligible in itself" (*Meta.* 7.3.1029b7). But, does this latter statement not presuppose that the most intelligible in itself is initially the least intelligible for us?

Let me try to explain. It is the coincidence of the order of knowledge with the order of being that must be clarified first before we can even think of laying bare the conditions for the possibility of first philosophy. But this is to recognize that the problem of beginning takes precedence over the problem of origins: first philosophy, as a properly human vocation, necessarily presupposes an isomorphic relation of the order of knowledge to the order of being; consequently, although we can initiate a "transcendental deduction" of the conditions for the possibility of achieving first philosophy, we would eliminate this very possibility if we did not first inquire how to begin philosophizing authentically. The problem of beginning is the properly human affair; and it is this *initiation* into the philosophic life that is denied to the divine, for to begin to philosophize is to presuppose that the divine has always already and henceforth been philosophizing *sub species aeterni*, which is to say, to begin to philosophize is to presuppose that philosophy is the one vocation denied to the divine. But that the origin of the divine way of life can be only presupposed means that it can never be recuperated: the beginning occludes the origin; yet it is at the same time the attempt to recover the origin from out of the obfuscation the beginning imposes upon it.

The problem of beginning poses itself in analogous terms when it is a question both of epistemology and of ontology. In both cases the impossibility of an infinite regress introduces an absolutely first term: in the first case it is a premise not deduced from any other that is therefore the indemonstrable; in the second case it is an uncaused cause that is the unmoved Prime Mover. But then, how is this principle or ἀρχή to be apprehended? If, being fundamental to all knowledge, it ought to be more known than that which it permits to be known, and if, however, it is not an object of science, since every science demonstrates by proceeding from principles already known, it would perhaps be better to admit a mode of knowledge distinct from science and superior to it: "If we possess no other kind of knowledge than science, it remains that it is *Nous* that will be the beginning of science" (*Post. Analyt.* 2.19.100b13).

I believe Aristotle means by this last statement that *Nous* is only the cognitive correlate of the principle, its mode of being known: it is that without which the principle cannot be known, if it is at least in some sense knowable. The term *Nous* is invoked as a primitive in order to show that first philosophy should be, in principle, humanly possible.

Aristotle occasionally enjoins us to reflect on the relation of divine *Nous* to the human estate, saying, for example:

> If, then, God is always in that good state in which we sometimes are, this compels our wonder; and if in a better state this compels it yet more. And God *is* in a better state. (*Meta.* 12.7.1072b12ff.)

This passage, however, is reminiscent of a statement Aristotle makes in the *Nicomachean Ethics*:

> But such a life would be too high for man; for it is not in so far as he is man that he will live so but in so far as something divine is present [ὑπάρχει] in him. . . . (*Nico. Eth.* 10.8.1177b26ff.)

And he says in the *De Anima* that

> *Nous* is not at one time thinking and at another time not. But only when it is separated is it alone that which it is, and this is the only time when it is immortal and everlasting. (*De An.* 3.5.430a21 ff.)

The suggestion here is that, whereas divine *Nous* is eternal, separable from matter, unchanging and therefore necessary, its entry into the human estate is problematical: it is temporally conditioned, that is, not necessary, but contingent and accidental. In fact, it would seem that its actualization within human existence is not even guaranteed. But if the contemplative life is not necessarily available to us, beginning to live it is doubly problematical, while what we call its origin—the life of the divine *Nous* thinking itself as thought—is doubly necessary. The fall into time of *Nous* does not necessarily engender its own ascension into divine self-thinking thought; and even if this ascent is possible, it does not necessarily mean that the philosopher attains to the eternal repose and composure of the divine form of life but may fall back away from this mode of existence, while the origin of first philosophy necessarily enjoys an eternal and unchanging nature and is necessarily free from the exigencies and afflictions of human existence.

It is here a question of the relationship between necessity and possibility. Aristotle himself discusses this relationship in *De Interpretatione*, concluding that there are two types of possibility (*De Int.* 12.23a8f.), with one relating to what actually is and the other to what we could call ideality. In this light Aristotle notes:

> *In the individual*, potential knowledge is in time prior to actual knowledge but on the whole it is not prior in time. (*De An.* 3.5.430a20–21)

He also notes that:

> The thing that is may be yet may not be. But if we suppose for a moment it either must be or must not be, we rule one alternative out, and 'no need is there that it should not be' (which equally holds of what must be) must follow, therefore, from 'it may be.' (*De Int.* 13.22b22–25)

And:

> In conclusion, then, as the universal must follow upon the particular, so will the possible follow on that which exists of necessity, although not in all of its senses. (*De Int.* 13.23a18–20)

These several passages point to an ambiguous relationship between the necessity of divine *Nous* and the possibility of its realization in human existence. This ambiguity suggests a difficulty in beginning the philosophic life: it is merely possible, yet, if begun, it shares in the necessity enjoyed by the divine form of life. One begins to philosophize truly at a point in time, but once one has begun, one attains existential truths that have always already been and will henceforth be, and in so far one achieves the eternal dimension to human existence. The paradox is this: what is merely possible will get to be seen as what will have been necessary. Alternatively, to participate in the divine life presupposes that we already understand what the divine life is; yet to understand what the divine life is presupposes a prior participation in it.

Easy *in title*, wisdom, although designated as first philosophy, is of all the sciences the most difficult *in fact*. Or rather, there is a wisdom *more than human* which is theoretically simple and easy since its object is of all objects the clearest and most exact, and a *human* philosophy that, moving itself at first to recover the originary presence of things, cannot, as we have seen, maintain this immediate relationship with first principles that Aristotle designates by the term *Nous*. This distortion, this distantiation, between an intelligibility in itself and an intelligibility for us was not novel with Aristotle. The old Parmenides had already objected to Socrates in the Platonic dialogue of that name. Are not the *Ideas*, which the *Cratylus* had posed as conditions for the possibility of knowledge, thus as the realities most intelligible, in fact the least intelligible for us? Is not the human estate the dispersal and distortion of these Ideas? If science is a relation such that the correlative terms are homogenous or at least isomorphic, there will no longer be some science *for us* of things *in themselves* (παρ' ἡμῖν), the science of the truth for us. The old Parmenides draws out the paradoxical conclusion that the divine is unable to know the things according to our standards (*Parmenides* 133aff.). Aristotle himself comments that it is of the nature of divine *Nous* to know only that which is most divine, and the knowledge of things according to our standards would be for it only "a change for the worse" (*Meta.* 12.9.1074b25ff.). Aristotle is also sensitive to the inverse of this paradox: how is the most exact science, the science of what is most manifest (φανερόν), that which is most hidden from us? How is the most intelligible in itself the least intelligible for us?

Again, referring to the aforecited passage (*Meta.* 6.1.1026a 23–32), in which Aristotle argues for the existence of a first philosophy, it would appear that the embarrassing contradiction between a first philosophy which is universal ontology and a first philosophy which, as theology, investigates only the divine substance did not exist for Aristotle: the peculiarity of first philosophy is that it is *at the same time both special and general*; first philosophy is theology of so special a kind that it is *as such at the same time* universal ontology. Aristotle is envisaging here a philosophical discipline that is both a first and a general philosophy, and a substance that is so superior to all other substances that it can at the same time in a certain sense be called substance in general. The underlying thought here is expressed with the quasi-formulaic words καὶ καθόλου οὕτως ὅτι πρώτη ("and universal in this way, because it is first," 1026a30). As Heidegger notes:

> This dual characteristic of πρώτη φιλοσοφία (ontology, theology) does not contain two radically different trains of thought nor should one be weakened or rejected outright in favor of the other. Furthermore, we should not be over-hasty in reconciling this apparent duality. Rather, through an analysis of the problem of "first philosophy" we must throw light upon the reason behind this duality and the manner in which both determinations are connected.[6]

Admittedly, it is not easy to "throw light upon the reason behind this duality," but this much is at least apparent: these two determinations of first philosophy, ontology and theology, essentially belong together and only their conjunction can adequately characterize Aristotle's "first philosophy." It is a question here of showing that a *metaphysica specialis* is at the same time a *metaphysica generalis*, as Kant understood these terms.[7]

---

6. Heidegger, *Kant and the Problem of Metaphysics*, 12.
7. See Immanuel Kant, *Critique of Pure Reason*, A845ff., B873ff. See also Kant, *Über die Fortschritte der Metaphysik seit Leibniz und Wolff*, *Werke*, 8:238, where Kant terms *metaphysica specialis* "true metaphysics," "metaphysics in its final purpose." However, Heidegger argues that the laying of the foundation of *metaphysica generalis* is precisely what guarantees the "intrinsic possibility of the metaphysical project" (cf. Heidegger, *Kant and the Problem of Metaphysics*, 124–29.

I myself wish to explore this riddle of the relationship between ontology and theology, between a *metaphysica generalis* and a *metaphysica specialis*, and I wish to do so by treating Aristotle as if he were being consistent, the various commentaries notwithstanding. I wish to engage Aristotle in such a fashion that the underlying connection between ontology and theology is exposed. That is to say, I wish to see if Aristotle's thought can be played out in such a manner that his "first philosophy" is determined as an autonomous language activity that therefore provides itself with its own intrinsic possibility.

In any event, the philosophical difficulty intonated in the classificatory title τὰ μετὰ τὰ φυσικά, this ambiguous venture designated by the term πρώτη φιλοσοφία, has the curious, nearly unintelligible logic of a koan. It is the great koan of the West. It is the koan of how a "science of being qua being" is possible.

This koan has the fourfold problematic:

1. The elucidation of the fundamental aporia investing philosophy with its possibility and necessity.
2. That "there is a science which studies being qua being."
3. Each science bears upon a determined genus.
4. But being is not a genus.

The problem is one of securing a science the condition for the possibility of which both is determined intrinsically from that science yet is the impossibility of there being such a science.

First, it is necessary to recount why being is not a genus.

It is not possible that that which is universal would be substance, for substance is always subject, while the universal is never anything but predicate. Therefore it is clear that the most universal would also be the least substantial. And being, being the predicate most universal, will also, of all terms, be the least susceptible to becoming the subject of a proposition. Being is said of all things, but nothing can be said rigorously of being. Moreover, if being were a genus, then this genus, being, could have no being, for otherwise this genus would participate in that of which it is the genus, but the genus cannot be predicated of itself: just as the genus animal is not another animal among animals, so too being, as we well know, is not a being among beings. And moreover, if being were a genus, it would comprise several differences, generative of species; but these differences would themselves be beings—since everything is being—and thus, in the case of being, the genus, we would have to conclude that it was attributed to its differences. It would be as if we said the rational, in "man is the rational animal," is itself an animal. But this is impossible. This impossibility, here presented as the immediate result of the very notions of genus and difference, is itself demonstrated in book 4 of the *Topica*. The reason invoked is that, if the genus were to be affirmed of its differences, it would have been affirmed of the species many times over: at first directly, then across the differences: thus, if the reasoning being were animal, it would be superfluous to define man as the reasoning animal, since rationality would always already imply animality.

Furthermore, consider this inverse of the absurdity first placed in evidence by Aristotle: if being were to be a genus, it would comprise differences. But the differences of being would not be beings (since it is not in differences that the genus is divided, but by differences, as Alexander of Aphrodisias noted); they would consequently be nonbeings. To make being a genus, by definition universal, is nothing but to deny the differences of being; this is to make of being an undifferentiated totality. That is to say, at the very moment that one was to have applied the vocabulary of genera, one would have already in advance suppressed being as genus, since genus is a totality always amenable to differentiation. So if being is not to be a genus, this is not because it is that to which one can enjoin no more differences; being does not exclude differences, but it includes all of them—it is absolute positivity—and this is why one can no more say anything of it, if it is true that the instance of discourse is always the composition of a subject and a predicate, where part of the predicate is a genus and the other part is a difference.

But for all that, what is to prevent us from hoping to discover a science of being qua being? Is there a fundamental lack in being that forestalls any and every attempt to say how it stands with being? Or is being, as I have intimated, such a plenum that this standing with being and this how of the standing with being are always already absorbed into being? Or is the lack in us, that we, the human, cannot say how it stands with being? Or perhaps it is the case that every saying says how it stands with being.

But the question is moot, since we are still, two thousand years after Aristotle, driven, driven ineluctably and inescapably, to say how it stands with being. Why must it be that the human estate must be secured in the divergence between the impossible discourse of ontology and the futile discourse of theology, the twinning of tautology and circumlocution, of empty universality and limited generalization? Why do we still think that it is essential to our fate to inscribe its meaning in the contradictory commingling of the impossibility of saying fully how it stands with being and the necessity of attempting this saying? Ontology, it would seem, before we have said anything, is both the forestalling of its own completion and the foreclosure upon its inauguration. Already, in advance of proceeding with ontology, we have fallen short of its discourse but nonetheless have somehow exceeded it. Excess and destitution: the ability to say how it stands with being is always already divided within itself in a mystifying doubling which any saying is now—before it gets said—of two sayings radically excluding each other, namely, the enunciation of how it stands with being and the denunciation of this enunciation. All we can say is that these two sayings destroy the possibility of each other yet grant each other their own proper possibility.

Perhaps we should ask what a "science of being qua being" would be like for it to be a science.

The passage from the particular to the universal is presented as a progression from the infinite to the finite; and this progression is constitutive of science as such, for only the finite is truly knowable, if only to satisfy the scientific demand of stability and certitude: "Again, the more particular the causes are, the more they tend to form an infinite regress, whereas universal demonstration tends towards the simple and finite; and causes qua infinite are not knowable, whereas qua finite they are knowable. Hence causes are more knowable qua universal than qua particular; and therefore universal causes are more demonstrable" (*Post. Analyt.* 1.24.86a4–10). The universal alone can possess true individuality, since it is, alone, the perfectly determined. In finding our passage from the particular and specific to a science of being qua being we court a dual danger: either we lack scientificity by remaining at the level of the particular, in asking what this particular entity is as this particular entity, or we ask after being-in-general and get ourselves caught in a discourse that is both general and empty.

Aristotle was quite sensitive to the fact of each and every science, each and every possible science, that such is the nature of science that any science can easily degenerate into idle speculation, into rococo, evanescent legerdemain. This paradox he resolved by saying that each science is of a universal but there can be no universal science. And, with greater emphasis, there can be no science of all things, for then there would be a science of sciences, but these are infinite, yet a science of the infinite is impossible. Being qua being is not the totality of beings, but "what is common to all things"; it is neither an empty generality nor a discrete particularity.

Moreover, whereas each science proceeds from principles that are appropriate to it and not shared by other sciences (read: genera), these principles are derived from an anterior science. So no science has itself as its own proper foundation; that is, no science is presuppositionless. So there can be no universal science that every other science presupposes. But this is just what the science of being qua being would have to be. This is just what this science would lay claim to being.

Here we begin to suspect that a science of being qua being would necessarily be unlike any other science. It would be infinitely more indirect, suggesting not the linear progression of the other sciences, but rather something like a Chinese box of references back to itself as the principle from which it proceeds. Being is nothing in particular; yet it is nothing in general. So the science appropriate to it would be radically different from those sciences proceeding from generic principles to explanations of particulars. This science would be, rather, a science the sole content of which would consist in demonstrating its own possibility. This would be a science that would examine, to the exclusion of everything else, the principle from which it would proceed. Such would be this science of being qua being that to proceed from the principle appropriate to it would be simply to establish that it is possible to proceed from this principle. The principle, then, from which the science of being qua being proceeds is the principle the nature of which is that all proceeding from it is simply a conscientious attempt to demonstrate that this is the principle from which it is possible to proceed. This is to say that the science of being qua being has only one principle the nature of which is that the proceeding forth from it becomes the principle from which it proceeds recursively back to the original principle. Alternatively said, every proceeding forth is instantly reabsorbed into the principle from which it was to have proceeded, generating in this way an infinitely recursive series of instantiations of proceeding from this principle, yet without having ever actually proceeded from it. Given this recursivity, it would in principle be impossible to stop establishing that this is the principle from which a science of being qua being can proceed. But by virtue of the fact that this recursivity is an inverted one—viz., the next step in the series is a step back to the previous step—it would also be in principle impossible to start proceeding from this principle.

It would appear, were we to pursue the discourse of πρώτη φιλοσοφία, that our inquiries into the problem of establishing such a discourse, which would be begun with exuberant confidence, would end up such that at each level of insight to which we would attain, we would encounter an exponentially increased impasse, an exponentially intensified impassability. The science of being qua being has a ruthlessly aporetic character.

But let us see. And in the process perhaps something unexpected will come to light about our postmodern concern with questioning the legitimacy of the metaphysical vocation, that the postmodern world not only bears an inward dialectical relationship with the properly metaphysical but is itself a troubled term of that relationship, divesting itself of the metaphysical by investing itself with it and investing itself with the metaphysical by divesting itself of it.

So then: the problem is certainly well known. But what can be said in favor of an attempt to dissipate its aporetic character? or barring this, of making this aporia the affirmation of metaphysics, its final cause and not just the condition for beginning to do it?

II

> And so, whether we speak of the metaphorical character of metaphysics or of the metaphysical character of metaphor, what must be grasped is the single movement that carries words and things beyond, *meta*.
>
> Paul Ricoeur, *The Rule of Metaphor*

The problem has the form of trying to determine whether or not the conditions for the possibility of metaphysics are intrinsic to it. It is a question, as Kant wrote in a letter, of the possibility of "a metaphysics of Metaphysics."[8] It is a question of the necessity of effecting a transcendental deduction of the intrinsic possibility of metaphysics, a deduction, Kant reminds us, that can only be *quid juris*. And this deduction, this "metaphysics of Metaphysics," has the inverse structure of the deduction of the impossibility of a meta-metaphorics carried through in "White Mythology."[9] Inverse of it, we may claim, but a deduction the standards and strategies of which are the same as that which in advance renders impossible any and every meta-metaphorics. A "metaphysics of Metaphysics"

---

8. Kant, *Werke*, 9:198.

9. Jacques Derrida, "White Mythology: Metaphor in the Text of Philosophy."

attempts to secure within its own order of discourse the intrinsic possibility of that order, thereby guaranteeing the autonomy of speculative discourse, that is to say, its own self-grounding; but a meta-metaphorics is impossible since it would be derivative with respect to the discourse over which it would claim ascendancy— since it is both impossible to explicate philosophical metaphor from a position external to that discourse and impossible to derive a philosophy of metaphor from within, inasmuch as philosophy deprives itself of what it gives: the one metaphor the more or less, the one metaphor the more that is at the same time the one metaphor the less, the "metaphor of metaphor."[10]

III

And aporicity evokes, rather than prohibits, more precisely promises *through* its prohibition, an other thinking, an other text, the future of another promise. All at once, the impasse (*the dead-end*) becomes the most 'trustworthy', 'reliable' place or moment for reopening a question which is finally equal to or on the same level as that which remains difficult to think.

Jacques Derrida, *Memoires for Paul de Man*

The failure of ontology is manifested, not on one plane, but on two: on the one hand there is no single λόγος of ὄν; on the other, since being qua being is not a genus, there is not even an ὄν that would be one. If we can repeat *a propos* of ontology what we said above of theology, to know that it exhausts itself, but at the same time realizes itself, in the demonstration of its proper impossibility, and thus that the negation of ontology is confounded with the establishment of a negative ontology, we can add here that this ontology is doubly negative: from the first it is negative in its expression, but also in its object. The negativity of ontology expresses not only the impotence of human discourse, but the very negativity of its object. The consequence is that here these two negativities, far from being taken together in order to make of ontology nothing but the shadow of a shadow, end by setting

---

10. Ibid., 17–18.

each against the other: the difficulty [*l'embarras*] of human discourse on being becomes the more true expression of the contingency of being. Being is no longer this inaccessible object that would be beyond our discourse; rather, it reveals itself in the very gropings that we make in order to reach it: being, at least this being of which we speak, is nothing other than the correlate of our difficulty. The failure of ontology becomes ontology of contingency, that is to say, of finitude and failure. It is this overturning that lets itself be recognized in the fact that *aporia* is itself the measure of philosophizing: the infinite repetition of the question "what is being?" becomes the image resembling most a being that is never quite what it is and in the end, therefore, never coinciding with itself. The absence of path (πόρος) becomes the plurality of ways: the incapacity of human discourse to extricate the unique signification of the word *being* does not lead to denying of it all signification, but rather leads to letting arise the irreducible plurality of the categories where it reveals itself. One could say of philosophy what Sophocles says of man, that he is a παντόπορος ἀπόρος (Antigone, v. 360), a being so much the richer in resources than it is destitute.

Pierre Aubenque, *Le Problème de l'être chez Aristote*

The procedure throughout the *Metaphysics* never becomes deductive; it always remains aporematic. . . . Aristotle's frequent description of metaphysics as the science of principles itself suggests that it is not meant to get beyond principles to conclusions.

W. D. Ross, *Aristotle's Metaphysics I*

How, then, to begin the conception and enactment of metaphysics? How, then, to give to it its own name, the name of the Orphic seal and signature of being? With wonder, of course, for Aristotle tells us, "It is through wonder [θαυμάζειν] that men now begin [ἤρξαντο] and originally [τὸ πρῶτον] to philosophize" (*Meta.* 1.2.982b12–13); for philosophy begins by "wondering that things should be as they are" (*Meta.* 1.2.983a13). He also tells us, in the *Nicomachean Ethics*, that "the beginning [ἡ ἀρχή] is admittedly more than half the whole" (*Nico. Eth.* 1.7.1098b7).

The correlate of this wonder, this astonishment that things are that they are what they are, is termed ἀπορία for Aristotle, by which he means *perplexity, bewilderment, impasse*, literally *loss of* passage. Both the difficulty of beginning philosophy and the carrying through of the philosophic venture and vocation, ἀπορία is, for Aristotle, the essential moment of philosophical inquiry. Ἀπορία is just one of a threefold consisting of ἀπορεῖν, διαπορεῖν, and εὐπορεῖν: "Now for those who wish to get rid of perplexities and impasses [ἀπορουμένα] it is a good plan [εὐπορῆσαι] to go into them thoroughly [διαπορῆσαι]" (*Meta*. 3.1.995a26); "for the subsequent certainty [ὕστερον εὐπορία] is a release [λύσις] from the previous perplexities and impasses [ἀπορουμένων]" (*Meta*. 3.1.995a28): "For to solve a difficulty is to find the answer to a problem" (*Nico. Eth*. 7.2.1146b7: ἡ γὰρ λύσις τῆς ἀπορίας εὕρεσίς ἐστιν); ". . . those who start an inquiry without first considering the difficulties [ἄνευ τοῦ διαπορῆσαι] are like people who do not know where they are going; besides, one does not even know whether the thing required has been found or not" (*Meta*. 3.1.995a34).

Ἀπορία, then, is central to the investigation of being qua being. Philosophy is not born out of a spontaneous *élan* of the spirit, but from the pressure of the phenomena. Things manifest themselves, impose themselves upon us as contradictions and contradictories. They force us, in spite of ourselves, to work our way through their contradictoriness, to find our way in a pathless realm. In his historical studies Aristotle speaks often of a "constraint of the truth [ὑπ' αὐτῆς τῆς ἀληθείας . . . ἀναγκαζόμενοι]" (*Meta*. 1.3.984b9) and of the necessity of the philosopher to "follow the phenomena [Παρμενίδης . . . ἀναγκαζόμενος δ ἀκολουθεῖν τοῖς φαινομένοις]" (*Meta*. 1.5.986b31). Yet the constraints imposed by the phenomena do not eliminate the intractability of experience but constitute its advent, for they are of themselves invested with a contradictoriness: we are constrained by the ever-present pressure of things because they dwell in a mute resistance to disclosure, in an irreconcilability and impermeability within themselves. However we respond to the phenomena—either by listening to them speak for themselves or by saying their nature— it is clear that we will have to chart our passage through a malignant and lingering aporia.

Astonishment in the face of the fact that things are is not a question; it also cannot be expressed as a question; and therefore there is no answer to it. It is the *self-manifestation* of the limit of intelligibility. This limit manifests itself *from within* intelligibility. It is this we initially designate as *aporia*. In this sense 'aporia' is the expression in the form of a question of what conceals this aporia. In our astonishment we think there is something deep, something hidden, about the fact that things are; we look for something behind things, we look for something "deeper" than the simple description of what is, than its bare intelligibility. 'Aporia' here signifies that we are always trying to say more than we know, more than we can know, that we mistake the solution for something that looks as if it were only a preliminary step to it. We want constantly to go behind the immediate intelligibility of things. But what might be behind the immediate intelligibility of things cannot itself be made intelligible. The unintelligible, of course, does not make itself known, cannot make itself known, unless *that* fact is what makes itself known. And *that* is the experience of aporia. *Aporia* is the approaching of unintelligibility. But unintelligibility never arrives, for the disclosure of the unintelligible would be its reduction into intelligibility. In this sense *aporia* is the *heterogeneity of signification* that draws one toward the point where meaning and sense collapse and vacate themselves. We are fascinated with the uncanny possibility of apprehending what precedes intelligibility.

Let us suppose, then, taking our cue from these aforementioned passages, that human existence would be naturally in a state of aporia, that it would in fact be deprived of νοῦς, even if the latter belongs to its essence: the preliminary philosophical investigation will become an indefinite contest waged against an aporia that is always threatening to take over and the advent of true knowledge that will be indefinitely deferred.[11] In this vein Aristotle tells us that it is incumbent upon the science of being qua being to "render intelligible for us that which is intelligible in itself" (*Meta.* 7.3.1029b7), for what is intelligible to us is that

---

11. Cf. Aubenque, *Le Problème de l'être chez Aristote: essai sur la problématique aristotélicienne*, 59–63.

when we try to understand what is intelligible in itself we become infinitely perplexed.

But if aporia initiates, enables, and empowers the investigation of being qua being, then, as a preliminary or prolegomena, it would be necessary to understand this term or concept *aporia*. Here there is hesitancy; here there is uncertainty; for it would seem that at this stage in the investigation the word 'aporia' can only be understood aporetically, according to its own aporetic structures of dispersion and deflection and defection. It would seem that the question concerning aporia is itself part of the aporia. It would be a misunderstanding to try to hold to a literal understanding of the word, that it is an absence of path, a paralysis before roadblocks, the immobilization of thinking, the impossibility of advancing, a barrier blocking the inbreaking of new possibilities. That is to say that the attempt to understand the word or concept 'aporia' is necessarily a self-eliminating process: if aporia can be understood at all, then it cannot be understood at all, for the understanding of it would dispel and ultimately abolish the very thing that is to be understood; yet if aporia cannot be understood, then this is precisely what is understood and so is itself understood to be what cannot be understood. The question of the nature of aporia makes of the very question an instance of aporia and so does away with this question. That is to say, the question of the nature of aporia is self-eliminating. But it is self-eliminating to the extent that even the insight into this self-eliminating nature of the question is itself eliminated. Aporia is, then, the paradox of its own auto-implication.

The discourse on aporia necessarily betrays aporia, making of it something from which thinking can advance, turning it, then, into what it is not, its opposite; yet aporia undoes this discourse, renders it impossible. It is as if no thought could suffice to think aporia. It is, in this sense, inexperienced; it is what escapes the very possibility of experience.

Like God for Descartes, aporia is not anything subjectivity could have thought up on its own, for, in exceeding our capacity to think it, it discloses, not itself, but the inability of subjectivity to account for itself. *Aporia* names not so much a difficulty of passage but the rite of passage, that subjectivity, in coming to terms with itself, discovers itself to be a term of a relationship the other term of which is the undermining of this relationship. In wanting to come to terms with itself, subjectivity wants to define itself on its own terms and in its own terms. But if subjectivity is itself the attempt to establish a relation to itself, then there is always already an irreparable duality—necessary, essential, and fundamental—within subjectivity. Without such a division within subjectivity, the relation to itself that constitutes subjectivity would be structurally impossible. Subjectivity is, then, the activity of putting itself out of phase with itself. But if this is the case, then subjectivity could never define itself in its own terms, could never come to be what it is on its own terms or in its own terms.

Again, insofar as subjectivity attempts to relate itself to itself, that is, to relate to itself on its own terms and in its own terms, it puts itself out of phase with itself. And this activity of putting itself out of phase with itself in order to consolidate itself opens up within this self-dirempting the purely aporetic event of being, namely the non-self-coincidence that is subjectivity. *Aporia*, then, names, not so much this or that difficulty, but rather the essence of subjectivity, that it can never be on equal terms with itself, that, in trying to come into itself fully in its own terms and trying to relate to itself on its own terms, it is always coming into itself in terms other than its own, and it is always relating to itself on terms other than its own. Subjectivity, insofar as it is self-dehiscence, cannot comprehend the terms of its contract with itself: it comes to itself *otherwise than* on its own terms, *otherwise than* in its own terms, in terms of *something else entirely*, by virtue of what is without term.

But this *otherwise than itself*, this *something else entirely*, by which subjectivity is established is not anything that subjectivity could discover on its own, for this *otherwise*, this *something else entirely*, is itself revealed in terms other than subjectivity, in terms of something else entirely than subjectivity, in terms, therefore, of what is without term. That subjectivity could never discover this on its own is what is indicated by the term *aporia*. *Aporia* designates, then, that even this insight into the inability of subjectivity to define itself in and on its own terms is itself eliminated in the process of being elaborated: this insight cannot be experienced or disclosed, yet it must be presupposed. But if it is presupposed, then everything becomes infected with a factor of *otherwise than itself*, of *something else than itself*.

Aporia, consequently, designates the inapprehensibility of aporia. Yet the term *aporia* nonetheless signifies. And if it signifies its own inapprehensibility, it does so as the intrigue in subjectivity of an unaccountability, that, even if there is nothing but the accountability of subjectivity to and for itself, this accountability is itself unaccountable, unaccountably unaccountable. The term *aporia* designates the existential basis of the understanding, that there is a blind spot, a corner it cannot look around, a "that" which it cannot get around, namely, understanding itself and understanding itself in terms of its existential basis. The understanding of this problematic of unaccountability precludes realizing it existentially, for in understanding it it becomes accountable. But realizing this problematic existentially consists precisely in abandoning every attempt to understand it, in which case it no longer is at issue and so gets eliminated as a problem. *Aporia* designates that for beings to be the beings that they are they must be seen to be what they are when no one is looking at them; it designates what things look like without us looking at them. In terms of subjectivity, the term *aporia* signifies that, in order to see what I really am, I must see what I look like when I am not looking at myself. But since this is impossible, *aporia* names the impossibility of apprehending things *otherwise than* we always already have and the impossibility of apprehending *something else* than what we always already have.

Yet this impossibility is something we come upon. It is, to quote Aristotle, a "knot" (*Meta.* 3.1.995a31) in the things themselves. This impossibility is a breaching of the intelligibility of things, a disaster that precedes beings being the beings they are. Aporia, the silent rupture of the fragmentary, the interruption of the incessant, overcomes thought, comes over thought as a disaster that has always already taken place in an immemorial and irrecuperable past. Aporia is the unheedable unlimited; it cannot be measured in terms of failure or as a pure and simple absence of passage. It does not have the ultimate for a limit; it bears the ultimate away in and into aporia.

But not only does the discourse on aporia necessarily betray it in attempting to make sense out of it; the discourse of aporia is *itself* betrayed by aporia: understanding essentially misunderstands itself if it attempts to understand the term *aporia*—for this term undoes the understanding. Yet understanding essentially misunderstands itself if it does not attempt to understand this term.

For these reasons it should be apparent that the meaning of the term *aporia* can be experienced only, but it can be experienced only in the most indirect way, as a breaching promising the thinking of a path, as a breaching promising the thinking of the very possibility of what still remains unthinkable or unthought, impossible. But if aporia can be experienced indirectly only—and not thought as such—then this is because this term outstrips any and every attempt to think it, overturning thought in general in the process.

If I begin to question by being overcome with aporia, aporia nonetheless does not put me or anything else into question, but annuls the question while showing or by showing the inexhaustible questionability of everything. Aporia annuls the question, makes it disappear—as if, along with the question, "I" too disappeared in an aporia that could never appear. The fact of disappearing is precisely not a fact, not an event; it does not happen, not only because it eliminates the "I" that would undergo the experience but also because aporia always takes place as having already taken place, and so precedes the experience of it. Aporia presupposes itself, not before it is encountered, but in that it can be encountered. The encountering of aporia presupposes that it has been encountered in an aporetic way; but this aporetic encountering is itself something that can never be encountered as such.

But if aporia is the foundering of thought, it is so only because it is at the same time the funding of thought. Things make sense. It is impossible not to make sense out of things. That things make sense is the very impossibility of things not making sense. So things make sense only insofar as aporia makes none. In not making sense, aporia signifies that things make sense, signifies that everything can be made sense of. In making sense, things make nonsense out of the very term *aporia*. Yet that there even is the word or concept *aporia* means that not-making-sense is a possibility that can overtake anything and everything, that can overturn it, denature it, turning it into the ruination of itself.

To understand the term *aporia* is not simply to understand the not-making-sense of things, but rather it is to understand that *it is possible* for things not to make sense—even if they always already have been made sense of. But to understand this is to concede that before they were made sense of, things did not make sense. But the time when things did not make sense is a time that precedes every recuperable past, a time that is more remote than any time, that is time immemorial: things always already and in a thoroughly passive way have been made sense of. Aporia, then, designates an immemorial and irrecuperable past, a time prior to the possibility of experience.

Yet there is the term *aporia*. That there is this term indicates that at the limit of their making sense is the possibility that things ultimately cannot be made sense of. It is when we are at the limit of making sense of things that we are concerned with how it is that things make sense. And so the issue of how it is that things make sense is therefore precisely that moment when aporia breaks in. If aporia is the paradox of its own auto-implication, it is also the paradox that the intelligibility of things is simply an allegory of their unintelligibility. As the threat of an inbreaking of infinite nonsense, aporia is that *from* which thinking properly *emerges*, *toward* which thinking tends, and *against* which it is shattered.

Just as Aristotle says that it is impossible to hold a false view of the law of contradiction, so is it impossible for things not to make any sense.

The law of contradiction is the most certain of principles,

for it is that about which one cannot be mistaken (*Meta.* 4.3. 1005b11–20; 11.5.1061b34–36). "Hence all men who are demonstrating anything refer back to this as an ultimate belief; for it is by nature the starting point of all other axioms as well" (*Meta.* 4.3.1005b32–34). Now, in order to refute this principle one must subscribe to it, for to argue that the same thing can at one and the same time be and not be is to assume that this statement itself is both true and false. But if it is true, then this statement is itself both true and false, and to that extent it is false; yet if it is false, then it could never be true. Moreover, if nothing can be truly affirmed, then this very statement—that there is no such thing as a true affirmation—will itself be false.

Analogously, and on a perhaps more fundamental or ontological level, it could never make sense that things do not make sense, for if anyone asserts that things do not make sense, then he would have conceded that they do make sense, namely, the sense it makes to assert that things do not make sense.

Since *aporia* raises the issue of sense, aporia is felt as a phenomenological pressure first and foremost in the case of the enownment of word and world to one another. According to Werner Jaeger,[12] Aristotle was the first "to break the bond between the word and the thing, between the λόγος and the ὄν" and the first to elaborate a theory of *signification*, that is, of the separation *and* the relationship between language as *sign* and being as *signified*. His theory of language can be summed up in two propositions:

1. We use names to refer to things.
2. Nonetheless, there is no complete resemblance between the names and the things they signify.

These two propositions show that language is not so much an "image" or an "imitation" of being, as the sophists thought, but solely a "symbol," which ought to be defined as a sign in order

---

12. W. Jaeger, *Aristoteles: Grundlegung einer Geschichte seiner Entwicklung*, 395–96.

to bring out its conventionality. Or better: the force of Aristotle's meditations on language is the discovery that language does not manifest (οὐ δηλῷ), but signifies, not as a natural instrument of signifying but by convention (κατὰ συνθήκην). As signification, language presupposes an ontological distance between the word and the thing—but only in order to suppress this distance. Yet this distance can never be completely suppressed. This is graphically displayed in Aristotle's refutation of the naive confounding of word and thing: words are limited in number while things are infinite in number. One and the same word necessarily signifies a plurality of things, and the equivocity, which Aristotle calls homonymy, far from being a simple accident of language, appears from the start as an essential vice.

Yet, as Derrida notes, that a word may have several senses is a fact which

> has no right in language except to the extent that the plurality of meaning is finite, that the different meanings are limited in number, and above all sufficiently *distinct*, each one remaining single and identifiable. Language is what it is— language is language only to the extent that it can control and analyze plurality of meaning. And without remainder. A spread which cannot be controlled is not even a plurality of language: it belongs outside language.[13]

The suggestion is that since words, though necessarily homonymous, have an identifiable and finite number of meanings, they do not actually give us the being named, which after all is one among an infinite number, but simply its invocation into the linguistic world. The suggestion is that the infinitely many things cannot enter into the linguistically enhorizoned world, but rather can only be invoked in order to serve as their own tokens and indices.

Aristotle certainly recognizes this in his discussion of equivo-

---

13. Derrida, "White Mythology," 49.

cation in Book Gamma of the *Metaphysics*, a text that will provide us with great insight to aid us in declining an autonomous order of discourse.

> And it makes no difference even if it be said that "man" has several meanings, provided that they are limited in number; for we could only assign a different name to each formula [λόγῳ]. For instance, it might be said that "man" has not one meaning but several, one of which has the formula [λόγος] "two-footed animal," and there might be other formulae as well, if they are limited in number; for a particular name [ἴδιον ὄνομα] could be assigned to each formula. If, on the other hand, it be said that "man" has an infinite number of meanings, obviously there can be no discourse [λόγος]; for not to have one meaning is to have no meaning, and if words have no meaning there is an end of discourse with others [διαλέγεσθαι πρὸς ἀλλήλους] and even, strictly speaking, with oneself [κατὰ δὲ τὴν ἀλήθειαν]. Because it is impossible to think of anything if we do not think of one thing; and even if this were possible, one name must be assigned to that which we think. (*Meta.* 4.4.1006a34–1006b13)

And again:

> . . . for between names and things there is no complete resemblance: the names are limited in number, so also then the plurality of definitions, whereas the things are indeterminable in number [τὰ δὲ πράγματα τὸν ἀριθμὸν ἄπειρά ἐστιν]. It is inevitable that several things would be signified and these by one definition and by one and the same word. (*Soph. Refut.* 1.165a10ff.)

It is not necessary to believe that "that which happens in names happens in things" (*Soph. Refut.* 1.165a9).

Every case in which a multivocity of meanings is irreducible, in which there is not even a promise of a unity of sense, is a case, it would seem, in which we are beyond language. While the philosopher is by his own word taken beyond signs and names in his quest for truth, and the sophist manipulates empty signs and derives his effect from the contingency of signifiers (hence his taste for the equivocal and in the first place for homonymy), the poet on the other hand makes play of the multiplicity of things signified in order to come back again to a univocity of meaning. As Aristotle puts it:

> Homonyms are chiefly used to enable the sophist to mislead his hearers. Synonyms are useful to the poet, by which I mean words whose ordinary meaning [κύρια, not ἴδιον] is the same. (*Rhet.* 3.2.1404b37–1405a1; also cf. *Meta.* 11.5.1062a14ff.)

The suggestion is, then, if we read these words carefully enough, that the philosopher occupies a third place in language, one in which plurivocity of meanings is irreducible by an endeavor to achieve a sort of escape velocity in and from language. The third place would be one where language would be pressed to infiltrate the alien world of things, a spy in the house of things covertly supplying a clandestine and complicit commentary.

If, then, the analysis of language guards us against overlooking the inevitable equivocity of words, the reality of communication brings us, on the other hand, to see in univocity the *telos* aimed at by philosophical inquiry, since without it all rigor would be impossible. From this perspective the contingency of signification confounds itself with the demand for unity within signification. But the question is: how are we to reconcile this unity of signification with the indeterminate plurality of signifieds? To develop a response to this question, a question that is decisive for determining the autonomy of philosophical discourse, I first note that Aristotle distinguishes between the ultimate *signified*, which is multiple and in the final analysis infinite, since language signifies individuals, and *signification*, which is that through which the signified is pursued. Although this distinction perhaps may not be made explicitly by Aristotle, it results from the comparison between two series of remarks: on the one hand, we find that the same word "signifies several things [πλείω σημαίνειν]" (*Soph. Refut.* 1.165a12); on the other hand, it "has many significations [πολλαχῶς λέγεσθαι]" (*Meta.* 7.1.1028a10; 6.4.1028a5; 5.7.1017a24). In the first case the accusative indicates that it is a question of the *quid* of signification; in the second, the adverb indicates that it is a question of the *how* of signification.

I also note that, on the basis of these remarks, signification would seem to presuppose a relative permanence to essence as the foundation of the unity of sense: words have a sense only because things have an essence. But this implies that not only is the principle of identity posed by language but it is supposed by language as that which is on this side of all language, because it is the foundation of it: the principle, not only logical but ontological, of contradiction is from the first recognized by Aristotle as the condition for the possibility of language.[14] But the principle of identity concerns the nature of being; so that what language presupposes as its condition of possibility is, as it were, the exchange rate between the word and the thing: that things are in principle identifiable. But this is precisely what prevents language from enjoying direct commerce with the world of things. Instead, all is infiltration and covert commentaries on the impossibility of maintaining a fair and bilateral exchange rate.

But if the principle of identity holds sway over language and even holds language together, it would seem clear that there is an ontology at the basis of language. But how, then, can this ontology be elicited, if Aristotle's contribution to the theory of language has been to clear the distance separating λόγος from ὄν? This would seem to discourage any and every ontological adventure.

We speak. We speak about something, and we understand each other. This is to say that we speak within being, or rather, that "we speak" implies that being is always already supposed by

---

14. Aubenque, *Le Problème de l'être chez Aristote*, 128–30.

language, and a fortiori philosophical language, as its "objective" horizon. Not only is all language immediate discourse about being, but it is a discourse that can be constituted only if being is supposed as the ground of its intelligibility. The Aristotelian theory of language presupposes an ontology.

But not only is there an ontology, the possibility of which is guaranteed by the intelligibility of discourse, this ontology is reflected in all discourse. In elaborating a theory of language Aristotle was, for this reason, led to posit the existence of objective unities of signification that he called essences. "But to signify a substance means that the essence is that and nothing else [Τὸ δ' οὐσίαν σημαίνειν ἐστὶν ὅτι οὐκ ἄλλό τι τὸ εἶναι αὐτῷ]" (*Meta.* 4.4.1007a27).

The unity of signification expresses and supposes the incompatibility of these essences, but the equivocity inherent in language disrupts and disperses the unity of each of these essences, casting over the entire ontological project an indefiniteness and indeterminacy. Because of the plurivocity intrinsic to language it would seem that the ontological venture is always defeated in advance of itself. There just doesn't seem to be much controlling the slip-sliding shifting of sense that animates discourse. By this, authentic philosophical discourse would be rendered impossible, mute, moot.

The problem is to preserve the plurivocity of the signification of being while (or in) vouchsafing its unity of sense. Whereas the sophists, in the name of usury and utility, rendered impossible an ontology that would be coherent, and whereas the Megarics, in the name of the ontological injunction of Parmenides, rendered impossible an ontology that would be fecund, Aristotle, by appealing to the aporia conditioning human experience, sought an ontology that was both coherent and fecund—and this by noting that "being is said in many ways [τὸ ὂν λέγεται πολλαχῶς]" (*Meta.* 4.2.1003a33). Being is a polyvalence.

But a decisive question poses itself here as to the legitimacy of the ontological project: how can being have multiple significations without human discourse falling into nonsense and even denying itself in that way as signifying discourse?

If the unity of signification appears as the condition for the possibility of an intelligible dialogue and of a coherent thought, as we have seen (*Meta.* 4.4.1006b7), does not the multiplicity of signification—which we are constrained to recognize—to the most fundamental word of all, the word *being*, go to risk ruining this dialogue and this thought? But this is an impossible consequence, in truth, because it is controverted by fact; and this is also an absurd consequence, because it is the analysis of the conditions of possibility of discourse that has led us to the distinction of the significations of being. Here we have the first intimation of that of which the science of being qua being would have to be constituted: such a science would study the conditions for the possibility of that which denies its own possibility. But, then, the condition for the possibility of such a science would be the impossibility of instituting such a science, for such a science would deconstruct scientific discourse, destroying the possibility of scientific discourse. In this way such a science would put its own intrinsic possibility radically into question, with interminable reiteration, such that, as we have seen, to proceed from the principle establishing such a science is to proceed back to the establishing of this science, with the effect of indefinitely deferring the establishment of this science. Since to proceed from the principle establishing this science is to establish that this is the principle from which it is possible to proceed, the science of being qua being disestablishes itself in ascertaining that it has properly established itself, for it never could become the case that it is possible to proceed from this principle. There is no actual proceeding from this principle, only that, in principle, this is the principle from which it is possible to proceed.

It is necessary, then, to interrogate the status of the multiple ways of saying being. Being, we have seen, is a πολλαχῶς λεγόμενον (a being-said-in-many-ways). But what does this πολλαχῶς imply? Does it indicate that the word considered is said of several different subjects? But if it were, every name—save for the proper name—would be said πολλαχῶς in virtue of this statement. We have also already seen that the things are singular while language is general. There is, in this sense, a fundamental and irreducible ambiguity to human discourse, and it is natural that the word ὄν, the most general of all, bears, more than all others, this indeterminate relation to an indenumerable plurality of subjects. But it is one thing to signify several things, quite another to signify in multiple fashion: it is to the adverbial form of πολλαχῶς and πλεοναχῶς (multiply), more than to the idea of multiplicity, that it is necessary to adhere. The word *being*, as in the general way of πολλαχῶς λεγόμενα, does not only signify different things, but it signifies them in different ways; and we can never be sure that it has the same sense each time. It is a question here of a plurality of significations, and not just of a plurality of signifieds; it is a question here of the plurivocity in the relationships, already ambiguous, of the sign to the signified.

IV

. . . if we are to understand Aristotle correctly, we should not oppose the two apparently contradictory definitions of 'first philosophy' and attempt to decide in favor of one or the other, but should rather try to understand the assertion that these two definitions essentially belong together and that only their conjunction adequately characterizes Aristotle's 'first philosophy'. Our understanding of this basic theme naturally depends in turn upon our success in comprehending that metaphysical relationship in virtue of which what is true of the 'first' is true universally, or—to phrase it in a less Aristotelian way—in virtue of which reasoned judgments about the whole domain of being can be provided by a science that deals with a determinate part of that domain.

Günther Patzig,
"Theologie und Ontologie in der 'Metaphysik' des Aristoteles"

It is the ontology of Aristotle, and not his theology, that should be understood as *metaphysica specialis*, metaphysics of particularity, of

> the exception, no longer this time highest or fullest, but deficient, that constitutes, by relation to essential being [*l'Etre*], the being of the sublunar world.
> Pierre Aubenque, *Le Problème de l'être chez Aristote*

> It is theology, and not ontology, that is disclosed as the theory of any being whatsoever, of a being of which there is nothing to say; it is on the contrary ontology that, insofar as it seeks a unity within the scission is constituted as metaphysics of finitude and of the accidental, responds to the astonishment before what is not of itself.
> Pierre Aubenque, *Le Problème de l'être chez Aristote*

We have seen in detailing the problems attendant upon classifying Aristotle's πρώτη φιλοσοφία that Aristotle appears to recognize a quite peculiar relationship of part to whole—at least when posed in ontological terms. But I have just suggested that Aristotle's theory of language, that is, his formal logic, presupposes an ontology. So it would seem necessary to elaborate precisely this ontological relationship of part to whole, for it would seem to be at the basis of all of Aristotle's philosophy—and that means, above all, at the basis of the metaphysical yearning to give a comprehensive account of the all.

But what of this relationship of part to whole? Of being in the first instance to being in general? We have seen that Aristotle codifies this relationship of *metaphysica specialis* and *metaphysica generalis*, of theology and ontology, as καὶ καθόλου οὕτως ὅτι πρώτη ("and universal in this way, because it is first") (*Meta.* 6.1.1026a30). The part in some way supplies the content and principle of the whole. If language and logic presuppose an ontology, if the philosophical disciplines depend upon ontology, then we might expect to find this metaphysical relationship between privileged part and whole in the other philosophical disciplines. In fact, Aristotle provides us with a large array of such cases; and, as we might suspect, this metaphysical structure, which is given the name πρὸς ἕν λέγεσθαι ("be so called in relation to some one thing") in the *Metaphysics*, has a not inconsiderable standing among Aristotle's modes of arguments.

The simplest example appears in book 2 of the *Metaphysics*. At the end of the first chapter (993b23–26) fire is described as being "most hot" (μάλιστα θερμόν) in the sense that everything else that is called hot only possesses this quality by virtue of the fire contained in or working on it. In this way, fire has a special position in the class of hot things; it is both itself a hot thing and the cause and principle of heat in other things.

Furthermore, in book 4 of the *Metaphysics*, where Aristotle expressly posits the existence of the "sought-for" "science of being qua being," he notes:

> The term 'being' is said in many ways, but with reference to one central thing and one definite nature, and not merely as a common epithet. Thus the term 'healthy' always relates to health (either as preserving it or as producing it or as indicating it or as receptive to it), and as 'medical' relates to the art of medicine (either as possessing it or as naturally adapted for it or as being a function of medicine)—and we shall find other terms used similarly to these—so 'being' is said in many ways but always with reference to one principle [τό ὂν λέγεται πολλαχῶς μέν, ἀλλ' ἅπαν πρὸς μίαν ἀρχήν]. (*Meta.* 4.2.1003a33–1003b6)

Thus, clothing is called—and is—healthy if it preserves health; medicine if it restores it; healthy complexions indicate health, etc. Things that are, and are called, healthy stand in differing relationships to health itself. Health, Aristotle is here arguing, is the source of healthiness in everything else; it is both healthy itself and the cause and principle of being healthy—it is the "first healthy thing" (πρῶτον ὑγιεινόν). In both these cases, Aristotle only adduces these concrete examples as graphic models for abstract relationships: the case of fire is supposed to illuminate the dependence of everything true on what is "truest by nature"; the examples of health and of the medical are supposed to clarify how "being is said in many ways," of how being has many senses. From here Aristotle elaborates how things are said to "be" because they are substances (οὐσίας), and then modifications of substances, or processes toward substance, or privations or destructions or qualities of substance, or productive or generative of substance or of terms relating to substance. Qualities, substances, processes, and relations are fundamentally different from each other as beings. But Aristotle says:

> For it is not only in the case of things which are according to one way of saying [οὐ γὰρ μόνον τῶν καθ' ἕν λεγομένων] does the investigation belong to one science, but also in the case of things which are related to one common nature; for even these have in a sense one common nature. (*Meta.* 4.2.1003b12–15)

It is, then, precisely this καθ' ἕν and this πρὸς ἕν that forms the kernel of the problem of the relation of *metaphysica specialis* to *metaphysica generalis*: in what sense is the first first? Aristotle naturally suggests that "in every case knowledge is principally concerned with that upon which other things depend and in virtue of which they get their name" (*Meta.* 4.2.1003b16). Thus ontology, although it is the science of being qua being and universal, is nonetheless the science of the "first being."

As further evidence that this relationship of some favored part to the whole was a natural element in Aristotle's thought, we have his celebrated *mots* in the *De Anima* (3.8.432a1–2) that "as the hand is the tool of tools so reason is the form of forms and perception the form of sensible things." It is not simply a question here of the hand being superior as a tool than all other tools; Aristotle does not mean simply that. Rather, the human hand is only an illuminating image for the obscure relationship that obtains between human nous and the other forms or εἴδη: the hand is a tool among other tools, and yet it is also true that these latter tools are only raised to their status as tools through the activity of the hand. Aristotle says in *De Partibus Animalium*: "Take the hand: this is as good as a talon or a claw or a horn, or again a spear or sword, or any other weapon or tool: it can be all of these because it can seize and hold them all" (*PA* 4.10.687b2–5). Without a hand to use them, all other tools could no longer properly be called tools. Tools are, ontologically speaking, a function of the human hand— the human hand is the ἕν to which all tools bear a reference. This analogy can perhaps illumine the famous and controversial words that follow in Aristotle's text: νοῦς, human reason, is the "εἶδος of εἴδη," the "form of forms" (*De An*. 3.8.432a2).

Without specifying in detail how Aristotle came to regard the Prime Mover as the "first" in the study of being, I think we can see how his thinking was tending toward the idea that ontology is at the same time theology. Alexander of Aphrodisias has the felicitous expression for this: he says that in his ontology Aristotle treats the substance of the Prime Mover προηγουμένως—"with special preference."

Another way of considering the duality involved in elaborating first philosophy, that ontology and theology are the conditions for each other's possibility, can be developed by considering Aristotle's idea of "the good." In the first place let us note that Aristotle devotes arguments to the question of the ontological nature of "the idea of the good." These arguments are logical in nature and are designed to display the contradictoriness of the idea of the good. In *Eudemian Ethics* Aristotle notes a strict parallel of the good with being: "οὐδὲ τὸ ὂν ἕν τι ἐστὶ περὶ τὰ εἰρημένα . . . [being is not one thing in all that we have spoken of (and neither is the good)]" (*EE* 1.8.1217b33). This argument precludes any being-for-itself (χωριστόν) of the idea of the good. But in saying this Aristotle has committed himself it seems, not only to the impossibility of a science of the good but also to the impossibility of a science of being as such (1.8.1217b34). Obviously the *Nicomachean Ethics*, as well as the *Magna Moralia*, seeks to avoid this consequence. Hence, when the *Nicomachean Ethics* uses the same arguments, it speaks only of the good and rules out that it could be "something universal corresponding to a single idea [κοινόν τι κατὰ μίαν ἰδέαν]" (*Nico. Eth*. 1.6.1096a28).

The kind of arguments that follow is taken from the sciences and based on the notion that the good is not a category, not a genus. According to it, knowledge of the good disappears among the particular arts (τέχναι). Aristotle here rejects the possibility of a science of the good: σχολῇ αὐτό γε τὸ ἀγαθὸν θεωρῆσαι μιᾶς (there can hardly be a sole theorizing about the good itself) (*EE* 1.8.1218a1) or ἦν ἂν μία τις ἐπιστήμη (there would have to be [but cannot be] a single science) (*Nico. Eth.* 1.6.1096a30).

The second argument offered in the *Eudemian Ethics* is designed to demonstrate that the good cannot be both something in common and something for itself (κοινόν καὶ χωριστόν). Just as there are no ideas of the numbers because there could be no idea of number as such (because if the idea of number, number per se, were what is first, the first number would no longer be the first number), there also can be no idea of the good: the good is only of each thing; it discloses itself as a concrete reality. There can be no "good in itself," no "good itself," except in the functional sense of the οὗ ἕνεκα, the *hou heneka*, the "that for the sake of which."

Let these remarks serve to indicate a parallel line of argument Aristotle entertained of the impossibility of there being an idea of being, "being itself" or "being in itself." Being, the argument implies, cannot be separated from its concrete embodiments; "being itself" or "being in itself" is precisely the disclosure of the particular entity in its particularity. But, as I shall argue, being is nonetheless irreducible to being this or that particular thing.

Thus in a relatively obscure but absolutely central passage in the *Posterior Analytics*, Aristotle, after arguing that knowledge of the essence of something (its τὸ τί ἦν εἶναι, "that which was to be" the thing), implies a precursory knowledge of its existence, yet knowledge of its essence and knowledge of its existence are two different things, notes that

> Εἶτα καὶ δι' ἀποδείξεώς φαμεν ἀναγκαῖον εἶναι δείκνυσθαι ἅπαν ὅτι ἔστιν, εἰ μὴ οὐσία εἴη. Τὸ δ' εἶναι οὐκ οὐσία οὐδενί· οὐ γὰρ γένος τὸ ὄν. (*Post. Analyt.* 2.7.92b12–14)

Before we attempt to read this passage, allow me to situate it in its context. It occurs after Aristotle asks how one can prove the essence of something (Ἔτι πῶς δείξει τὸ τί ἐστιν) (92b5), the "what is" of something or the "that which is" of something. He goes on to note that to know *what* something is one must also know *that* it is: questions about the τὸ τί ἐστιν of something imply concomitant questions about the ὅτι ἔστιν of that thing. He argues that of that which is not no one can know *that* it is, so no one knows *what* it is. He then notes that what a thing is is a different matter from that a thing is. Here he uses τὸ εἶναι instead of ὅτι ἔστιν.

Now we are in a position to read the aforecited passage. Before we do so let me cite Ross's translation. It reads:

> Next, we say it is necessary that everything that a thing is should be proved through demonstration, unless it is its substance. But being is not the substance of anything; for what is is not a genus.

There are, I would like to argue, certain difficulties with this translation, difficulties that ultimately render the translation unacceptable. First, there is the word 'should', or 'should be able to', suggesting, as it were, that Aristotle is enjoining us to observe the moral imperative of going about demonstrating of each thing everything that that thing is. I do not think Aristotle actually thought that each of us take each thing one at a time and demonstrate of it everything that it is. Second, Ross understands the ὅτι ἔστιν of line 92b13 to be the neuter ὅ τι ἔστιν, "the what it is." This seems wrong, given that the paragraph before this one (92b4–11) is unequivocally about ὅτι ἔστιν and τὸ τί ἐστιν. Third, although οὐσία is used, say, in book 9 of the *Metaphysics* as 'substance', the τόδε τι, it is well to recall that the *Analytica Posterior* is an early text in the Aristotelian corpus; and here he is just in the process of codifying his technical terms, basing them upon Plato's language. But in Plato, οὐσία means 'essence'. Moreover, it is clear from the context that Aristotle is interested in distinguishing between *essence* and *existence*. In fact, this passage is a pivotal one for the tradition, for Avicenna finds in it precisely this distinction between *essentia* and *existentia*, a distinction which was to provide a focal point for speculative thought for almost two thousand years.

But without further ado, but with well-considered reservations, I now offer my translation of the aforecited passage. In fact, I offer two different translations; I do so in an attempt to elicit the most significance from the passage.

(1) Next we say by demonstration everything that is must be proved to be, unless it be essence. And it is not the essence of anything to be; for being is not a genus.

(2) Next, we say that *it is* by demonstration *that* everything that is must be proved to be, unless it be essence. And it is not the essence of anything to be; for being is not a genus.

What is striking upon first considering this passage is the sheer number of forms of the verb 'to be', and this in a language that generally can do without any form of that verb. There are a full seven different forms, with four of these being technical terms in the Aristotelian lexicon.

Next, I have offered two different translations in order to elicit where the weight of the thought falls. In the first translation, (1), the thrust of the first sentence asks that we consider "everything that is" and prove "by demonstration" that everything is. The suggestion is that we are to take all beings and take them as a whole and demonstrate what is meant in noting that all beings taken as a whole *are*. In the second translation, (2), the thrust of the first sentence consists in noting that *whenever* we want to say of something that it is, we must demonstrate that it is. Here the emphasis is on taking "everything that is" serially one at a time; here the 'everything that is' is used distributively.

In this light the emphasis in this passage is on the ἅπαν; ἅπαν is the topicalized term. Ἅπαν is an ancient word, a Homeric term, and it is not privileged much in Attic Greek. It is a word composed of ἅμα and πᾶς. Ἅμα means 'at the same time', 'simultaneously'; while πᾶς means 'all', 'everything'. While ἅπαν can mean the same as πᾶς, there is the difference of the ἅμα embedded in the ἅπαν and not in πᾶς. The question is that, whereas πᾶς means 'everything' and is used distributively, similar to the French *'tout'*, ἅπαν means 'everything all at the same time', 'everything all together'; it is similar to the French *'le tout'*. Furthermore, when Aristotle presents his analysis of time in the *Physics*, this ἅμα, this 'at the same time,' occurs with such startling frequency that it becomes *the* topicalized term, even if it is not and cannot be made the theme of the analysis.

If, as I am arguing, ἅπαν is the topicalized term in this passage, is there any way that we can decide on whether the proper translation is 'everything', used distributively, or whether it is 'everything all together all at the same time'? To develop the proper sensitivity to the question we now ask What is it Aristotle is intending with this 'everything'? Is he intending 'everything' globally or serially, everything all together or everything one at a time? We are to prove of everything that is that it is, and prove this by demonstration. But how could we ever go about proving of something— whether of anything or of everything—that it is? Is not each thing, insofar as it is, the demonstration that it is? Is not each thing the sole possible demonstration that it is? If we seek to demonstrate that something, everything or anything, is, do we not just appreciate in silence that it is that it is, that it is that it may be?

Let us recall that Aristotle opens book 2 of the *Posterior Analytics* by noting that there are four kinds of questions that we ask about something, corresponding to the kinds of things that we know: τὸ ὅτι, τὸ διότι, εἰ ἔστι, τί ἐστιν (*Post. Analyt.* 2.1.89b24–25). Translated, these four ways of seeking what is are: the that it is (or its facticity), that by which it is (its cause or reason), if it is (its existence), and the what it is (the question of essence). He goes on to say:

> Ὥσπερ οὖν λέγομεν, τὸ τί ἐστιν εἰδέναι ταὐτό ἐστι καὶ διὰ τί ἔστιν. τοῦτο δ' ἢ ἁπλῶς καὶ μὴ τῶν ὑπαρχόντων τι, ἢ τῶν ὑπαρχόντων οἷον ὅτι δύο ὀρθαί, ἢ ὅτι μεῖζον ἢ ἔλαττον. (*Post. Analyt.* 2.2.90a32–34)

This translates as:

> As we said, then, to know what something is is the same as to know that by means of which it is. This is so whether the subject is *simpliciter*, apart from being any of its attributes; or whether it is one of its attributes, e.g., having the sum of its angles equal to two right angles, or greater or smaller.

After the aforecited passage at 92b15, Aristotle concludes that "neither by definition nor by demonstration can we acquire knowledge of what something is" (2.7.92b38–39). He then notes, after calling for a "fresh start," in what way demonstration is possible:

> It is when we are sure of the fact that we look for the reason; sometimes we become aware of them at the same time, but it is quite impossible to recognize the reason before the fact. Clearly in the same way the essential nature of something [τὸ τί ἦν εἶναι = 'that which was to be'] cannot be known without knowing that it is; it is impossible to know what a thing is if we do not recognize [ἀγνοοῦντας] if it is. (*Post. Analyt.* 2.8.93a17–21)

Aristotle is arguing that our knowledge of what something is depends on our awareness that it is; and this "that it is" comprises both its facticity, its τὸ ὅτι, and if it is, its εἰ ἔστιν.

So if it is a question of demonstrating of everything that is that it is—whether globally or serially—then we must comport ourselves, not to what it is, but rather to its facticity and to if it even is in the first place. If we understand the ἅπαν as everything taken distributively, then it is a matter of reflecting on our precursory awareness of whether and that something is before we conduct our inquiries into what it is. That is to say that, relating to the fact that something is in order to know what it is requires that we hold open the question of whether it even is. This holding open the question of whether something in particular even is lets that particular thing of itself come forward from itself, lets that particular thing show itself forth from itself. In asking if this particular thing is, what we are asking about is whether this thing is, as opposed to it not being. But asking whether something is is to anticipate that it is as the coming forward of itself, that it is as the giving of itself. In anticipating that something in particular is, we make a decision to ask after its existing (τὸ εἶναι), not as this or that thing in particular, not as the particular thing that it is, but rather simply and ἀλλῶς (*simpliciter* or absolutely) that it is, that it gives itself as the 'there is' of itself, that it comes forward as what is there whenever it is. But what is anticipated here is not something peculiar to this particular thing. Rather, it is what everything that is has in common, namely, that everything of itself comes forward as what there is whenever there is anything at all. Everything is the affirmation and proof of its own existence and so is the affirmation and proof that there is something and not rather nothing, that there is the 'there is'.

So to ask, in the first place, if something in particular is is to ask what is there that there is this something in particular rather than there not being this something in particular. But in asking this, we are not asking what is there other than this particular thing, but rather, what is there that there is not rather nothing. This is to raise the possibility that it might not have been. Thus we are led to consider: Why is this something in particular torn away from the possibility of not being? Why does it not simply keep slipping back into simply not being? How is it that it has established itself over against the possibility that it might not have been, that it itself is the emergence of what overcomes this possibility and renders it impossible? In this way we are forced, upon asking whether this something is, to see it as the decision for itself over against the possibility of it not ever being, as being itself the dispensation for it to be and so being itself the foreclosing on the possibility that it might never have been. But that it might not have been, that it, at the very least, might not be what it is and as it is, is something it itself elicits as a possibility inscribed in the fact that it is; it has never itself entirely (ἁπλῶς) caught up with or overcome the possibility of not being.

So to ask if something in particular is is ultimately to ask why there is something and not rather nothing, for it is to ask what is there when there is not nothing. This is, then, to ask after that wherewith there is something, and so to ask after the wherewithal of there being something. Aristotle names this wherewithal of being τὸ εἶναι. Τὸ εἶναι is a verbal substantive formed by placing a particle before the infinitive form of the verb 'to be'. The infinitive is the *modus infinitivus*, the mode of unlimitedness, indeterminateness, and indefiniteness in the manner in which a verb accomplishes and indicates its significative function and direction. The infinitive signifies an indefinite emptiness of detail; the infinitive indicates lack of any tense, person, and mood that are found in other forms of the verb. So in asking whether something is, we are not inquiring into how it is this or that; we are not inquiring into its particular way of being. Rather, we are asking about τὸ εἶναι, that there is something and not rather nothing, that there is anything at all; we are inquiring about being in its pure indeterminateness, without regard for any of the specific determinations in and by which something in particular makes itself manifest.

Moreover, to question the facticity of something in particular, its τὸ ὅτι, is nothing less than to hold open a relation to the givenness of that thing. This is not a relation to this particular thing *per se* but rather a relation to the particular thing *in its particularity*, in its *givenness* as a particular thing. But, again, this relation is not established just for this particular thing, but rather, inasmuch as it relates to this particular thing *in its particularity*, it discloses particularity in general, givenness in general, that is, what must be encountered for there to be given anything at all.

This relation discloses that being is always given as a particular being. But if we are relating to particularity in general, to the givenness of being—that being gives itself as particular being—then we are no longer relating to any particular thing but rather to anything that is, that it is as given.

After discussing the aporia involved in considering whether the first principles are the highest genera (*Meta.* 3.3.998b14–999a23), Aristotle raises another aporia, "one which is the hardest and yet the most necessary of all to investigate [καὶ πασῶν χαλεπωτάτη καὶ ἀναγκαιοτάτη θεωρῆσαι]" (3.4.999a24–25). This aporia consists in this, that if nothing exists apart from individual things, and these are infinite in number, how then is it possible to obtain knowledge of the numerically infinite? That is to say, how is a science possible if nothing other than singulars exist? The Greek here reads:

εἴτε γὰρ μὴ ἔστι τι παρὰ τὰ καθ' ἕκαστα, τὰ δὲ καθ' ἕκαστα ἄπειρα, τῶν δ' ἀπείρων πῶς ἐνδέχεται λαβεῖν ἐπιστήμην; (*Meta.* 3.4.999a26–28)

Here the key words are the formulaic καθ' ἕκαστα and ἄπειρα, ἀπείρων. Ἕκαστος means every, every one, each, each one. Καθ' ἕκαστα means each one singly. Ἄπειρα is the privative of πέρας, meaning 'end', 'limit'. Ἄπειρα means, then, boundless, endless, countless. The topicalized term appears to be the formulaic καθ' ἕκαστα. This aporia, the eighth of Book B, represents another version of the fifth aporia of the same book, namely the aporia involved in wondering whether or not sensible substances alone should be said to exist (*Meta.* 3.2.997a34–998a19).

The aporia is this: if nothing exists outside of individuals, since they are numerically unlimited, science would be impossible, since it cannot exhaust their unlimitedness. The assumption is that if all there are are particulars, then we can know only by taking each one singly (καθ' ἕκαστα). The assumption is necessary since knowledge of the individual is possible only insofar as we can refer it to something one and identical. But this is to refer it to the universal. If, therefore, it is necessary that the universal exists in addition to the individuals, then it is necessary that there exists, besides the individuals, the genera—whether they be first genera or ultimate genera. But the existence of genera was seen in the preceding aporia to be absurd (*Meta.* 3.3.998b14–999a23).

Moreover, to admit that nothing exists besides the singulars would make of the "sought-for science" a contradiction, for if only singulars were to exist, that is, the sensible particulars, then all existing things would be sensible, and so intelligible entities would not exist. Consequently there could be no knowledge of anything. But this is absurd, for if only sensible particulars exist, that they exist is nothing that could be known, and so we could not even say that sensible particulars exist. In fact, as Socrates noted in the *Theaetetus*, if only particulars exist, not only could this not be said, but there could be no discourse at all.

It is to this aporia that I think Aristotle refers in the term ἅπαν in the *Analytica Posterior*: being cannot be said καθ' ἕκαστα; the science of being qua being is not of particular beings, considering each one singly. In fact, Aristotle, in enumerating the aporiai in Book B, speaks of the "sought-for science" as an inquiry concerning the στοιχεῖα τῶν ὄντων (the first elements of the beings) (*Meta.* 3.3.998b10), of the ἀρχαὶ τῶν ὄντων (the principles of the beings) (*Meta.* 3.3.998b19; 4.999b32; 5.1002b24), and of the οὐσίαι τῶν ὄντων (the substances of the beings) (*Meta.* 3.4.1001a6; 5.1001b29; 1002a28). Thus, it is not, it would seem, to be a matter of inquiring into the principles of any *particular being*, but of inquiring into the principles of *all beings* (τῶν ὄντων). These phrases, then, indicate that it is a matter, not of inquiring into particulars qua particulars, but rather of inquiring into the particular*izing* giving of itself of being, that being gives itself particularizingly, that *there is* the particular.

In this light it should be clear that the ἅπαν in the aforecited passage at 92b can only be understood as ἅμα πᾶν, as, that is, 'everything taken as a whole', 'everything taken together all at the same time'.

The problem of taking beings as a whole invites a discussion of the Kantian thesis that "being is not a real predicate." Kant notes this in the last third of the *Critique of Pure Reason*, in the section entitled "On the Impossibility of an Ontological Proof of the Existence of God" (A592 = B620). The passage in question reads:

> 'Being' is obviously not a real predicate; that is, it is not a concept of something which could be added to the concept of a thing. It is merely the positing of a thing, or of certain determinations in and of themselves. (A598 = B626)

He then continues:

> Logically, it [being] is merely the copula of a judgment. The proposition, 'God is omnipotent', contains two concepts, each of which has its object—God and omnipotence. The small word 'is' adds no new predicate, but only serves to posit the predicate *in its relation to* the subject.

Here the suggestion is that there is another significance to "being" and "is" besides the "logical" one. The suggestion is that in a sentence such as "God is" the significance of the "is" goes beyond the concept of God and brings to this concept the thing itself. Thus, in an undated note (*W. W. Akadamieausgabe* XVIII, n. 6272) Kant briefly summarized this extralogical use of "is":

> By the predicate "existence" I add nothing to the thing, but rather add the thing itself to the concept. I go in an existential sentence, therefore, beyond the concept, not to a predicate other than what was thought of in the concept, but rather to the thing itself with just the very same predicates, not more, not less.

Now, these reflections by Kant carry us back to a note Aristotle makes in *De Interpretatione*:

> Verbs by themselves, then, are nouns, and they stand for or signify something [σημαίνει τι], for the speaker stops his process of thinking and the mind of the hearer acquiesces. However, they do not as yet express positive or negative judgments. For even the infinitives 'to be' [τὸ εἶναι], 'not to be' [μὴ εἶναι], and the participle 'being' [τὸ ὄν], are indicative only of bare particulars, if and when something further is added [προσσημαίνει]. They signify nothing themselves but imply a synthesis [σύνθεσίν], which we can hardly conceive of apart from the things thus combined. (*De Int.* 3.16b20–26)

By uttering verbs for themselves, they *mean something*, but they do not say that what they mean *is* or *is not*. Rather, verbs, taken by or for themselves, *consignify*, signify *along with* the principal meaning, signify as προσσημαίνει. Being, Aristotle says, has no independent meaning, but προσσημαίνει, it implicates being in thinking how something is predicated of something. 'Being' signifies that being is implicated whenever we think of something; being is not itself a being among beings but is implicated in our thinking of any being whatsoever.

There is agreement here between what Kant says and what Aristotle says. Thus, when Kant says, "Being is obviously not a real predicate," he does not mean that being is not really a predicate. The "real" here is what can be predicated of a '*res*'. Being does not belong to the substantive content of a *res*; *that* something is can never be explained by *what* it is, i.e., by a concept. Thus, Aristotle says, "It is not the essence [or substance] of anything to be." For Kant, in saying that something is, we go beyond the concept of that thing and bring to this concept the thing itself.

For both Aristotle and Kant existential predication (and the passage at 92b15 of *Posterior Analytics* is the *locus classicus* of existential predication) "demonstrates" that being is not a factual predicate; being is not thing-like, is a no-thing, is not a being.

In 92b15 Aristotle distinguishes ontologically between ordinary predication (τὸ τί ἔστιν) and existential predication. Whether we understand the ἅπαν of "everything that is" globally or serially, it is still a question of seeing how being cannot be reduced to the being of which it is existentially predicated—even though all there are are particular beings; being cannot be reduced to a being-this or a being-that, to being a particular. This is the force of the words "by demonstration." In demonstrating of "everything that is" that it is—whether this is understood globally or serially—what we are doing is allowing everything to show itself forth, to show forth from itself that it is; demonstration sets forth that it is, brings forward that it is, makes manifest, not the particular being, but rather, *that* the particular being *is*. To demonstrate of "everything that is" that it is is to let everything be its own self-exposing, its own self-exposition, within the horizon of the exposition of the thing, of what the thing is.

But let me ask the question again: which of the two translations that I have offered is the better, i.e., is "everything that is" to be taken globally or serially? This is to ask in what sense "is there" being? Parmenides says: ἔστιν γὰρ εἶναι (there is, namely, being) (frag. 6). That we can say of anything that is that it is means that something like being must in some sense be. But, as we have seen, being cannot be reduced to a being-this or a being-that; besides there being a being-this and a being-that, there is also the *fact* that there is a being-this and a being-that. Being is the affirmation and proof that this particular being is and that that particular being is. Being is what is there whenever there is anything. Now, whatever is the sense of ἅπαν here, it should be clear that for Aristotle even to use it in this passage indicates that there is a sense of being that is not only not reducible to a being this or that but also irreducible to the meaning of the word or concept 'being'. If "being is said in many ways" (τὸ ὄν λέγεσθαι πολλαχῶς), this is because being is not reducible to any or even all of its ways of being said: being is always said προσσημαίνει; there is always, in addition to naming this or that being or this or that way of being, the *fact* that there is this or that being or this or that way of being; there is always, in addition to naming a particular being, that there is the being being said, that there is the 'there is being' (ἔστιν γὰρ εἶναι, Parmenides frag. 6). Being is not reducible to its being-said. It is, rather, implicated in being said yet irreducible to it.

For Aristotle there is no "idea" of being. But this is not to say that there are just particular beings. Rather, implicated in there being just particular beings is *their being just particular beings*. The 'that everything that is is' belongs in a certain sense to what is, yet is not itself anything that is, yet belongs to us who take note of the fact that everything that is is yet is not anything that we are. This is the properly transcendental dimension to being, for it means that being cannot be explained by *what* anything in particular is or *that* anything in particular is; being is always what is left out and left over in being said. For all these reasons I would like to argue that by ἅπαν Aristotle could only have meant 'everything all together all at the same time'. And I would like to argue for this reading, the rest of the Aristotelian corpus notwithstanding, for if we are to understand that something in particular is, we can understand that it is only by a precursory comprehension of the fact that it is a being among beings. But to anticipate it being a being among beings is to decide in favor of it being rather than not being. Yet, to repeat, this decision is not just about this particular being being the particular being that it is, but it is rather about this particular being even being, and so is about the fact that there is being in the first place, that there is something, anything at all, rather than nothing. Again, what is understood in deciding how it stands with this being being this particular being is that by virtue of being it makes a decision for being over against not being, and this is itself not anything that is.

In this way we can appreciate even more what a "science of being qua being" would have to be like. Given that being is irreducible to the particular beings that are yet is not anything that is, the "science of being qua being" could only be a science of the particular, not as such, but rather as *the disclosedness of its particularity*. Such a science would not be about anything in particular but rather would be about the fact that being always gives itself in, through, and as particular beings; it would be about the fact that being gives itself in, by, through, and as particular particularizations of itself. Such a science, then, would be about particular beings only insofar as each particular being is a particularizing giving of itself of being. This science, were it to be instituted, would not be about the particular as *this* particular particularization of being, for, as we have seen, to inquire as to if and that something in particular is is to inquire into the properly transcendental dimension of being, namely, that being, while irreducible to particular particularizations of itself, nonetheless always gives itself as particular particularizations of itself. In this way, a science of "being qua being" would inquire into the particular only insofar as it is, not so much *this* particular particularization of being, but rather insofar as it is *a* particular*izing giving of itself* of being.

But such a science, then, would undercut itself, for there can be no science that studies the particularizing giving of itself of being: the particular as a particular particularizing giving of itself of being is precisely that which cannot be amenable to scientific inquiry; it is precisely that which cannot be subsumed under an idea of itself; it is precisely that which thinking cannot get around and against which thinking disappears into itself, dispersing conceptualization in general. The particular as a particularizing giving of itself of being would seem to be, not just the abrogation of thought, but the self-refusal of the particular to give itself as itself and so the self-elimination of the idea of this particular particular. Again, by 'the particular as a particularizing giving of itself of being' we mean precisely its existence, *that* it is, and precisely this is what can never be reduced to a concept. Moreover, it is precisely this that can never become an object of scientific inquiry. By undermining itself in this way such a science would have to return to establishing its own possibility. But in that event the "science of being qua being" would need to establish that it is possible to proceed from this guiding and grounding insight that there can be no idea of being, only the disclosedness of beings.

However, to proceed from this principle would be to renounce the scientific demands of the problem in favor of a mystical appreciation of each particular particular as a particular particularizing giving of itself of being. Every proceeding forth from the principle that establishes the "science of being qua being," the principle that establishes that there can be no principle upon which such a science can be founded, eliminates itself and disestablishes this science: to execute a science of being qua being would require that proceeding forth with this science is necessarily a matter of proceeding back to the possibility of establishing this science, yet this science is made possible by means of a scientific demonstration that there can be no principle according to which this science conducts its investigation. In this way the science of being qua being is self-eliminating, and it is precisely this self-elimination that is the principle establishing this science. Paradoxes abound here with a fierceness and intractability that can only be described as infinitely exponentiating.

By '*a* particular*izing* giving of itself of being' I do not mean that being is a universal under which are subsumed particular beings; I do not mean that the "science of being qua being" inquires into the particular insofar as it is a particular manifestation or instance of being. Rather, I mean by this phrase that our "sought-for" science studies the 'there is' whenever and wherever there is a particular being; it has as its premier object the giving of being, and not just what is given as being. That is to say, the study of τόδε τι ούσία, of thisness, is not of a *particular* giving of itself of being, but of the particular*izing* giving of itself of being. Being is said primarily of τόδε τι ούσία, of "a certain this." But being, to repeat, is not predicated of this 'certain this'. Being is not itself a property of this certain this, but rather its 'thisness', that it is, that there is this. Here, it is not a question of demonstrating that this particular giving of itself of being is: "For this reason also there is no definition or demonstration of particular sensible substances, because they contain matter the nature of which is such that it both can be and not be [εἶναι καὶ μή]" (*Meta.* 7.15.1039b27–29; cf. also 1040a2–3). But as a particular giving of itself of being, as, that is, a particularizing giving of itself of being, the particular is itself what is given in the giving of itself of being. But the giving itself and that which gives of itself holds back with their own givenness: in the giving of itself of being, being does not give itself but rather gives itself *over* to a *particular* giving of itself; being gives itself over to a τόδε τι, a certain thisness, not a particular τὸ τί ἔστιν but a that there is the particular being, that being is always a particular*izing* giving of itself. The giving of itself of being is the bidding, itself unbidden, that bids beings to abide enbounded into particularity. This unbidden bidding is the abiding approaching of being, of the giving of itself of being; it is the abiding offering and opening up of what is. The bidding of being gives the enboundedness in which being is bidden as the bursting open of sudden yet abiding particularity.

But in what way can this "sought-for" science, the "science of being qua being" secure its object? It cannot study the particular insofar as it is a particular*izing giving of itself of being*, for there is nothing to say of the giving of itself of being except that there is a giving of itself of being as the particularizing into beings. Nor can this science study the particular insofar as it is a particular, that is, in its particularity, which is to say insofar as it is the exception, the accidental, the contingent, and therefore not for itself or of itself, for the accidental, the fortuitous, the contingent, the exceptional, and the conditional are precisely what no science can track, can keep track of. They are pure gratuity, *lagniappe*. Insofar as science inquires into the particular, it is both a *metaphysica specialis* and a *metaphysica generalis: metaphysica specialis* insofar as the particular is the exception to the theory of being in general—is the accidental, the contingent, the gratuitous, the fortuitous; *metaphysica generalis* insofar as the particular discloses itself as what there is when there is anything at all and not rather nothing, as, therefore, a peculiar or particular giving of itself of being.

And if this "sought-for" science is an ontology because it is a theology yet is a theology because it is an ontology, then it now becomes a question of relating the discourse on the divine to the discourse on being in general. Here Aristotle provides us with a clue: "There is demonstration only of the necessary" (*Meta.* 7.15.1039b34). He also defines what he means by the necessary: "We say of that which cannot be otherwise that it is necessary"

(*Meta.* 5.5.1015a32–33). But, as we know, the god is necessary but also separable, immutable and imperishable, that "which is first in complete reality" (*Meta.* 12.5.1071a37). Aristotle, in arguing for the existence of the god, argues for its *necessary* existence, i.e., that it is necessary that there is an actuality, that it is necessary that there be a being the substance of which is actuality (*Meta.* 12.6.1071b20–28), and that this "which is both substance and actuality" is eternal (*Meta.* 12.7.1072a25–26). This being "exists out of necessity."

That the god exists necessarily and eternally and exists as pure actuality means that for Aristotle ontology is properly a theory of the god—for here there is no contingency, no accidentality, and no possibility of not being; but for the same reasons theology is properly a theory of being in general. In the transparency of its self-manifestation the god *is* not anywhere given in the giving of itself of being; the god nowhere appears. In particular, the god is not given in particular. But this is to say that the god is the pure particularizing of being, for with the god οὐσία is παρουσία; the god is pure presence that has always already accomplished its own actuality. That the god exists means that it is necessary that there be being; the god *is* that there is a giving of itself of being before there is anything given. Thus Aristotle argues:

> Since we have seen that there are three kinds of substance, two of which are natural and one immutable, we must now discuss the last named and show that *it is necessary that there be some substance which is eternal and immutable.* Substances are the primary reality, and if they are all perishable, everything is perishable. But motion cannot be either generated or destroyed, for it always existed; nor can time, because there can be no priority or posteriority if there is no time. (*Meta.* 12.6.1071b3–9)

The god, then, is what is there when there is anything at all and nothing in particular. But what there is when there is anything at all and nothing in particular is not, of course, a τόδε τι οὐσία, but rather the 'there is', *Anwesen*, presencing, *that* there is the giving of itself of being, that there is the 'there is', the *'es gibt'*.

V

> For philosophical problems arise when language *goes on holiday*.
> Ludwig Wittgenstein, *Philosophical Investigations*

> Walking measures the ground; talking measures language; thinking is peripatetic. But the thinker also finds that thinking is beyond *measure*, or that man is not the measure, not even of his language. He discovers that where he thought he was on solid ground—whether terra firma or presuppositions or whatever you name the substratum—he is (also) on language; then, that language is not a ground but a groundless veiling of the hypothesis (itself a grounding term) of the ground.
> Geoffrey Hartman, *Saving the Text*

For Aristotle a name is a proper name when it has only one sense. Or rather, it is only in this case that it is properly a name. To be univocal would then seem to be the τέλος of language. Or at least this ideal has almost always received confirmation from philosophy. It would seem to be philosophy, this attempt at univocity, this wrestling language into univocity. Derrida even goes so far on this score as to say that univocity constitutes philosophy "*as such.*"[15] The abrogation or aberration of this idea serves to solicit a meaning of philosophical discourse that can site metaphysics into a closure by determining it in its discursive autonomy.

In the opening lines of the *Categories* Aristotle distinguishes the different forms that this new relationship between sign and signified—the relationship of plurivocity to essential and irreducible determination—takes. He recognizes three different kinds of names.

"Things are named 'equivocally' [ὁμώνυμα] when, though they have a common name, the definition corresponding with the name [τοὔνομα λόγος τῆς οὐσίας] is different from it." He then

---

15. Derrida, "White Mythology," 19.

defines univocity: "Things are said to be named 'univocally' [συνώνυμα] which have both the name and the definition answering to the name in common [τό τε ὄνομα κοινὸν καὶ ὁ κατὰ τοὔνομα λόγος τῆς οὐσίας ὁ αὐτός]." Finally he defines a third kind of naming, distinct from the other two, but whose relation to them is not immediately clear: "Things are said to be named 'paronymously' [παρώνυμα] which derive their name from some other name. Thus the grammarian [τῆς γραμματικῆς] derives his name from grammar or writing [γραμματικός, a word itself derived 'paronymously' from the difference between writing, γράμμα, and trace, γραμμή]."

One could make two remarks concerning this tripartite distinction. The first is that this distinction concerns immediately the things, and not the words: it is not the word that is said homonymously, synonymously, or paronymously, but the things that the word signifies. Second, homonymy, synonymy, and paronymy concern the relationship of a unique sign to a plurality of signifieds. The difference between these three relational forms is to be sought neither in the name nor in the signifieds but in the intermediary standard of signification, which is designated in the *Categories* by the expression ὁ κατὰ τοὔνομα λόγος τῆς οὐσίας, which we might, somewhat forcingly, translate as "according to the word expressed in being possessed by being."

It remains to ascertain just what is the importance of this tripartite distinction by which Aristotle, according to the tradition, opens his philosophy. With the notable exceptions of Günther Patzig and Paul Ricoeur,[16] all the recent major commentators[17] have neglected the third division of naming, that of paronymy. That they

---

16. Paul Ricoeur, *The Rule of Metaphor*. Günther Patzig, "Theologie und Ontologie in der 'Metaphysik' des Aristoteles."

17. Notably Pierre Aubenque, W. Jaeger, and Franz Brentano, *Von der Mannigfachen Bedeutung des Seienden nach Aristoteles*, trans. Rolf George as *On the Several Senses of Being in Aristotle*, and, of course, Trendelenburg and Bonitz. Joseph Owens, in his *The Doctrine of Being in the Aristotelian "Metaphysics"*, does, contra the others, mention the status of paronymy in Aristotle's texts, but only to note that paronyms them-

have might prompt one to suspect a kind of systematic neglect and forgetfulness, given the current climate of hermeneutics. But if there is anything systematic to their oversight, about this we are not yet able to speculate. Moreover, how could there be anything systematic in how we have traditionally overlooked something? Should we not rather see if by precisely focusing on this third and neglected division of naming, paronymy, we might elicit some unexpected insight into the nature of philosophic discourse?

We have already seen a suggestion of the significance of this tripartite division. It occurs in the *Rhetoric*. To repeat: "Homonyms are chiefly used to enable the sophist to mislead his hearers. Synonyms are useful to the poet" (*Rhet.* 3.2.1404b37–1405a1). If homonyms are the proper property of the sophist and if synonyms are the proper province of the poet, then, according to this division, perhaps the philosopher is concerned with paronymy. The problem is to clarify this concern, especially insofar as it has been neglected by those commentators who wish to find in Aristotle's first philosophy the prototype of science.

Being, we have said, following Aristotle, is said in many ways. That *being*, the highest and most general concept, is not a strict genus but a unity according to analogy we can adduce from a passage from book 5 of the *Metaphysics*, the book on definitions:

> Again, some things are one numerically, others formally [κατ' εἶδος], others generically [κατὰ γένος], and others analogically [κατ' ἀναλογίαν]: numerically, those whose matter is one; formally, those whose definition is one; generically, those which belong to the same category; and analogically those which have the same relation as something else to a third object [κατ' ἀναλογίαν δὲ ὅσα ἔχει ὡς ἄλλο πρὸς ἄλλο]. In every case the latter types of unity are implied in the former: e.g., all things which are numerically one are also one

---

selves can be said synonymously or homonymously. However, Owens does develop a notion of "focal meaning" to account for and resolve the same problematic that I am addressing here.

formally, but not all which are one formally are one numerically; and all are one generically which are one formally, but such as are one generically are not all one formally, although they are one analogically; and such as are one analogically are not all one generically. (*Meta.* 5.6.1016b31–1017a3)[18]

The decisiveness of Aristotle's last remark becomes at once apparent if one admits that being has the unity of analogy. Aristotle explicitly does so, for example, in the fourth book of the *Metaphysics*:

The term "being" is used in many senses, but with reference to one central idea and one definite characteristic, and not just equivocally [τὸ δὲ ὂν λέγεται μὲν πολλαχῶς, ἀλλὰ πρὸς ἓν καὶ μίαν τινὰ φύσιν, καὶ οὐχ ὁμωνύμως]. Thus as the term "healthy" always relates to health (either as preserving it or as producing it or as signifying it or as receptive of it), and as "medical" relates to the art of medicine (either as possessing it or as naturally adapted for it or as being a function of medicine)—and we shall find other terms used similarly to these—so "being" is used in various senses but always with reference to one principle [ἅπαν πρὸς μίαν ἀρχήν]. (*Meta.* 4.2.1003a33–1003b6)

Although we should perhaps be tempted to think that being is said paronymously, since in these two passages Aristotle tells us that it is not said synonymously (since it "is said in many ways") nor homonymously, we should be cautioned from rushing to too ready conclusions, if only because textually there is very little support: Aristotle gives "being" the logic of neither/nor—neither univocally nor equivocally do we speak when we speak (about) being.

But this much we might want to say: perhaps the tradition has denied paronymy its own voice for the same reasons that Aristotle's πρώτη φιλοσοφία has come to be interpreted according to

---

18. Also cf. *PA* 1.5.645b26; *Meta.* 14.6.1093b19.

its indicial name of τὰ μετὰ τὰ φυσικά. Keeping in the tradition of those looking back upon the tradition in order to recover hitherto hidden possibilities that pronounce its end, we might be tempted to think that perhaps this neglect of paronymy, despite what would seem to be Aristotle's overt intentions, and which has been systematically passed over since the days of St. Thomas, is the means and measure by which the truth of Aristotle has receded into forgetfulness by virtue of the force of the tradition. But let's be content with asseverating that, at any rate, the role of paronymy in ontology *is* puzzling.

The tradition has responded to the demand imposed by Aristotle's meditations on "being" and being, their difference and their belonging together, by citing an obscure but famous passage in the *Nicomachean Ethics*. This passage evokes the necessity of developing a logic of nonaccidental homonymy:

> But in what sense then are different things called good? For they do not seem to be a case of things that bear the same name merely by chance [ἀπὸ τύχης ὁμωνύμοις]. Possibly things are called good in virtue of being derived from one good; or because they all contribute to one good. Or perhaps it is rather by way of a proportion [κατ' ἀναλογίαν]: that is, as sight is good in the body, so intelligence is good in the soul, and similarly, another thing in something else. (*Nico. Eth.* 1.6.1096b26–30)

While denying paronymy in explicit defiance of the *Categories*, the tradition acknowledges the essential undecidability involved in the meaning of being, to the extent that it appeals to nonaccidental, but also nonessential, homonymy. But the problem still persists: how to clear out a space for the intermediary position between synonymy and homonymy that the meaning of being invokes.

Now, the *Categories* does not itself invoke the term *analogy*, but by reference to paronymy, suggests a nonpoetic model of equivocity and thus suggests the necessary conditions for a nonmetaphorical ontology, an ontology neither parasitic upon poetry, since it is not based upon univocity, nor for this same reason, an ontology parasitic upon scientific orders of discourse.

The search for this nonmetaphorical theory of being that Aristotle attempts to initiate has carried philosophy at least up to Kant and Hegel. Speculative discourse, it used to be said, stands or falls on the basis of the legitimacy of this theory. For the *Categories* raises its question of the connection between the meanings of being only because the *Metaphysics* poses the question that abruptly breaks with poetic discourse as well as with ordinary discourse, the question, τί τὸ ὄν, τοῦτό ἐστι; "what is being?" (*Meta.* 7.1.1028b2).

As we know, this question exceeds all relative and specific linguistic determinations. For this reason, when the philosopher is confronted by the koan that "being is said in many ways," and when, in order to rescue the diverse meanings of being from dispersal, Aristotle establishes between them a relation of reference to a first term that is neither the univocity of genus nor the mere chance equivocity of a simple word, the *plurivocity* that is thus brought to philosophical discourse is of a different order from homonymy and synonymy inherent in any other discourse. The first term—οὐσία, Aristotle informs us—places all other terms in the realm of meaning outlined by the question: what is being? The decisive thing is to establish a nongeneric order among the multiple meanings of being. The lack of a common point of contact between the ordered plurivocity of being and poetic metaphor is attested to indirectly by the charge that Aristotle levels against Plato. Ordered plurivocity is to replace Platonic participation, which is only metaphorical: "And to say that [the Forms] are patterns and the other things share in them is to use empty words and poetical metaphors" (*Meta.* 1.9.991a19–22).

That there is no small significance attached to the tripartite division of naming opening the *Categories* is evinced in the second paragraph of this treatise that opposes and combines two senses of the copula *is*, namely, being predicable of a subject without ever being present in it (τὰ μὲν καθ' ὑποκειμένου τινὸς λέγεται ἐν ὑποκειμένῳ δὲ οὐδενί ἐστιν), and being present in a subject without ever being predicable of it, as for instance when "a piece of grammatical knowledge is there in the mind as a subject but cannot be predicated of any known subject whatever [οἷον ἡ τὶς γραμματικὴ ἐν ὑποκειμένῳ μέν ἐστι τῇ ψυχῇ καθ' ὑποκειμένου δ' οὐδενὸς λέγεται]." These two senses of the copula, along with the attendant progressive dispersions and deviations, are not related to one another either synonymously or homonymously: they are derived from one another paronymously; and the progressive diffractions of the copula are paronyms attendant upon the difference between these two. A correlation suggests itself, then, between the distinctions made in the *Categories* on the level of morphology and predication and the famous passage in Book Gamma of the *Metaphysics* on the reference of all categories to a first term (aforecited, cf. *Meta.* 4.2.1003a33–1003b3). This correlation is set forth in Book Zeta of the *Metaphysics*, the boot camp for metaphysicians that subjects substance to a rigorous and definitive analysis and which explicitly relates the various forms of predication—and hence the categories—to possible equivocation in regard to the first category, ousia.

> For it must be either by equivocation [ὁμωνύμως] that we say that these things *are* [ταῦτα φάναι εἶναι ὄντα], or by adding and subtracting qualifications, as we say that the unknowable is known [known to be unknowable: τὸ μὴ ἐπιστητὸν ἐπιστητόν]; since the truth is that we use the terms neither equivocally nor in the same sense, but just as we use the term "medical" *in relation to* one and the same thing [πρὸς τὸ αὐτὸ μὲν καὶ ἕν]; but not *of* one and the same thing, nor yet equivocally. The term "medical" is applied to a body and a function and an instrument, neither equivocally nor in one sense, but in relation to one thing. (*Meta.* 7.4.1030a32–1030b4)

Aristotle here admits the analogy of being is neither a matter of equivocalness nor a matter of a univocal term serving as a genus containing all its equivocations.

Yet Aristotle does not call analogy what has just been seen to be a relation of progressively extended derivation. What is more, if the table of categories formed by "adding and subtracting from the meaning of 'to be'" does permit us to order the series of alleged terms, it does not show us why there must be other terms than the presumed first nor why they are as they are. If we read the canonical text of Gamma 2[19] we see, as already noted, that the other categories are so termed with reference to one central point (πρὸς ἕν), one definite kind of thing (κατὰ μίαν φύσιν). But we do not see that the multiple meanings form a system. Aristotle may well declare that the lack of notational unity does not prevent there being a *single* theory of the multiple senses of being. He may well affirm that terms that "are related to one common nature" give rise to a *single* science, for "even these in a sense have one common notion" (*Meta.* 4.2.1003b14). For, in this case, "*science deals chiefly with that which is primary, and on which the other things depend, and in virtue of which they get their names*" (*Meta.* 4.2.1003b16–18). Despite the enigmatic character of dependence that Aristotle alleges, there is *prima facie* evidence that Aristotle is dealing with a paronymous logic and therefore attempting to elaborate a paronymous ontology, for, as he notes, it is a question of the derivations, the deviations and dispersions, the diffraction of sense that a science of being qua being must resolve.

An "aporetic" reading of these statements does serve to suggest strongly that a solution to the multiple meanings of being with all their dependencies on an original sense and name might be gained by a development of a science of paronymy—a science, as we are beginning to suspect, of the origin that has always already erased itself in the production and play of differences and derivations; a science of the dissimulation and dissemblance of the primordial and the essential; a science of the surplus and

---

19. ". . . so 'being' [τὸ ὄν] is used in various senses but always with reference to one principle. For some things are said to 'be' because they are substances; others because they are modifications of substance; others because they are a process towards substance, or destruction or privations or qualities of substance, or productive or generative of substance or of terms relating to substance, or negations of those terms or of substance" (*Meta.* 4.2.1003b5–10).

overdeterminability of naming, along with the indeterminateness of the named that is involved in the plurivocity of sense. In a word, what I find suggestive in these remarks of Aristotle is the possibility of a science of the *forgetfulness of origins* at work in the basic movements and moments of the Western experience. Or to be precise, a science of the *self-forgetfulness* of origins in principle. Moreover, I find the provocation in these passages of Aristotle to enter into a kind of playfulness that would allow the intractable reserve, the inexhaustible excess, and the overabundance of being to come into the play of thinking through an unchecked but nonetheless rigorous paronomasia.

All this and more I find suggested by the possibility of a science of paronymy that Aristotle intimates, even if he, as Patzig argues, recoils from carrying it through, and which he unwittingly enunciated in his quest for a science of being qua being, given that such a "science deals chiefly with that which is primary and on which other things depend, and in virtue of which they get their names." This aporetic reading is an attempt to establish the intrinsic possibility of a "science" of paronymy that would enable us to think philosophically the meaning of being in all its plurivocity and polyvalency.

But on what conditions would a science of paronymy be possible? Given that Aristotle ultimately discloses that philosophy is irreducible to a science, it would seem that the fundamental condition for a science of paronymy would be the undoing and abrogation of the scientific attitude in the quest and questioning of being. For this reason, this condition of possibility turns into a condition of impossibility. If it were to be instituted, it would risk destroying the very concept of science.

It is a seemingly perilous necessity at stake here—as Derrida has footnoted and which I shall discuss shortly. The same necessity, just as perilous, it would seem, as the necessity to *delimit* the origin, state, and estate of metaphysics (given the ascendancy of somewhat confusing talk about the "end" or "closure" of metaphysics, of the "metaphysics of representation" or of the "metaphysics of presence"). It would seem to be the necessity of marking the *limit* of metaphysics. It would seem to be a matter of marking off the limit by which metaphysics would be delimited, the delimitation in which metaphysics unfolds from its limit. It is a question, after all, of determining whether this necessity can be seen as necessary, or whether it may not be just apparent, just virtual. So the issue becomes, then, one of determining on what conditions a science of paronymy is possible.

So: on what conditions would a science of paronymy be possible? On the condition of knowing what paronymy is and that the plurivocity of its objects is irreducible. But this is a question of origins and essence.[20] But a science of paronymy, if it is to be anything at all, is precisely the science of the self-occultation of origin in the free production of paronomasia; it is, if anything, the science of the forgetting of origins and of the self-dissimulation of the essential. It would be a science of the self-forgetfulness of the

---

20. This is Derrida's programmatic *apologia*. Cf., e.g., *Of Grammatology*, 74:

"On what conditions is a grammatology possible? Its fundamental condition is certainly the undoing [*sollicitation*] of logocentrism. But this condition of possibility turns into a condition of impossibility. In fact it risks destroying the concept of science as well. . . .

"When venturing up to that perilous necessity, and within the traditional norms of scientificity upon which we fall back provisionally, let us repeat the question, on what conditions is grammatology possible?

"On the condition of knowing what writing is and how the plurivocity of the concept is formed? Where does writing begin? When does writing begin? Where and when does the trace, writing in general, common root of speech and writing, narrow itself down into 'writing' in the colloquial sense? Where and when does one pass from one writing to another, from writing in general to writing in the narrow sense . . . ?

"But the question of origin is at first confounded with the question of essence."

It should be clear at this point that what I have invoked as the science of paronymity is another metaleptic reformulation, in a long list of reformulations that have no prior formulation from which they are derived, of grammatology. But: there are, we can rightly suspect, differences.

origin. The science of paronymy, if it is at all possible, would be the study of the beginnings and dispersions which conceal the origin and the essential. Its possibility can only be established in accordance with the elaboration of its necessity; and the conditions on which it is possible can only reveal themselves in the course of illuminating the state and estate of metaphysics. It is, as Derrida says,[21] a matter of showing how the impossibility of beginning at the beginning of a genealogy of a science, as this is understood by the logic of transcendental reflection, refers us to the originarity of a paronymity that erases origins and diffracts essences yet nonetheless maintains them by a constant deconstructive reference to their originality and essentiality. It is, briefly, one in the indefinite and undermining chain of substitutions, the most notorious of which is called "grammatology." It is the "paleonomic"[22] quest that subverts even while situating the request for the originary name.

The possibility of a science of paronymy can only be established according to the articulation and elaboration of the necessity of an aporetic reading. It is this necessity that is so keenly felt, for whatever the status of the arguments that finally develop all the reasons, well known from Aristotle, for which being is not a genus,[23] adding as well those curious reasons Kant gives which determine that Aristotle's table of categories cannot form a system but must remain in a state of "rhapsody";[24] it nonetheless remains that the aporia in question results from an aim, a requirement, an exigency, the original character of which ought to be acknowledged, even if it necessarily escapes any and every attempt at

---

21. Cf. ibid., 75.
22. Cf. Derrida, *La Dissémination*, "Preface: Hors Livre."
23. Cf. *Meta.* 3.3.998b23ff. and especially *Meta.* 11.1.1059b33ff.: "But inasmuch as, if being and unity are to be regarded as generic, they must be predicated of their differentiae [διαφοράς], whereas no genus is predicable of its differentiae, from this point of view it would seem that they should be regarded neither as genera nor as principles."
24. Kant, *Critique of Pure Reason*, §10 ("The Pure Concepts of the Understanding of the Categories"), immediately following "The Table of the Categories."

formulization/formalization. It is because ontology aims at a nongeneric science of being that even its failure is specifically its own. And it is because ontology fails according to its own standard of the πρὸς ἕν (with reference to one thing), that a science of paronymy is seen as not only possible, but even necessary. For it should be clear that such a science, if it could secure its own intrinsic possibility, would provide the basis for a particularly philosophical study of the multiple meanings of being.

What is at stake here is the institution of a regime that would prevent confusing this ἀπορία with an ἀποφράδες, both the ineffability of a doctrine of the analogy of being as well as the holiday which language takes in coming to the irreducibility of the plurivocity of the term 'being', a holiday that in fact is a day of great misfortune, for it is the day upon which the dead, in this case the dead metaphors, return to reinhabit the houses in which they had lived and thereby darken the lives of the living, the living paronymity.

VI

> To respond affirmatively to these questions would be to mistake [*méconnaître*] all of that which is of the aporetic in the Aristotelian doctrine of the categories, which, as we have seen, authorizes less a hierarchized vision and unitary completion than it does of expressing the necessarily fragmentary character of our discourse on being.
> Pierre Aubenque, *Le Problème de l'être chez Aristote*

To establish the prescientific character of metaphysics, let us look at an opening remark of the *Metaphysics:*

> In general, to investigate the elements of existing things without distinguishing the various senses in which things are said to exist is a hopeless task; especially when one inquires along these lines into the nature of the elements of which things are composed. For (a) we cannot surely conceive of the elements of activity or passivity or straightness; this is possible,

if at all, only in the case of substances. Hence to look for, to suppose that one has found, the elements of *everything* that exists is a mistake. (b) How *can* one apprehend the elements of *everything*? (*Meta.* 1.9.992b19–26)

But since science deals with genera and species, and substance is in every case a determined individual, philosophy designates a term for which no science exists. This belongs properly to the transcendental in human experience. This transcendental element or dimension which Aristotle attempted to articulate in an elaboration of a "doctrine of the analogy of being," as it has come to be known by the tradition, and which I have invoked in the name of the possibility of a "science" of paronymy, can never be recognized as the *object of a science*, for it can never appear *as such*, even though it makes its presence felt throughout human experience. This is precisely its transcendental quality: it transcends every attempt at objectification, yet it is the horizon of objectivity in general. This transcendental dimension to the linguistically enhorizoned world can only be approached by a playfulness, a polymorphous and polysemic playfulness that admits the play of the world in all its dissemblance, dissimulation, and occultation. It designates the resolute refusal to subject being to a systematic totalization of rigorous determination.

Again, this playfulness was given voice by finding unexpected significance in the first paragraph of the *Categories*. To say that there are not two classes of things to name—synonyms and homonyms —but three classes, with the insertion of paronyms, is to open up a new domain of discourse that permits the autonomy of philosophy to be based on the existence of what has traditionally been called *nonaccidental homonymy*. From this point on there is a continuous chain formed from the paronyms in paragraph 1 of the *Categories* to the reference πρὸς ἕν in *Metaphysics* 4.2, 4.1, and 7.4. The new possibility of thought opened up in this way was that of a nonmetaphorical, unscientific, and properly transcendental resemblance among the primary significations of being. Based on the difference between paronymy and poetic analogy, the nongeneric bond of being can be—and without a doubt must be—thought according to an order that will no longer owe anything to analogy as such but rather can best be expressed by the middle voice, for it precedes and sets up the opposition between activity and passivity that produces the *play* of differences and derivations. This play of differences and derivations can never be fully mastered, so it must be marked out in a strategic and risky way. It signals the possibility of errancy without which there could be no thinking.

Before, however, a theory of paronymy can be fully elaborated, we must first make provisions to secure the possibility of a science the condition for the possibility of which is the impossibility of there being such a science, and the object of which has, as we have seen, its condition of possibility in the impossibility of discourse about it. We must ask after a number of things, not the least of which is the deconstructive significance of passing over the term 'paronymy', both by Aristotle in the *Metaphysics* and by the tradition that gives us this text. We must ask after the suppression of 'paronymy' in the *Metaphysics*. That is to say, we want to master as best we can what Aristotle designates by the phrase "the science of being qua being," in particular, in its relation to the πρὸς ἕν and to πρώτη φιλοσοφία and in its bearing upon the fact that although every science concerns a specific genus, being is not a genus. The general situation is like this: Aristotle asserts something about the nature of being that undermines the possibility of making a coherent discourse about being. This self-canceling nature of speculative discourse is brought to light by an analysis of the ἕν of the πρὸς ἕν.

The ἕν, we are told, is substance: πρώτη οὐσία, τόδε τι, ὄν ᾗ ὄν, ἕν ᾗ ἕν, and to speak with rigor, ὄν καθ' αὑτό, as well as καταγορούμενον καθ' αὑτό, being according to itself, being in itself, and being predicable of itself. From πρώτη οὐσία—of which everything is predicated but which can itself never be a predicate, and consequently is the nameable per se, for it is precisely that which can receive names—from πρώτη οὐσία come paronymic derivatives: being as mobile; being as living;

being as figure, etc. From πρώτη οὐσία, the name Aristotle gives to nominalizability—and not the nominalized—is generated a progressive diffraction, dispersion, and derivation of sense. This progression is what I term paronymity. It should be added here that οὐσία, as the name for the process of nominalization, can only be left unnamed, or rather, can only be named apophantically as that which has no strict and rigorous name. In this sense we can say that the ἕν is said paronymously, for there is no rigorously privileged first term, but rather a progression of diffractions, dispersions, and derivations of a term spoken paraleptically. The ἕν is not one thing, does not stand by itself or unto itself. The ἕν, rather, is only insofar as it bears the reference to itself of the diffraction of sense. In this way the ἕν names, not the one, but the fragmentation of the one, its progressive dispersal.

The problem, then, is this: if the appeal to being authorizes the instituting of analogy, analogy can evidently not be applied to the case of being, for want of a more fundamental series with which the series of significations of being can be put in relation. Or otherwise said, the πρὸς of the πρὸς ἕν remains always ambiguous in the strong sense, that it is undecidable which of its polyvalent uses has gained ascendancy at any one particular time: although the main sense appears to be causal, it can never be decided which of the four causes the ἕν is. And the problem of Aristotelian ontology remains entire: if being is equivocal or if, at least, its unity is suspended by a relation which is itself equivocal, how are we to institute a discourse on being?

Even though being is said plurivocally, Aristotle does not seem to put in doubt the possibility of a *coherent* discourse on being when, at the opening of Book Gamma of the *Metaphysics*, he affirms without hesitation the existence of a science of being qua being (*Meta.* 4.1.1003a21). This apparent contradiction between the affirmation of a radical plurality of significations of being and the confidence in a unified, or at least unifiable, discourse is astonishing—at least to the extent that the commentators have attempted to render this contradiction either innocuous or inconspicuous by programmatically steering a reading away from any discussion of paronymy. This contradiction appears already in his declarations of principle: all happens as if Aristotle, at the very moment where he presents the founding of the science of being qua being, multiplies arguments in order to demonstrate the impossibility of such a founding. Such a science would then have to accede to its limitations, the most notable of which is that, although urgent and necessary, it is also self-subverting since it can never free itself of questioning its own intrinsic possibility, given that its object is precisely what cannot be tracked scientifically. But this obligation to subject itself to the most exacting questions is not so much a limitation as it is the *de*limitation of the science in and by which it would unfold from its limit. The risk this science would run in exposing itself to its own impossibility is at the same time the opening of its own intrinsic possibility; to found this science is to expose the ever-present possibility of its foundering, and to expose this possibility of its foundering is to find its founding and funding.

This much is clear, that the science of being qua being would be other than the particular sciences. Now, every science is particular, but no science can itself justify its proper particularity: a science concerns a determined region of being, but it can found itself only by the elucidation of its relation to being in its totality. But this is a paradox of sorts, or at least a koan: Aristotle is the one who announces the constitution of a science of being qua being defined directly by its nonparticularity (*Meta.* 4.1.1003a23) and who demonstrates that every science inasmuch as it is science is necessarily specific.

To start with, the science of being qua being seems to be the legacy of the universalistic and synoptic vocation that is bound, as is testified to at the beginning of the *Metaphysics*, to the idea generally conceded to philosophy (*Meta.* 1.2.982a7); for being qua being is "that which is common to all things" (*Meta.* 4.3. 1005a27), that which is "said *par excellence* of the totality of all things" (*Meta.* 3.3.998b21), and the science of being qua being is defined expressly by its opposition to the particular sciences (*Meta.* 4.1.1003a21).

More precisely, the study of the common principles or axioms is incumbent upon such a science, that is to say, of those principles that, not being proper to any particular science, but nevertheless presupposed by all, enhance the competence of neither the mathematician nor the physician (*Meta.* 4.3.1005a21–1005b1), nor of any particular knowledge. And, finally, these common principles are at the same time the first principles, for their possession is necessary in order to know any being whatsoever; for "that which a man must know if he knows anything he must bring with him to the task" (*Meta.* 4.3.1005b15). In this sense, the science of being qua being claims to realize another of the characters recognized as part and parcel of wisdom: the "theoretic science of first principles and first causes" (*Meta.* 1.2.982b8) looks at being.

In understanding that being is not a genus, we also see that being is not a substance: "No universal can be a substance [Εἰ δὲ μηδὲν τῶν καθόλου δυνατὸν οὐσίαν εἶναι]" (*Meta.* 10.2.1053b16) (since substance is always subject, whereas a universal is nothing but predicate; cf. *Meta.* 7.13). It is clear, then, that that which is most universal will also be the least substantial. But, as we have seen, this is being. Being has no substance: "Being itself cannot be a substance in the sense of one thing existing alongside the many (since it is common to them), but only as a predicate [κατηγόρημα]" (*Meta.* 10.2.1053b20).

The term *being* designates a radical lack, a radical lack of substance. In a word, then, in claiming that there is a science of being qua being, while nevertheless maintaining that every science is concerned with a determined genus and that being is not a genus, Aristotle asserts something about the nature of being that destroys the possibility of any coherent discourse about it.

We have seen that the πρός of the πρὸς ἕν is essentially undecidable as to which of its polyvalent meanings has gained mastery at any one time. We have seen that there is a necessarily fragmentary and dispersed character to any discourse on being. This can be expressed by saying that although Aristotle says in book 4 of the *Metaphysics* that being, being said πρὸς μίαν φύσιν, is assimilated "in a certain manner" to "things that have a common character [λέγεται καθ' ἕν]" (*Meta.* 4.2.1003b14), nonetheless πρὸς ἕν λέγεσθαι must be strenuously opposed to καθ' ἕν λέγεσθαι, for to conflate these two ways of speaking is not to resolve the koan but rather to suppress all the difficulties incumbent upon entering into the logic of this koan. Moreover, a little further on Aristotle presents substance, οὐσία, considered in its relation to the other significations of being, as the "premier," that upon which all things "depend" and "by means of which [δι' ὅ] they are named as being what they are. If being is said in terms of οὐσία or by means of οὐσία, this nevertheless does not name a simple relation of dependence or even of production. Πρός is not reducible to διὰ for the same reason that it is not reducible to κατά. The deconstructive significance of the πρὸς ἕν—as opposed to καθ' ἕν and δι' ἕν—is that the ἕν can never be named as such, rather it is the principle of nominalizability, in that it directs experience *toward* the naming of things, or better, it directs us to experience things in the pursuit of naming them. The one thing that all beings, in being said, bear a reference to, is that being gets nominated in, by, and through, the name.

"Being is said in many ways," but it cannot be defined and, in fact, designates the radical lack of substance (οὐσία) and therefore of name. It can only be a radical lack of name that could give itself over to the process of nominalization; for, given the distinction I drew out for the Aristotelian corpus between the ultimate *signified* and *signification*, between πλείω σημαίνειν and πολλαχῶς λέγεσθαι, it is not so much the meaning of "being" that Aristotle is interested in as it is the meaning of being.

Now, the tradition, in suppressing and excluding the paronymity of being, has found the ἕν to the πρὸς ἕν to be substance, for "substance in the truest and strictest, in the primary sense of the term [κυριώτατά τε καὶ πρώτως καὶ μάλιστα λεγομένη], is that which is neither asserted of nor can be found in a subject" (*Categ.* 5.2a11). The claim is that substance is the primary, originary mode of being. In Book K of the *Metaphysics* Aristotle asserts that οὐσία *is* τὸ ὂν ᾗ ὄν. But if so, then being is displaced from the origin and is subordinated to substance. That the ἕν of the πρὸς ἕν is expressly named substance, οὐσία, the self-subsisting, can only be considered philosophically correct if we keep in mind that οὐσία is the name for the process of nominalization that occurs as the progression of sense.

VII

> Philosophy, in its very diachrony, is consciousness of the breakup of consciousness.
> Emmanuel Levinas, *Otherwise than Being, or Beyond Essence*

By suppressing and excluding paronymy, the commentators have sought to give an original and unique name to the ἕν of the πρὸς ἕν, and have found this source word in οὐσία. But if the term *being* designates the radical lack of substance, it designates that the origin is absent, that there is no center, and that the quest for the original and unique name for being displaces every name. Since being cannot be defined, it designates that the ἕν of the πρὸς ἕν is *but the apophantic name for the process of paraleptic nominalization*—that is, there is no speaking strictly about being, there is only the parabolic reading of what can only be omitted from thematizing discourse, but by being omitted or passed over gives voice to the name. There is no privileged term, only a series of derivatives. This is just what I mean by a science of paronymy, the science of the (self-) forgetfulness of origins by means of the free play of differences and derivations. The science of paronymy, as I would wish to propose it, would be the study of how things lack a definitive meaning; it would pursue the elision and erosion of sense, its slippaging and seepaging away from a definiteness and determinativeness into a diffraction and diffusion and defection. But this movement away from determinative sense toward a dissipation and dispersion of that sense is not a simple movement but rather one that is dialectical: the definitive sense is not simply diffracted and diffused into a series of paronyms; rather, the process of diffraction and diffusion is simultaneously the obliviating of the privileged first term in the series to the extent that it is in principle irrecuperable, in principle forgotten and forgotten that it has always already been forgotten. Again, the obliviating of the first term is also the obliviating of this obliviating of the first term; nothing could arouse the suspicion that a definitive meaning has always already been diffracted into a series of derivative terms. Nonetheless, sense is putatively derivative, ostensibly derivative, presupposing its derivation but without demonstrating its derivativeness; rather sense is itself the supposing of derivativeness. Thus, given the derivativeness of a series of paronyms, everything is charged with the search for a first term.

According to the analysis of πρὸς ἕν equivocals, the originary is both the first term in the series and also the principle generative of that series. With the insight into the paronymous character of this series, we find that the principle generative of the series is the principle determining sense to be essentially diffractive. So the principle of diffractiveness, since it is a term of the series, is itself diffracted, broken up, dispersed. It collapses into itself, disappearing into diffractedness. Thus, what is generative of the series is the dispersal of any generating principle. The terms stand alone, undetermined, ungenerated, unsupported. Again, the principle generative of sense, accordingly, determines sense to be the supposition of *its* own derivativeness. But since this principle is itself the originary sense, it is itself the supposition of *its* own derivativeness, and so is its own undoing: the principle determining sense determines itself to not be the principle determinative of sense and so determines sense to stand alone, undetermined and ungenerated.

Furthermore, each term of the series carries a reference back to a prior term that generates the diffractedness of the terms of the series. What generates this diffractedness is, as I have suggested, the obliviating of any definitiveness or determinativeness of sense. So every term of the series, including the putative first term, is itself the reference back to a term obliviated in, by, and as the generation of the series. The reference back that each term of the series carries, since it is a relation to what is assumed to have already been obliviated, cancels itself out as a relation and so is itself dispersed, broken up, dispelled. It is purely a presumption, like the ghost limb of an amputee. The reference back is, in this sense, the indeterminate opening up upon the lapsing into indeterminateness: the diffractedness of sense implicates a determinativeness only as something that is being obliviated by the emergence of sense, only as something that has always lapsed into indeterminativeness. Sense emerges by determining itself to be the assumption of a prior lapse into indeterminateness. Since by definition every term of the series carries a reference back to a term obliviated in and as the generation of the series, this term is, of course, always implicated, but *only* implicated, nothing more. The reference back is itself the obliviating of a putative first term. But in that case, the reference back is a dissolution of itself; that back to which the reference back is a reference back dissolves the referencing back.

But: the implication of a term that has always already been obliviated is merely the presumption of that term, for it does not bring the term out of oblivion. Rather, the implicating of the obliviated term is itself the assumption of an obliviated term and so for that reason is the obliviating of the obliviation of the term. This is, however, not the same as the emergence of the term back into the series. The implication of a term that has always already been obliviated implicates that term in such a way, then, that the terms of the series are released from their reference back to this putatively originary term.

Now, the originary is what is referenced back to yet is itself this referencing back. This referencing back is, however, the obliviating of the originary. Consequently the originarity of the originary consists in the obliviating of the originary. But if the originary is itself the obliviating of the originary, it nevertheless is still the originary and can be so only by the obliviating of this obliviating of itself. That is to say, if the obliviating of the originary is itself the originary, then this obliviating is itself obliviated. But if this is the case, then it should be clear that everything and nothing is originary. The diffractiveness of sense that follows upon this movement of double obliviation is itself the resurgence or resumption of the originary. Originarity is always *re*surgence, with no prior upsurgence, the *re*sumption of what has never been assumed. But this means, then, that the originary is irretrievable. I do not just mean that the originary has become completely obliviated, obliviated to the extent that it has disappeared without a trace. Rather, the originary is irretrievable precisely because everything and nothing is simply the resurgence and resumption of the originary. All there is is resurgence; all there is is the upsurgence of the resurgence of originarity. In this way the science of paronymy is the restoration, the restitution, of sense: everything returns to being what it already was, but now can be seen for what it is.

Again, if each term of a paronymous series carries within itself a reference back to an originary term, this reference back is itself the obliviating of the term referenced back to. That is to say, the principle generative of the series is precisely this reference back that obliviates what is being referenced back to just as it is dissolved by that back to which it is a reference back; the principle generative of the series is the disappearing into the terms of the series of precisely this principle. Another way of saying this is to note that the reference back to the term presumed to be generative of diffractiveness is itself the diffracting of sense.

The science of paronymy, then, as I would wish to propose it, is not simply the elaboration of the deconstructive insight that the originary is lacking or has always already been covered over by the derivative and parasitic. It is not simply a question of how the derivative and parasitic effect their own valorization over against a presumed originarity. If there is an obliviating of the originary, there is also the obliviating of this obliviating. This is to say, the science of paronymy would demonstrate that the quest for the originary is in principle defective and defeasant, delinquent, not so much in and of itself, but rather because such a quest is self-eliminating: given that, according to this proposed science, everything and nothing is equally originary just as it is equally derivative, the telos of this quest undermines the whole point of the quest, namely, that it is a quest. The quest overlooks and passes over what it is seeking precisely by seeking it. That is, the intention of such a quest entirely vitiates itself, for, since it presumes a progression of sense that can be traced back to an originary sense, it is not able to discern that everything (and nothing) is already equally originary (as well as derivative), and so by searching for the originary, it deprives itself of it. The quest for the originary—which we might say is the movement of classical philosophy—is self-eliminating to the extent that it even eliminates the insight into its self-eliminating nature.

It is this dialectic that the science of paronymy would realize. The science of paronymy would demonstrate that a term gets privileged only insofar as there is a forgetting that it has gotten privileged *as well as* forgetting that its privileging has itself already been forgotten. Accordingly, the science of paronymy would disengage us from the quest for the originary by affirming a certain originary derivativeness of sense. But this affirmation is itself dialectical, for what would be affirmed by the science of paronymy would be a certain inadequacy of language in the task it assigns itself. But this inadequacy is not a *simple* determination of language, that it is, say, not completely transparent in its intention, or that it cannot fully realize its sense, or that it does not completely disappear in the fulfillment of its sense. Rather, to affirm a certain inadequacy to language not only makes this inadequacy itself inadequate, so showing that it could never be inadequate enough, but in so doing makes of this inadequate inadequacy the perfect adequation of language to its task. If the task of language, as far as philosophy understands it, is the recuperation of the originary constituting of sense, this language already does so by default, provided that this recuperation is not something that has to be specifically undertaken. For to undertake to find in language the recuperation of the originary constituting of sense is already to have missed the point; it is already to have already passed over and overlooked what is always already immediately there. The originary constituting of sense is the incessant recommencement of sense that is language.

But there is, along with this incessant recommencement of sense, the suspicion that language is not the transparent disclosure of sense that it presumes to be. Language itself gives rise to this suspicion. Language, in saying its other, says something about itself, but says it with masterful, almost undetectable irony; language is its own *défiance*—defiance *of* language, effected *by* language, and situated *in* language, and which finds within itself the terms of its own critique.

But if the science of paronymy arises from the self-suspicion and self-defiance and self-defection of language, nonetheless, in its elaboration it would preserve the integrity of sense; it would release language back into the transparency of its intention. But it could do this only through deconstructing itself. Its elaboration is its self-deconstruction. For if a definitive or determinative sense is shown to be lacking, leaving only the elision and erosion of sense into diffractedness and diffusion, the science of paronymy determines that the definitive and determinative sense is irrecuperable, obliviated to such an extent that its obliviation is itself obliviated, leaving nothing to be recuperated—but, then, precisely for this reason this sense *could never be suspected to be lacking, could never be suspected to be missed, and so could never be missed.* And if the science of paronymy determines sense to be diffracted, this diffractedness *could never become apparent*, for the diffractedness of sense is itself self-dispersing, and it is self-dispersing to the extent that even the insight into its self-dispersing character is itself dispersed. In light of this, we can no longer affect surprise that the tradition has "systematically" overlooked paronymy and the speculative effects a meditation on it might have initiated. For it is by virtue of this very paronymy that philosophy is blind to anything like a science of paronymy, even though such a science would not only account for its being overlooked but also could alone account for philosophic insightfulness in general. Any philosophic insight, on this account, would be blind to the paronymy generative of its insightfulness.

Thus, discourse on the principle of paronymity affirms the impossibility of coherent discourse upon the diffractedness of sense by venturing to realize this impossibility by the very discourse on this impossibility. What the science of paronymy demonstrates is in contradiction with the demonstration. This science, then, would be self-refuting. That is to say, the science of paronymy demonstrates a principle—the principle of the dissipation and diffractedness of sense—the very possibility of which is denied by the fact of its demonstration. The formulation of this principle disappears into the diffractedness of sense, is completely taken over and absorbed into this diffractedness.

Yet the science of paronymy is not self-contradictory, for the demonstration and what is demonstrated are not simply correlative. The demonstration could never be contemporaneous with what is demonstrated.

In this way, the science of paronymy is the return from its own self-refutation. Again, it refutes itself by putting its thesis into contradiction with the conditions for any thesis. But this does not turn it into pure nonsense, for the principle of paronymity, inasmuch as it is an indirect refutation of itself makes a special kind of sense, even if it is doubtful that this sense that it makes can ever be made sense of. Let me see if I can explain this sense that the principle of paronymity makes. The erosion of sense is, of course, the sense that the principle of paronymity determines sense to make. And, as the exposition of this principle demonstrates, a special kind of double forgetfulness is at the source of sense. This doubly dialectical forgetfulness promotes an indifference toward the essence of sense while indicating a *something else*, an *otherwise* than sense, a *beyond essence*. The science of paronymy is the opening up of the otherwise than sense. But, then, how does this otherwise than sense makes sense? It makes sense by making of sense an *in other words*. One cannot conceive the making of sense otherwise than what makes sense. But one can conceive otherwise than as making sense the obliviating of the making of sense. The principle of paronymity exposes the resumption of sense from out of the obliviating of the making of sense. Making sense is the very impossibility of things not making sense;

yet there is constantly recommencing behind our attempt to make sense out of the fact that things make sense the anonymous muffling rustling of senselessness.

The relationship to sense that the principle of paronymity expounds, which formulates the experience of sense, is not itself experienced, does not itself make sense. For this principle determines the defectiveness and diffractedness of sense, and this determination of defectiveness and diffractedness always disappears into the sense being determined as defective and diffracted. As a coherent discourse formulating the diffractiveness of sense, the science of paronymy would render itself the cause and proof of its own impossibility even while destroying the very possibility of its object, the diffractedness of sense.

Moreover, the positing of the principle of paronymity, that is, the instituting of the formal inquiry into the diffractedness of sense, not only destroys its object just as it is undone by it, but also disrupts and disperses the subjectivity doing the positing. Subjectivity finds within itself an intrigue and investment of *something else*, of an *otherwise*, a something else and an otherwise that not only remains unaccountable in terms of subjectivity, but also could not even be suspected.

According to its basic precept, the science of paronymy would exclude self-identity; it would indirectly dissolve the coherency of self-definition. If the principle of the diffractiveness of sense appears coherent, it can do so only by virtue of the self lapsing into a kind of incoherency, where it is conscious only of the breakup and dispersion of its presumed self-definition. The principle of the diffractiveness of sense is not incoherent; rather it is so perfectly coherent that it excludes me at the very moment I realize it. I become incoherent in relation to the coherency of this principle. That is to say, it is precisely the integrity of selfhood that is obliviated by the diffraction of sense.

Whereas, before the discovery of the principle of paronymity, the sole content of the ego consisted in identifying itself as itself, with the realization of this principle of diffractiveness, the ego consists entirely in the dissolution of its content, leaving only a kind of pure intentionality without correlates. Here intentionality collapses into its objective correlate. But if this is the case, then its subjective correlate also disappears into its objective correlate. Now, to speak of the ego and its contents here is not to relapse into the prephenomenological metaphor of a mental container with its contents. Rather, I am intending with this metaphor to indicate that the ego is precisely the activity of identifying with its contents, that is, with its states, thoughts, moods, feelings, and so on, an activity that, in its preparonymical awareness of itself, consists in the ego being absorbed wholly into its states, thoughts, moods, and feelings.

To be precise, if the science of paronymy exposes the obliviating of the originary in the doubly dialectical way I have attempted to analyze, then intentionality, according to the principle of paronymity, is precisely the self-forgetting of the ego. This does not mean so much the dissolution of the ego *simpliciter* as it does the disappearing of the ego into its contents, its losing itself in and by wholly identifying with its contents, forgetting itself, its singularity, in this diversion.

One's sense of inwardness, however, is irreducible to one's "immanent" objects, for there is always the recommencing of this identification; the identification of the ego with its contents is precisely the recommencement of this identification. But this means, then, that the ego can, in principle at least, always interrupt this process of identification, break away from it and recuperate itself from out of its self-forgetfulness. The ego then becomes the other in the same. It is itself the interruption of the incessantly same, the exception to the same excepting itself from its identification with the same.

The identity of the same in the ego comes to it despite itself, as an election, in the form of the singularity of someone assigned. This is someone who, in the absence of anyone, is called upon to be someone, and cannot evade this assignation. This assignation is borne as a mortal wound, that left alone the ego is a wound that cannot heal. We neither can evade such laceration nor find in it ourselves. The ego is inseparable from this appeal or this election, which cannot be declined. The ego, in attempting to recuperate itself from its identification with its contents, experiences itself as being someone assigned to be this ego, to be its substitute, its proxy, as someone called upon for whom no one else can substitute. It can never desert this assignation, yet it can never fulfill its obligation. Accordingly, the ego takes refuge or finds exile in its identification with its contents. This exile or refuge is without conditions or support; the ego stands alone as the incessant recurrence of refuge and exile; it is its own hostage. Yet the ego finds refuge and exile only insofar as it is always wanting with respect to itself, always wanting to catch up with being itself, in deficit of being itself. This is its self-forgetfulness, this divestiture of itself that is never sufficient, this restlessness and insomnia. In this light, as the science of paronymy would indicate, the recuperation of the ego from out of its self-forgetfulness is simply the resumption of this selfsame self-forgetfulness.

According to the principle of paronymity, this self-forgetfulness of the ego constitutes what is classically understood as consciousness: the intentionality that aspires to fulfillment, the centripetal movement of a consciousness that coincides with itself, recovers, rediscovers itself without remainder or reserve, rests in the certainty of itself, confirms itself, doubles itself up, consolidates itself, becomes the congealment into a substance. Yet all this as what "consciousness" has always already and thus henceforth forgotten about itself.

For the ego that has absorbed itself, or has been absorbed, into its contents, consciousness is the very locus of the reverting of the facticity of individuation into the *concept* of the individual, which is to say into a universal, in which its singularity is lost in its universality. In such consciousness no supplementary specific difference, no negation of universality can extract the ego out of universality. This is the ego as it stands in its self-forgetfulness.

But, then, the activity or actuality of the self-forgetfulness of the ego, the activity of its identifying with its contents, cannot itself be anything universal, cannot itself be thought, for in order to be thought there would have to be the thought that thinks the process of this identification rather than its content—but then, this too would be identified with, this too would become the content of this identification. The actuality of self-forgetfulness is not a conjuncture of concrescence in being, and it is not a concept; it is pure transcendence, transcendence without correlate. Yet this transcendence is not a transcendental unity of apperception, nor is it the undeclinable transcendental ego which constitutes sense. Rather this transcendence can be said to be, if indeed anything can be said of it, the implication of a *something else*, an *otherwise than oneself*, something intractably unintelligible even while enabling intelligibility per se. Needless to say, this *something else*, this *otherwise than oneself*, cannot be posited, cannot be identified, for it is the abnegation of positing and identifying. It is what is there when there is no positing, no identifying.

VIII

Both instinctively and for logical reasons, I find it hard to believe that principles can exist which make no difference in facts.
William James, *The Varieties of Religious Experience*

124. Philosophy may in no way interfere with the actual use of language; it can in the end only describe it.
For it cannot give it any foundation either.
It leaves everything as it is.
Ludwig Wittgenstein, *Philosophical Investigations*

It is along these lines that a "science" of paronymy would be able to decline and delimit itself, would be able to demonstrate its own autonomous character, since this "science" would be able to account for its own genesis and genealogy. Such a science, and only such a science, could account for the fact that it was systematically overlooked, neglected, and suppressed by a tradition intent on naming the origin of the all in a totalizing discourse, a discourse designed to constitute a kind of comprehensive certainty about the all, its origin, and its genealogy. Only such a science of the (self-)forgetfulness of origins would be able to account for the systematic forgetfulness of the possibility of such a science, for it is only by being the forgetting of origins that this science could forget that its origin lies in it being systematically forgotten; and in forgetting that the condition for its possibility is the forgetting that it is possible it would thereby render itself the condition for its own possibility. In this way the science of paronymy would establish its autonomy.

Like the term *aporia*, the science of paronymy presupposes itself, obviously not before it is posited, but in *that* it is posited: it can be elaborated only as the presupposing of itself; that is, as presupposing that there is an essential science the possibility of which has been essentially forgotten, and this science is itself the science of the dispersion and defection involved in forgetting the possibility of just this very science. Like aporia, the science of paronymy is itself the paradox of its own auto-implication: the paradox consists in the fact that once the dispersion and diffraction of sense is opened up to inquiry, it is seen to be essential, so essential, in fact, that any theory of the dispersion and diffraction of sense would be, in advance of its elaboration, always already dispersed and diffracted, would be, in a word, the undoing of just such a theory. That is to say, in developing a theory of the dispersion and diffraction of sense, this theory is seen to have always already been almost completely dispersed and diffracted; the object proper to the science of paronymy eliminates the very possibility of elaborating such a science. The theory of paronymy, then, is the recuperating of itself from out of its own necessary dispersion; yet it is the incessant lapsing and relapsing into its dispersion and diffraction. If the science of paronymy presupposes its own intrinsic possibility as the condition for its elaboration, or presupposes that the condition for its possibility is intrinsic to itself, then it does so only in order to become the proof and cause of its impossibility.

So if the origin of the science of paronymy consists in forgetting the possibility of such a science, yet this science is a science of the forgetting of origins, and so a science that describes in particular how forgetting the possibility of just such a science gives rise to this very science, this science, then, would contain within itself its own origin, for, in being the general interpretation of how origins efface themselves in the play of the dispersing and dissemination of sense, it would itself be an interpretation of how it itself must necessarily have always already been forgotten. Not only would the science of paronymy be a theory of the genealogy of sense and of theories of sense, it would also be generative of the elimination of all theories of the general conditions for the upsurge of theories, including a fortiori itself. The paronymous solution to the question of the meaning of being not only annuls that question, deactivating its questionability, but terminates in the radical dissolution of itself, and so terminates in principle in the radical dissolution of every attempt to interrogate the meaning of being. The "house of being" is a rundown ramshackle runamok shanty sinking into the mire of its own ruination of rumination.

The science of paronymy would eliminate itself in the process of elaborating its own intrinsic possibility. As soon as it posits itself as the condition for its own possibility, just as soon would it have forgotten that it is possible. The science of paronymy is like one of Jean Tinguely's self-constructing-self-consuming artifacts, the only purpose of which, once activated, is to construct itself by dismantling itself and to dismantle itself by constructing itself.

In the end, this project proposes a theory of philosophic sense the *only* effect of which would be to destroy the possibility of proposing just such a theory. In the end, this project is its own radical erasure. In the end, unlike at the beginning, the problem, then, is not so well known.

PART II

THE CUNNING OF BEING

The Amphiboly of Being
in *Being and Time*

> Because something ontical is made to underlie the ontological, the expression '*substantia*' functions sometimes with a signification which is ontological, sometimes with one which is ontical, but mostly with one which is hazily ontico-ontological. Behind this slight difference of signification, however, there lies hidden a failure to master the basic problem of Being. To treat this adequately, we must 'track down' the equivocation *in the right way*.
>
> Martin Heidegger, *Being and Time*

> . . . 'the Being of beings' in the essential ambivalence of subjective genitive and objective genitive. The ambivalence of the preposition 'of' occurs within the ambiance of the ontological difference, but does not think this difference.
>
> Martin Heidegger, *The Essence of Reasons*

> At the same time 'Being' has long stood for 'beings' and, inversely, the latter for the former, the two of them caught in a curious and still unraveled confusion.
>
> Martin Heidegger, "Letter on Humanism"

Thus it is that we begin to philosophize when we realize that philosophy is itself the activity of having already and all along closed off upon its own essential and intrinsic possibility, leaving itself waylaid back along the way of its self-obliviating waywarding but without ever leaving itself behind. We do not come out of this waywarding, we do not come out of it at the other end, it having never come to an end for having never been able to begin, having never been able to begin for having already and all along come to its end. But if we do not come out at the *other* end of philosophy, out into the *other* of philosophy, this is because with it we do not ever come to an end even though we are all along at the end. Rather, we look to begin at the end, and then to begin again at the end, to begin in the end, to find in the end the way to begin, in the end to begin, beginning to begin by putting an end to the end.

> But what if that which is early outdistanced everything late; if the very earliest far surpassed the very latest? What once occurred in the dawn of our destiny would then come, as what once occurred, at the last (ἔσχατον), that is, at the departure of the long-hidden destiny of Being. The Being of beings is gathered (λέγεσθαι, λόγος) in the ultimacy of its destiny. The essence of Being hitherto disappears, its truth still veiled. The history of Being is gathered in this departure. The gathering in this departure, as the gathering (λόγος) at the outermost point (ἔσχατον) of its essence hitherto, is the eschatology of Being. As something fateful, Being itself is intrinsically eschatological.[1]

Coming at the end of the end we begin and begin to begin and begin to begin again. With being. Begin being with being to the end of being with being.

> Therefore, it lies in the *very nature of a beginning* that it be being and nothing else. To enter into philosophy, therefore, calls for no other preparations, no further reflections or points of connection.
>
> Consequently, whatever is intended to be expressed or implied beyond *being*, in the richer forms of representing the absolute or God, this is in the beginning only an empty word

---

1. Martin Heidegger, "The Anaximander Fragment," 18.

and only being; this simple determination which has no other meaning of any kind, this emptiness, is therefore simply as such the beginning of philosophy.

This insight is itself so simple that this beginning as such requires no preparation or further introduction; and, indeed, these preliminary, external reflections about it were not so much intended to lead up to it as rather to eliminate all preliminaries.[2]

Of course, these remarks mark the beginning of the end, which is to say, the end to beginning.

I

That difficulty lies in language. Our Western languages are languages of metaphysical thinking, each in its own way. It must remain an open question whether the nature of Western languages is in itself marked with the exclusive brand of metaphysics, and thus marked permanently by onto-theo-logic, or whether these languages offer other possibilities of utterance—and that means at the same time of a telling silence [*des sagenden Nichtsagens*].

Martin Heidegger,
"The Onto-theo-logical Constitution of Metaphysics"

Ample to the point of believing itself interminable, a discourse that has *called itself* philosophy—doubtless the only discourse that has ever intended to receive its name from itself, and has never ceased murmuring its initial letter to itself from as close as possible—has always, including its own, meant to say its limit. . . . this discourse has always insisted upon assuring itself mastery over the limit (*peras, limes, Grenze*). It has recognized, conceived, posited, declined the limit according to all possible modes; to dispose of the limit, it has transgressed it. *Its own limit* had not to remain foreign to it. Therefore it has appropriated the concept for itself; it has believed that it controls the margin of its volume and that it thinks its other.

Jacques Derrida, "Tympan," in *Margins of Philosophy*

---

2. G. W. F. Hegel, *Hegel's Science of Logic*, 72, 78.

Near the end of his career Heidegger submitted a paper to appear, translated, in a collected volume entitled *Kierkegaard vivant*. This paper, which was originally a lecture, was entitled "The End of Philosophy and the Task of Thinking."[3] At first blush this seems a strange lecture indeed, for how can we presume that philosophy has come to an end? Is not this itself a philosophical question? Are we not now engaged in something that at least seems to resemble philosophy? Is not philosophy that form of life that poses itself as its own limit in order to possess this limit? Is not philosophy that form of life the sole content of which consists in identifying the concept of its limit as the limit of its self-concept? Is not philosophy, in other words, that form of life that has, having always already come to an end, struggled to begin anew, by incorporating its end, its completion, into itself as a new beginning? Is not the question Has philosophy come to an end? *the* philosophical question, not just for our day, the latter-day of metaphysics, but for any and every day that dawns for philosophy, inasmuch as philosophy always and everywhere demands that it give itself an account of its own self-adjudicating legitimacy, that it validate itself as that which gives itself its own name, a name that soars and sounds throughout the human estate, laying a claim upon us that it is the only authentic name, the true Orphic seal and signature of being? And if philosophy has come to an end, what can be left for thinking aside from the manipulating of entities into unconditionally objectified calculable stock, something to be done with the aid of a computer? This logistic, technological prowess of thinking embodies, Heidegger argues, the concretion of the completion of metaphysics, where the world is technologically mediated, enframed as the stockpile of disposable available resources.[4]

---

3. Martin Heidegger, in *On Time and Being*.
4. Cf. Martin Heidegger, "The Question concerning Technology." Further references are, of course, *The Question of Being* and *Identity and Difference*, where Heidegger introduces the terms "*Ereignis*" and "*Gestell*."

What, then, does Heidegger mean by "the end of philosophy"?

Before entering into the adventure of thinking, a thinking presumably guided and grounded by Heidegger's numerous assertions about the end of philosophy, perhaps I should first summarize the basis for his claim, even though this would seem to be a settled issue.

The end of philosophy is for Heidegger "that place in which the whole of philosophy's history is gathered in its most extreme possibility."[5] The end of philosophy is the completion of philosophy. It is not just the site of this gathering; it is itself this gathering; the whole of our history as a people, the people of metaphysics, reaches its foundering in this gathering. This gathering is not just a presentation of philosophy in the imperilment of its extremity; rather by this gathering is meant the exhausting of the most extreme possibilities intrinsic to the philosophic enterprise, where this enterprise has metaphysics at its basis. So the end of philosophy signifies the completion of the most extreme possibilities of metaphysics. It is the exhaustion of all the possibilities upon which metaphysics can play itself out.

Nietzsche, Heidegger constantly reiterates, was the first to understand how metaphysics has progressed into a "state of exhaustion." And Kierkegaard certainly had his suspicions as to the vitality of metaphysics after Hegel, for whom existence was taken up by thinking and then forgotten. However, Heidegger understands Nietzsche to have carried out the "consummation" of metaphysics, to have consumed the project of metaphysics by working out its most extreme, and thus final, possibility. But philosophy, we should insist, yet are still reluctant to do so, has always been concerned with its final possibility. It always begins after having intrigued itself with its final possibility. So philosophy can scarcely avoid being eschatological. It has its origin in subjecting itself to this final possibility, this extremity, as proof of its beginning anew

---

5. Martin Heidegger, "The End of Philosophy and the Task of Thinking," 57.

aright. "History," as Thomas Pynchon points out in *Gravity's Rainbow*, "is an aggregate of last moments."

We see all this dramatically staged in *Being and Time*. This work, which, as we all know, is blind to its own insight, is worked out within the traditional metaphysical matrix of problems, although it is engaged in an attempt to work itself out of its matrix into a new arena of thinking. Since *Being and Time* comes after the final and most extreme possibility of metaphysics—Nietzsche's thinking—it would seem not to have been an accident that it was never completed, and, as Heidegger remarks in passing on a number of occasions, essentially could not be completed.[6] Inasmuch as the way taken in the exposition of *Being and Time* begins along the way of "subjectivistic" metaphysics even in the venturing away from it, we say today that *Being and Time*, and not the thinking of Nietzsche, plays out the final possibility of metaphysics, and with such finality that this possibility can be brought forth only as a foundering of metaphysics. That is to say, not only is *Being and Time essentially* incomplete, it is *essentially* incompletable because its foundering was inherent in it: *Being and Time* is the end of that philosophy of which Heidegger speaks—it gathers subjectivistic thinking into its most extreme possibility, the possibility by which metaphysics comes into its own self-abrogation. For the final possibility of metaphysics is the foundering of metaphysics; and ultimately its transgression, its self-revocation and the abrupt but discreet foreclosure on itself.

At the beginning of his career Heidegger's exclusive concern was to lay a foundation for metaphysics. Repeatedly he insists on the urgency, the needfulness, of this concern. But as we know, his way was to be underway toward the thinking of the ground of thinking, until eventually he came to see that along this path the ground no longer mattered, for it is the path in the clearing that precisely suffices. But let us retreat for a moment to understand this term "metaphysics."

---

6. Cf. Martin Heidegger, "Letter on Humanism."

Metaphysics, whatever this term conjures up in the latter day of its law, receives its name from a fortuitous classification of select volumes of Aristotle. But as I have been arguing, the accidental is the essence of language, the essence of saying being. So if τὰ μετὰ τὰ φυσικά is the title of *the* basic philosophic difficulty, it can be no accident that this title is merely accidental and designates what escapes systematic classification, what is accidental with respect to systematic classification—yet nevertheless names what is essential to classifying in the first place, what permits the possibility of classification, enables and empowers it. So τὰ μετὰ τὰ φυσικά is the title of *this* basic difficulty, which involves the curious ambiguity in philosophy proper and so in discourse in general, that philosophy searches to say being as being, τί τὸ ὄν ᾗ ὄν;—what is being as being; yet this term, ὄν, designates the entity as well as what is common to all being, upon which beings find their principle and cause. Τὸ ὄν names the entity in its particularity as the entity that it is, but it also names the entitative order as such. As we have seen, this difficulty, although irresolvable, can be opened up by distinguishing between πρώτη φιλοσοφία and τὰ μετὰ τὰ φυσικά.

But without reviewing the difficulty involved in this ambiguity and in this paradox, this dueling duet between the highest being and the totality of being, between being-in-general and being-in-particular, between the entity in its particularity as the entity that it is and the entitative order as such, let us retreat a bit more into this strange and haunted term, this term ὄν.

The function of metaphysics, Aristotle would tell you, is to heed the summons of the question "What is being as being?" (τί τὸ ὄν ᾗ ὄν;). But to ask this question is to bypass any particular entity. It is to surpass every particular entity, to "pass beyond" particular beings. But passing beyond beings . . . to what? The "what" cannot, of course, be itself a being. It is, rather, a virtue that all beings share, namely, that that in virtue of being the beings that they are do beings enjoy being. But this "what" is also that that by virtue of being do beings enjoy being the beings that they are. To pass beyond beings is to pass over unto the virtue of being. This rite of passage is metaphysics, and through this passage beings as a whole are surpassed. Metaphysics is, then, the passage from beings as a whole unto their virtue of being, unto their virtue of being that they are what they are just as they are—beings *as* beings.

But if we are to meditate on the formula τὶ τὸ ὄν ᾗ ὄν; and endeavor thereby to disengage the interior structure of metaphysics we find an *essential* ambiguity: we fall into the amphiboly of being, a secret trapdoor in the beguiling disingenuousness of language through which we are hurled down into the metaphysical vocation and venture, hurled down until we teeter-totter on the brink of a thinksink.

"Beings as beings" means the whole of being considered in terms of that in and by virtue of which they are, that is, their "beingness." But the beingness of beings as a whole may be understood as either the "common denominator" of all things, or as some ultimate ground which lets the whole of beings be—beings. That is to say that in passing beyond beings as a whole that whereunto the passage passes may be either that *in* virtue of which they are—that they all enjoy being beings—or that *by* virtue of which they are—that it is by virtue of being that they enjoy being beings. Here the vision is split into two images, each the inversion of the other: it is in virtue of being the beings that they are that beings enjoy being; but it is by virtue of being that they enjoy being the beings that they are.

The term 'transcendence', or 'passing beyond', shares the same ambiguity. It can mean the passage from beings to the fact that they are or it can mean the passage from beings to their being how they are. But in any event, Heidegger tells us that metaphysics does not ask after being both in regard to *that* they are *and* in regard to their being *as* they are. It does not ask that beings show themselves from themselves as they are; rather, metaphysics is interested in the ground of beings, a ground that gives itself ground, that is, that calls entities to account as the entities that they are. As Heidegger tells us:

Metaphysics thinks being as such, that is, in general. Metaphysics thinks the Being of beings both in the ground-giving unity [*in der ergründenden Einheit*] of what is most general, what is indifferently valid everywhere, and also in the unity of the all that accounts for the ground [*in der begründenden Einheit der Allheit*], that is, of the All-Highest. The Being of beings is thus thought in advance as the grounding ground [*als der gründende Grund*]. Therefore metaphysics is at bottom and from the ground up [*im Grunde vom Grund aus des Gründen*] what grounds, what gives account of the ground, what is called to account by the ground, and finally what calls the ground to account.[7]

Heidegger uses three terms to express the nature of Western thinking, that it gathers itself toward being as its ground. The terms are *begründen* (to account for the ground); *ergründen* (to give the ground); and *gründen* (to ground). *Begründen* has to do with the entity and suggests that being "begrounds" itself in the entity, that being *is* only as the arrival of being in this particular entity or ontic region, where by "ontic" we mean "of or pertaining to an entity." *Begründen*, then, is ontic. Beings as a whole account for the ontological, for only by thinking beings as a whole does the fact that there is the entitative come into view. This is, properly speaking, the ontological, and it is itself nothing entitative. *Begründen* signifies, then, that it is in virtue of being the beings that they are that beings enjoy being. *Ergründen* is what *das Sein* achieves and, unlike *begründen*, is not what is achieved by considering the whole of the entitative order as such. *Ergründen* is a nonentitative activity. In fact, it is that activity that permits us to view the entitative order as a whole. *Ergründen* signifies that it is by virtue of being that beings enjoy being the beings that they are. Here, as before, the focus of this phrase is on the 'it is' of 'it is *by* virtue of . . . ' or 'it is *in* virtue of . . . .' This 'it is' desig-

---

7. Martin Heidegger, "The Onto-theo-logical Constitution of Metaphysics," 56–57.

nates the relationship that obtains in a being being, what I would like to call the *virtue* of being. It is, to follow Heidegger here, a *gründen*. So *gründen* signifies the relation of *begründen* and *ergründen*. It is the complicity that being and the entity bear to one another, that each refers us to the other, that "being" both signifies *to be* a being while naming a being. *Gründen* signifies that the disclosure of the ontological is possible only through the mediation of the ontic and the encountering of the ontic is accessible only through the mediation of the ontological. To be more precise: *gründen* signifies that beings are disclosed as *beings* pure and simple only in and through the encountering of them; yet beings can be encountered only on the basis of and in terms of their being beings. This is to say that the disclosure of being takes place in the ontical dimension and the encountering of an entity happens in the ontological dimension. As we try to think either term, there is an apparently irrecuperable shifting of foreground and background into each other, there is a slipping and sliding of the sense of both being and entity, there seems to be an eliding of the sense of one into the other, a slippage of sense, a gliding slippery slope slip-sliding, a *glissement*. In trying to think the ontic as such, we consider beings as a whole. But as soon as we do this, we find ourselves considering that there is the entitative order in its unity as a whole. Thereby the ontic is "ontologicized." But if we consider what gives the entitative order its unity in being taken as a whole, we find that each entity disappears into this unity, this as-a-whole, and therewith emerges the identity of the nonentitative order. But identity is a feature and function of the entitative order. The ontological gets "onticized."

But then, there apparently is an ambiguity at the heart of metaphysics. And this ambiguity lies in the nature of τὸ ὄν itself. Grammatically ὄν is a neuter singular present participle, and as such can serve as a noun or as an adjective with a verbal sense. As Heidegger writes in "The Anaximander Fragment," "In Plato and Aristotle [who expressly asks τί τὸ ὄν ᾗ ὄν;] we encounter the words ὄν and ὄντα as conceptual terms. . . . However, ὄν and ὄντα, considered linguistically, are presumably somewhat truncated forms of the Homeric ἐόν and ἐόντα. Only in the latter words is the sound preserved which relates them to ἔστιν and εἶναι. The epsilon in ἐόν and ἐόντα is the epsilon in the root es of ἔστιν, *est, esse, ist,* and 'is'. In contrast, ὄν and ὄντα appear as rootless participial endings," neither adjectival nor nominal substantives, neither standing on their own nor enabling anything else to stand, neither nominating nor predicating, as though they command us to think what is involved in "μετοχή, *participium,* i.e., those word-forms which participate in both the verbal and nominal senses of a word" (32–33). And the τό of τὸ ὄν does not only signify the singular form of ὄντα, "beings"; rather, the τό of τὸ ὄν indicates the singular as such, before all number, the singular matter for thinking, that τὸ ὄν says "being" in the sense of *to be* a being, while at the same time naming a being. In ancient Greek, the adjective used with an article customarily designated 'the thing that is (adjective).' To use an adjective with an article as an abstract noun was extraordinary. And that Plato would occasionally do so is simply not clear. Rather, I would like to suggest that he was exploiting the ambiguity inherent in the ordinary usage. This ambiguity is exemplary in the word τὸ ὄν. For in the duality of the participial significance of τὸ ὄν the distinction between "to be" and "a being" both obtrudes and remains overlooked in all Western languages. Τὸ ὄν does not so much name the enacting of being *and/or* a particular being as it does the riddle of the relationship between the two. Τὸ ὄν names the cunning of being found within the punning of 'being.'

So τὸ ὄν, "being," has the dual sense of being a substantive and an activity. It is intrinsically equivocal; it is a doubling dueling of sense, and this doubling dueling of sense, this sense-duello, is at the essence of metaphysics. This is what I term the amphiboly of being.

But if metaphysics has as its source the ambiguity of τὸ ὄν, and if its guiding and grounding question is τί τὸ ὄν ᾗ ὄν;, which lends itself to a fateful ambiguity, then the question of the meaning of being must be sensitive to this peculiar duality and auto-duello of τὸ ὄν. Moreover, it should be clear that being, and not just the concept or word 'being,' must be thought as that in and through which this ambiguity takes place, for the being of something is both that it is just what it is and the activity or enactment of this something being itself, both that it is a being and that it is by virtue of being, both that it is in virtue of being this particular being that it enjoys being and that it is by virtue of being that it enjoys being the being that it is. This ambiguity, this duplicity at the root of the Western linguistic experience, is possible only on the basis of an experience, however vague and unclarified, of some difference between these two senses of τὸ ὄν—"being" as substantive and "being" as the enacting of the substantive, between the substantive and the fact that there is the substantive. In this way the question of the meaning of being gets initiated, empowered, and enacted within the difference between the substantive and that there is the substantive. The point can be drawn more incisively: for there to be an ambiguity in τὸ ὄν, an essential ambiguity, there must be not just an experience of the different modalities signified by this word; rather this experience of an ambiguity in how being gets experienced is at the basis of being, and not just "human experience." Let me try to explain.

It is simple enough to elicit language as this amphiboly of being. Language is said to consist, on the one hand, of a system of signs designating beings, be they substances, events, or relations of substances. These signs designate identities, and therefore are a doubling of the beings they signify. But also, and with equal originality, language can be conceived as the verb, as the verbalization of being, in which substances break down into modes of temporalization. Here language does not double up the being of entities but exposes the silent yet resonant verbalization of the world. Being as the temporalizing sense to the world lets the "there is," and that there is the "there is," be seen, whereas being as the nominal brings the entity forth into its identity.

Although it might appear that this bonding together into the same of the nominalization and verbalization of being that is language is a product of subjectivism, it would perhaps be closer to the truth to say that it is the way of the world to fuse together into the same the congealment into identities and the annealing into modulations of temporality.

By virtue of the amphiboly of being invested in the ambiguity of 'being', being resonates in the sonorous saying to which philosophy has always attested and appealed. This saying is not just a saying of 'being', but the saying of being. Since originary saying says being, since being gives itself in its amphibolous figurations in the ambiguity of saying being, the phenomenon is itself a phenomenology, and phenomenology is itself a phenomenon. This saying is an exegesis, full of exigency and urgency, that is not just something laid onto the resonance of being; the resonance of being vibrates in the said of the exegesis. It is tuned in the attunement that is the amphiboly of being. In this amphiboly the resounding of being is on the verge of lapsing into a substantive, muffling the resonance of being, while the entity is on the verge of evanescing into the resonating of being. And it is the peculiar task of philosophy, its strange vocation and its uncanny place in the world, to name the resounding of the muffling of the resonance of being.

In the copula "is" scintillates and sparkles an essential ambiguity between the substantive being enchimed as a modulation of temporality and verbalizing being becoming encrusted and encollected into a substantive. The prefix "en" here signifies a reflexivity in being that is due to the reciprocal mutability in the amphiboly of being between being and entities, that being condenses into an entity and entities evanesce into being, that the presencing of the world presents itself within the world as what it is while what is present gets presented as the presencing of what is present. The presence of the present and the present of presence have an eerie way of transfiguring themselves each into the other. Heidegger constantly reiterates: in being the unconcealing of beings, being conceals itself as this unconcealing. When we consider the entitative order as a unified whole, another kind of figure is disclosed, or rather present, and this is that something conceals itself as the disclosability of the entitative order. It is this concealing of itself of the activity of unconcealing that comes to haunt the present, so that each entity disappears into this concealment of the activity of unconcealing, so that entities collapse into a murmuring, rustling muffling presence of the nonentitative. And it is to this murmuring, this rustling muffling presence, that the philosophers attest, bringing it out into view; and by nominating it in this way it gets nominalized, substantiated, entitated.

If there is this saying that draws being forth into its own exposition, then this saying belongs to being; it is its upsurge. It is, to use Heidegger's overknown phrase, "the house of being." But if there is a saying that says being, then it is philosophy that makes the astonishing adventure involved in this saying. It is philosophy that makes the astonishing adventure of showing and recounting being, of providing being with its own recitation. A philosopher's effort, and his or her unnatural position, consists, while showing the being on the nether side of the said, in immediately reducing that being to what gets deposited in and by the said, yet despite this reduction, retaining an echo of the saying that exceeds the said, an echo in which resounds the faint and fugitive figure of the amphiboly of being.

When Aristotle first asked τί τὸ ὄν ᾗ ὄν;, and answered τὸ ὄν λέγεται πολλαχῶς, "being is said in many ways," he attempted the saying that says being. He did not just want to understand the manifold meanings of the concept or word 'being'; rather he felt the urgent call to say what and that being is. As I have already noted, this is attested to indirectly in the Aristotelian corpus in the distinction he implicitly draws between the ultimate *signified*, which is multiple and in the final analysis infinite, since language signifies individuals, and *signification*, which is that through which the signified is pursued. Although this distinction perhaps may not be made explicitly by Aristotle, it results from the comparison between two series of remarks: on the one hand, we find that the same word "signifies several things [πλείω σημαίνειν]" (*Soph. Refut.* 1.165a12); on the other hand, it "has many significations [πολλαχῶς λέγεσθαι]" (*Meta.* 7.1.1028a10; 6.4.1028a5; 5.7.1017a24). In the first case the accusative indicates that it is a question of the *quid* of signification; in the second, the adverb indicates that it is a question of the *how* of signification.

The point of this excursus, even if it be uncomfortably obscurantist, is that it is problematic and perhaps even more obscurantist to argue that the amphiboly of being is only a condition of the Indo-European legacy of language and not a condition arising from the self-concealing enchiming-in of being. At the very least there is something astonishing about the amphiboly of being, something that Heidegger was beginning, in *Being and Time*, to open up to thought.

II

> A notion of subjectivity independent of the adventure of cognition . . . is required if signification signifies otherwise than by the synchrony of being, if intelligibility and being are distinguishable.
> Emmanuel Levinas, *Otherwise than Being, or Beyond Essence*

In and through the resonant granting of the "is" beings are. But also: in and through the resonant granting of the "is" there is the "is," there is being, the enchiming-in of the "is." We can think the entity as entity; we can also think the being of the entity, that is, the sonorous and resounding "is" in granting the entity its self-givenness. But we cannot think the "is" without thinking of the granting of being and the beings that are given in this granting, since to think the "is" in distinction from what is, is to think of what never and nowhere is. We cannot, it would seem, think being without thinking of entities. But it is Heidegger's contribution to philosophy to have elicited the negativity of being with respect to beings. To think being, *das Sein*, in its difference from beings is to think nonbeing or nothing: it is to think the primacy of the "not."

> Nothingness is the Not of being and thus is Being experienced from the point of view of being. The Ontological difference is the Not between being and Being. Yet Being, as the Not to being, is no more a nothingness in the sense of a *nihil*

negativum than the Difference, as the Not between being and Being, is merely a distinction of the intellect (*ens rationis*).[8]

We take it today that in and through human experience the ontological difference between being and the entity is opened up, insofar as such is the nature of human experience that an entity is encounterable only so far as human experience has a "precursory comprehension" of the being of this entity. Human experience is the giving to the entity the giving of itself as just this entity. It is by virtue of its encounterability that an entity can be encountered; it is in virtue of being encounterable that it can be encountered—and it is ζῷον ἔχον λόγον ('the rational animal', or literally, 'the living being that has logos') that is the attestation to the difference between the entity encountered and that it is encounterable. But this precursory comprehension, this giving to the entity the giving of itself, is possible only if human being can surpass not just this particular entity but all entities as a whole; and what is exhibited in having surpassed entities as a whole is itself nothing entitative. It is the nonentitative dimension of the world, the yonder of the entity toward which the philosopher is the yearning turning. As we know, Heidegger designates this yonder of beings as a whole as *das Sein*, the "*Nichts*" of beings. Thus Heidegger states:

> Holding itself out into the nothing, Dasein is in each case already beyond beings as a whole. This being beyond beings we call "transcendence." If in the ground of its essence Dasein were not transcendence, which now means, if it were not in advance holding itself out into the nothing, then it could never be related to beings nor even to itself.[9]

This nothing is the opening up of being in the experiencing of beings. In the encountering of entities the philosopher turns to-

---

8. Martin Heidegger, *The Essence of Reasons*, 3.
9. Martin Heidegger, "What Is Metaphysics?" 105–6.

ward the nonentitative dimension of the world, and in this yearning turning this nonentitative dimension comes forth and shines up the world so that entities are encounterable. But it comes forth only as the receding of itself. Yet this nonentitative dimension is disclosed only in and as the disappearing of entities from the entitative.

However: in truth, none of this could be said, for as soon as it is said, it cancels itself out, for it becomes necessary to say the difference of being from entities and of entities from being, a difference that is irreducible to either being or an entity—a difference that in no way appears as such. It is rather the disappearing of appearing, the receding of the arriving of the entitative, the as such as such that nonetheless undoes the as such of every entity. Though all language bears an inward reference to this difference, this difference, as soon as it gets instituted as an object of reference, diffuses itself into an evanescent trace of itself. So this difference can be said only in an unsaying of it, for every saying of it unsays it.

But enough of the litany. It is questionable, for reasons I am trying to trouble through, whether we can yet think through this doctrine. And this questionableness is not, I contend, an accident.

If the thoughtlessness with which I cite this litany is not just a slip of the pen, a dillydallying dalliance with the doctrinal in order to forestall having to continue slip-sliding the pen over the abyss enmiring the amphiboly of being, then it is because both the litany and my recitation of it play out the mutual mutability of being and entities into each other inherent in the amphiboly of being. In general, then, metaphysics works out the possibilities inherent in the fact that being is always an amphibolous figure of itself. Metaphysics is the immersion into this amphiboly in order to draw out the intelligibility of being, to stabilize the entity in the entitative, to impact it there, deeply, without the slippaging and seepaging into the ontological, yet fully fixing being, determining it as the real meaning of the entity, the wherewithal of its presence. In worrying itself through the interminable tension of this mutual mutability, metaphysics embarks on the near relentless stirring and striving to give an exposition of being, an exposition that would be being's own exposition of itself. So the amphiboly of being is the horizon within which this stirring striving takes place, that it sites itself in citing the recitation of being—metaphysics does not engage in making this amphiboly explicit, for, given that being always "gives itself" in an amphibolous figure of itself, the amphiboly of being could never admit to a disambiguating explication. Rather, metaphysics engages in the vocation of rendering being explicit in the light of its amphibolous being.

But the stirring striving of metaphysics is to hold open the intelligibility of being, to make the meaning of being fully transparent. Since according to this vocation, being implicates its own exposition, identifies with it, the ultimate goal of this venture is to achieve a radical coincidence of the intelligibility of being with being as such; it is to restore to being its own exposition, so that we can dwell in a world in which meaning and being coincide absolutely, the true human estate.

Yet because being always gives way to the amphiboly of itself, it contests the possibility of its own exposition; it will always invert it, turn it upside down and inside out. To think of a particular entity is to be referred to the fact that it is as it is, yet as soon as we try to think that it is, this "that it is as it is" loses itself in a conflation with the entity's being itself—an entity. Yet to go beyond beings as a whole in order to think this, that they are as they are, throws us ineluctably back upon and into particular beings, that they are . . . just particular beings. The entity is dispersed into the being of that entity and being congeals into the entity of being. Alternatively, by considering the entitative order as a whole, entities disappear in the void of that as-a-whole, and this as-a-whole thereby achieves its own entitative identity. Identities migrate back into a silent resonance while the modulating of this resonance becomes an identity. The presence of the present and the present of presence are quick exchange artists, with each conspiring to confound itself with the other. The onto-theo-logical difference is just what we mean by this confounding and conflating of being and entities; it does not hold them separate in a sameness yet to be thought. Rather, it is a rift, a *Riss*, the cleaving of being unto itself and into itself, and into itself and the entity, as well as cleaving within being from itself. And because being is itself amphibolous, language torments itself in attempting to expose the amphiboly of being; it becomes a self-effacing evanescing trace of this amphibolous character. It is certainly no accident that Heidegger, in attempting to name "the being of beings," can get no further than noting that the "of" here is both a subjective and an objective genitive.

Heidegger constantly reminds us that the sense of being is neither reducible to the word 'being' nor to the concept of being. In "Time and Being" he insists explicitly that it is necessary to think being without reference to beings. The force of this present essay is to understand this necessity, which, as soon as it is formulated, doubles as an impossibility, for no sooner is being conceived apart from entities then it degenerates into an entity. Heidegger, of course, was well aware of this predicament, which I have been calling the amphiboly of being.

If *Being and Time* represents the foundering of metaphysics, it is because, as I intend to show, the amphiboly of being is allowed to become more than just virtual, for metaphysics has always been the refusal to acknowledge this amphiboly, holding it in unavowed preterition. In fact, metaphysics originates from this refusal; yet it is guided and grounded, funded and founded by a covert appeal to what it denies, that being, in coming into the call of language, mutates into an entity, and the entity is elevated to being. In "The Anaximander Fragment" Heidegger offers terse commentary on this disdain on the part of metaphysics to think through the amphiboly of being. Most philosophers and critics are scandalized by the seeming exorbitance and excess that mark this essay. But perhaps this exorbitance is precisely its virtue, if there is to be any authentic attempt to think back behind metaphysics to its disavowal of the amphiboly of being. To that end I cite these passages without further comment.

What matter? The matter of the presencing of what is present. But to be the Being *of* beings is the matter of Being.

The grammatical form of this enigmatic, ambiguous genitive indicates a genesis, the emergence of what is present from presencing. Yet the essence of this emergence remains concealed along with the essence of these two words. Not only that, but even the very relation between presencing and what is present remains unthought. From early on it seems as though presencing and what is present were each something for itself. Presencing itself unnoticeably becomes something present. Represented in the manner of something present, it is elevated above whatever else is present and so becomes the highest being present. As soon as presencing is named it is represented as some present being. Ultimately, presencing as such is not distinguished from what is present: it is taken merely as the most universal or the highest of present beings, thereby becoming one among such beings. The essence of presencing, and with it the distinction between presencing and what is present, remains forgotten. *The oblivion of Being is the oblivion of the distinction between Being and beings.*

However, oblivion of the distinction is by no means the consequence of a forgetfulness of thinking. Oblivion of Being belongs to the self-veiling essence of Being. It belongs so essentially to the destiny of Being that the dawn of this destiny rises as the unveiling of what is present in its presencing. This means that the history of Being begins with the oblivion of Being, since Being—together with its essence, its distinction from beings—keeps to itself. The distinction collapses. It remains forgotten . . . even the early trace of the distinction is obliterated when presencing appears as something and finds itself in the position of being the highest being present.[10]

The oblivion of this distinction, Heidegger reminds us, *is the event of metaphysics.* I insist, again, that this oblivion is the de-

---

10. Martin Heidegger, "The Anaximander Fragment," 50–51.

ployment of the amphiboly of being; and metaphysics traces out the movement of this deployment. Metaphysics is the ploy by which being conceals itself in its own amphibolous being. To that extent, metaphysics is the proper and exclusive employee of this amphiboly; and this amphiboly is both the trace of the oblivion of being and the effacement of this trace. For this reason it is becoming clear that, since it disappears in its appearing, and since it is simultaneously traced and effaced in metaphysics, in the metaphysical text the amphiboly of being could be only virtual, never explicit. This is to say that the amphiboly of being has no essence: not only can it not allow itself to be taken up into the *as such* of its name or its appearing; it threatens the authority of the *as such* in general; it evanesces essence.

If by sense, then, we mean the appearing of that which has or makes sense, then the sense of the amphiboly of being is that as the source for all sense it is that which is intractable to sense. It is that which has always already receded from sense; it is that which is almost completely refractory to the process of sense making. It is that making sense cannot really make sense. The amphiboly of being is, in principle if not in fact, unnameable. Not because it is ineffable, but rather because as the effing of being the amphiboly of being effs away from itself, electing but never elected, electing not to elect itself, ineluctably inelectable, inelectably elucting (the) being from itself. In the name the amphiboly of being is involved, tucked away, and carried off, yet still the source of the ostensive, just as the false beginning or end of a game is still part of the game.

> Illumination of the distinction therefore cannot mean that the distinction appears as a distinction. On the contrary, the relation to what is present in presencing as such [!] may announce itself in such a way that presencing comes to speak *as this* relation.[11]

Being both opens up and effects its amphibolous being and is itself a term of this amphiboly; being is a relationship to beings

---

11. Ibid., 51.

and a term of that relationship. But being is also that exclusive relationship to beings that invests itself wholly in them, so that the relationship becomes absorbed in one of its terms.

It is in *Being and Time* that the amphiboly of being is for the first time exposed, but exposed *almost* in spite of the intentions of the text, by means of an indirect and indiscreet confirmation of this amphiboly's hidden history, contesting the force of its amphibolous character at the same time it subscribes to it, laboring it into the clear light of day while simultaneously keeping it almost totally tucked away in obscure sourcelessness and senselessness. As a text *Being and Time* reverberates with this seduction *of* the amphiboly of being (double genitive).

III

> . . . language splits the subject into an empirical self that exists in a state of inauthenticity and a self that exists only in the form of a language that asserts the knowledge of this inauthenticity. This does not, however, make it into an authentic language, for to know inauthenticity is not the same as to be authentic.
>
> Paul de Man, "The Rhetoric of Temporality"

Being and Time closes—prematurely—with a question that profoundly poses the dilemma involved in teasing the amphiboly of being to echo in a text its tracing out of its own effacing. The passage reads:

> Nevertheless, our way of exhibiting the constitution of Dasein's Being remains only *one way* which we may take. Our *aim* is to work out the question of Being in general. The *thematic* analytic of existence, however, first needs the light of the idea of Being in general, which must be clarified beforehand. This holds particularly if we adhere to the principle which we expressed in our introduction as one by which any

philosophical investigation may be gauged: that philosophy "is universal phenomenological ontology, and takes its departure from the hermeneutic of Dasein, which, as an analytic of *existence*, has made fast the guiding-line for all philosophical inquiry at the point where it *arises* and to which it *returns*." This thesis, of course, is to be regarded not as a dogma, but rather as a formulation of a problem of principle which still remains 'veiled': can one provide *ontological* grounds [*begründen*] for ontology, or does it also require an *ontical* foundation [*Fundamentes*]? and *which* entity must take over the function of providing this foundation [*Fundierung*]? (*Being and Time*, 436).

This passage, of course, already contains the kernel of the "*Kehre*," that fundamental ontology is "only *one way*," and one that must be abandoned in favor of situating thinking in the *Lichtung* of what of itself holds itself back within its own self-secluding reserve of self-refusal, in order not to clarify the *idea* of being in general, working out its exegesis, but in order to let go of language and of things, to leave be being. But what I find provocative in this passage is the suggestion that perhaps ontology rests on an appeal to an ontic foundation. *Being and Time* is an instance of "only *one* way" an investigation into the question of the meaning of being might take. Another way, Heidegger suggests, might be that an ontological grounding of the meaning of being may require being supplemented by laying "an ontical foundation." But what form would this ontical foundation take? It could only be that in the entitative order there is something that accounts for its grounding in the nonentitative, the ontological. This could only be the amphiboly of being, that the presence of the world is present in the world, and that what is present disappears into the void of its own presence. The suggestion is that the attempt to disambiguate being, to hold being and entities apart in their difference from each other, undermines itself, for each term in this difference repudiates itself *as a term* in this difference by denying a relationship to it of the other term, by, in fact, cutting off the relation of the other term to it by inverting itself into the other term.

This dilemma is suspected in the opening pages of Division Two of the published portion of *Being and Time*, where Heidegger puzzles as to the constantly reiterated "provisionality" of the existential analytic with respect to fundamental ontology and with respect to the question of the meaning of being in general:

> One thing has become unmistakable: *our existential analysis of Dasein up till now cannot lay claim to primordiality*. Its fore-having never included more than the *inauthentic* Being of Dasein, and of Dasein as *less* than a *whole* [*als unganzes*]. If the Interpretation of Dasein's Being is to become primordial, as a foundation for working out the basic question of ontology, then it must first have brought to light existentially the Being of Dasein in its possibilities of *authenticity* and *totality*. (*Being and Time*, 233)

But a casual perusal of the text reveals a conflict between this passage, an earlier passage, and a later passage. The earlier passage comes from §5, entitled "The Ontological Analytic of Dasein as Laying Bare the Horizon for an Interpretation of the Meaning of Being in General," the first section of the second introduction.

From the start Heidegger argues that it is only in its average everydayness and its flight from authenticity that Dasein can be revealed properly in the light of "working out the basic question of ontology." Thus he notes,

> Our analysis of Dasein, however, is not only incomplete; it is also, in the first instance, *provisional* [*vorläufig*]. It merely brings out the Being of this entity, without Interpreting its meaning. It is rather a preparatory procedure by which the horizon for the most primordial way of interpreting Being may be laid bare. Once we have arrived at that horizon, this preparatory analytic of Dasein will have to be repeated on a

higher and authentically ontological basis. (*Being and Time*, 17)

Needless to say, this repetition was abandoned in favor of thinking being itself, not its relationship to Dasein, a relationship that as early as page 12 of *Being and Time* is confirmed as remarkably ambiguous.

Zu dieser Seinsverfassung des Daseins gehört aber dann, daβ es in seinem Sein zu diesem Sein ein Seinsverhältnis hat.

To translate this passage, either of the following is offered by Macquarrie and Robinson:

This is a constitutive state of Dasein's Being, and this implies that Dasein, in its Being, has a relationship towards that Being—a relationship which itself is one of Being.

Or:

This is a constitutive state of Dasein's Being, and this implies that Dasein, in its Being towards this Being, has a relationship of Being.

Here its ontic nature is this "constitutive state," that "it is ontically distinguished by the fact that, in its very Being, that Being is an *issue* for it" (*Being and Time*, 12). That is, Dasein is that being that has an ontological comportment to its ontic nature. Understanding is, Heidegger insists, ontological. The first translation suggests that, for Dasein, part of being itself, and only part, is to be itself a relationship to itself; while the second translation suggests that the sole content of Dasein consists in identifying itself as that being which has yet to catch up to being itself, which has yet to work through the implications of its own self-understanding.

But in truth, both of these translations ignore the *Verfassung*.

A more telling reading might be: to this understanding of Dasein's being belongs the notion that in its being it has a relationship to that being, where this relationship is one of understanding. Alternatively: Dasein, in its being, is understood to enjoy a relationship to that being.

A later passage which enters into this conflict revolves around the word *vorläufig*, previously translated as *provisional*, but which reverberates throughout the second half of the text as *anticipatory*. The passage reads:

> Wenn im *Vorlaufen* zum Tode erst alle faktische *"Vorläufigkeit"* des Entschliessens eigentlich verstanden, das heisst existenziell *eingeholt* wäre?
>
> What if it is only in the *anticipation* of death that all the factical 'provisionality' [or: *'anticipatoriness'*] of resolving would be authentically understood—in other words, that it would be *caught up with* in an existentiell way? (*Being and Time*, 302)

The suggestion here is that the provisional character of philosophy is inescapable and that authentic existence is first encountered when we own up to the fact that, due to the unavoidability of "average everydayness" and the flight of inauthenticity from anxiety, the best we can hope for is authentically understanding this provisionality. It would seem that with the attempt to establish everydayness as a foundation inauthenticity triumphs over philosophy.

> But have we not at the very outset of our Interpretation renounced the possibility of bringing Dasein into view as a whole? Everydayness is precisely that Being which is 'between' birth and death. (*Being and Time*, 233)

Apparently philosophy is a phenomenon of inauthenticity, for the very identifying of the everyday takes too much philosophy.

IV

> The unconcealedness of Being is the truth of the Being *of* being, whether or not the latter is real. In the unconcealedness of being, on the other hand, lies a prior unconcealedness of its Being. Each after its own fashion, ontical and ontological truth concern *being in* its Being and the *Being of* being. They belong together essentially, by reason of their relationship to the difference between Being and being [*Unterschied von Sein und Seiendem*] (the Ontological Difference). The essence of truth, which is and must be bifurcated ontically and ontologically, is only possible given this difference.
> Martin Heidegger, *The Essence of Reasons*

> Being is, as such and in its every meaning, the being of being. Being is different from being, and only this difference in general, this possibility of distinction, issues an understanding-of-being. Put another way, in the understanding-of-being this distinction of being from beings is carried out. It is this distinction that makes anything like an ontology possible. We thus term this distinction that first enables something like an understanding-of-being the *ontological difference.*
> Martin Heidegger, *The Metaphysical Foundations of Logic*

But if ontology is ultimately the authentic understanding of its own essential provisionality, an understanding that consists wholly in owning up to its own tentative and reluctant provisions in applying itself to the question of the meaning of being, then this is because being comes into the call of language only in terms of its amphibolous figuration, so that any attempt to respond explicitly and unequivocally to the being can only lapse into an interminable ambivalence toward being, an ambivalence generated by the indetermination and undecidability enveloping being as it figures into and through its amphiboly. By giving voice to the metaphysical venture, being recedes and dissembles itself into and through its amphibolous figures, so that the attempt to recover being *simpliciter* ends up in a queasy uneasiness corresponding to this indetermination and this undecidability. The amphiboly of being is not only the source of metaphysics' inspiration; it is also its

"*Unumgänglichkeit*," in the face of which, Heidegger tells us, arises a certain willful and arrogant confusion. Moreover, any such attempt to respond to the amphiboly of being, rather than properly realigning the relationship of being to entities, a relationship which is itself one of being, and rather than evoking being, provokes the institutionalizing of this amphiboly. Such an attempt would be a provocation in which being becomes a fugitive from itself by escaping into entities, and entities are themselves refugees from themselves in their relationship to being. The exposition of being can only offer thereby a faint and fugitive, a cryptic and decrepit, corroboration of beings, that they are turned away from being, that they are apotropaically renouncing their relation of being to being. The metaphysical invocation of being is its revocation, its self-revocation, calling it back into its being amphibolous.

And if *Being and Time* was the first explicit attempt to *solicit* (*sollicitare*: to rend asunder) the amphiboly of being, it would seem necessary to document the failure on the part of this metaphysical text to disambiguate this amphiboly. This failure is due to the dialectical nature of the amphiboly of being, that the attempt to cleave being *from* beings contracts into the cleaving of being *to* beings, that holding apart the difference between being and entities involves a ceaselessly reiterative expulsion of each from the other by reason of converting each into the other.

In light of that, a deeper understanding would be possible as to why Heidegger felt the need to move back behind the metaphysical question of the meaning of being. That is to say, it would seem necessary to read *Being and Time* in a manner that is both faithful to it, wholeheartedly endorsing it, yet, nevertheless, by inhabiting it as a spy in the house of Being, would open out the play, the free play, of the amphiboly of being to which *Being and Time* is fatefully enjoined.

This is a three-dimensional problematic. It would require decomposing each of the following into the other two:

(1) Ontology arises from the recoiling of inauthentic everyday existence from resolutely facing the question of the meaning of being. As such, ontology is that adventure the condition for the

possibility of which is its own repudiation. The philosopher is like a paraplegic for whom the same illness constitutes both an obligation to walk and a prohibition against walking. He is forced to run ceaselessly in order to prove with each movement that he is deprived of movement. He is all the more paralyzed because of the fact that his limbs obey him. He suffers from the horror that turns his sound legs, his vigorous muscles, and the satisfying exercise he derives from them into the proof and cause of the impossibility of his progress. Ontology arises from an aversion to itself, from averting itself from itself. This is not so much a circle as it is an aporous Klein bottle.

(2) Ontology recapitulates the amphiboly of being—unwittingly and with a certain unavowed ambivalence. Ontology is the attempt at a complete resolution of the amphiboly of being, but a resolution, then, of a situation that would be only further compounded and confounded by any resolution. Yet as soon as this ambivalence becomes integrated into the ontological project and appears as the expression of the ontological venture, it denies the intention that has brought it into being, for the intention is to clear out all ambivalence and ambiguity and deliver being, and thus all being, over to univocity, to freeze-frame the sluicing and slicing through itself that is being. Where the enigma of the amphibolous nature of being shows itself as such, it vanishes. It is only an enigma when it does not exist in itself, when it conceals itself so deeply that it slip-slides away into what causes it to slip-slide away, when it directs the gaze to slip-slide over and away from this slip-sliding away. As enigma, the amphiboly of being elides its own sense: the solution to this enigma is not, as Nietzsche thought, the enigma of a solution, but no solution at all, being a dissolution, not of the enigma, but of itself. The solution, we will have learned upon understanding the later Heidegger, is to quit seeking a solution to this enigma, to let go into it. The ambivalence of the question of the meaning of being toward that which it interrogates responds to the amphiboly of being as if it were the language of an inscrutable messenger who tries to teach the philosopher what he cannot learn and who completes his instruction by warning

the philosopher that he is learning nothing of what the messenger is teaching him and that he will go on never learning anything from this teaching.

(3) Ontology is possible only as an owning up to its own inescapably hesitant, uncertain, and obscure provisionality; but this provisionality is precisely that which *in principle* could never be fully and wholly clarified and comprehended. That is, ontology is an owning up to what could never be owned up to and (from (1)) a not owning up to what it should own up to. Ontology, then, is a circular attempt to rid itself of its own self-obstruction. But since this self-obstructing is the basis for ontology, ontology is the incessant attempt to prove itself to be in principle impossible. In relentlessly questioning itself as to its own possibility, ontology proves itself the cause of its own impossibility. It is its own koan. Ontology is the declension of itself, in the etymologically pure sense of being the turning away from itself, the falling away from itself, tripping over away from itself. Ontology is that it irresistibly tends toward occluding itself, rendering itself the impassability that is at the plinth of an uncharted labyrinth.

In these three implosions we find something unexpectedly sighted: if the sense of being is not reducible to the meaning of the word 'being' or the concept of being, then this is because of the uncanny relationship of being to language embedded and embodied in the amphiboly of being. Every saying is a saying of being, but only a feinting, stuttering and muttering, muted response celebrating that the appearing of being without reference to beings consists wholly in the fact that nothing appears without reference to the amphibolous interchangeability of being and entities.

This ever-shifting, ever-destabilizing mutual mutability of being and entities presses us into the presence of absence, but to this presence as absence, to absence as affirmation of itself, affirmation in which nothing is affirmed save this affirmation itself. This presence is the impossibility of realizing a presence pure and simple without confounding the present of presence with the presence of the present. This presence is an impossibility that nonetheless is present, the shade and shadow of the present, stalking the present, that is there as that which doubles every present, a reflection of the present within the abyss. Within the hollow at the heart of this abyss the meaning of presence is the presence of meaning.

By naming being, the philosopher names the identification of the meaning of presence with the presence of meaning. But this name names the impossibility of naming anything but an order that, in its essence, forfeits an immediate relationship to Being pure and simple in favor of a commentary on the meaning of being, a commentary that is itself the being of meaning. As soon as the philosopher identifies the meaning of presence with the presence of meaning, entities appear only in the void of the reflection that is their meaning; entities disappear into their meaning, and meaning emerges as the entity proper. For this reason the entity becomes the distancing of itself into meaning; it turns into its own obfuscation. And for this reason being becomes the entity that is its own meaning. The entity obstructs itself from being itself so that its meaning can replace it.

To ask after the meaning of being is to seek to determine and conceptualize what is asked about. But this means that to ask the fundamental question about the meaning of being is to engage in rendering explicit, transparent, the *intelligibility* of being. Being as such is not (yet) questioned, just its meaning. What is sought is the intelligibility of being. That being *is* only insofar as it is intelligible is the theme of *Being and Time*. So much so that in naming being the philosopher seeks to make being and its intelligibility coincide. Thus it is that Heidegger, in passing judgment on *Being and Time*, says that "in Sein und Zeit how being *is* is to be understood chiefly from its 'meaning'."[12] And this is the case despite his protestations in *Being and Time* that

---

12. "Letter on Humanism," *Basic Writings*, 217. Heidegger refers to *Being and Time*, 230: "What does it signify that Being 'is' [*Was es bedeutet: Sein 'ist'*], where Being is to be distinguished [*sein soll unterschieden*] from every entity? One can ask this concretely only if the

The task of ontology is to explain Being itself and to make the Being of entities stand out in full relief.

Die Abhebung des Seins vom Seiendem und die Explikation des Seins selbst ist Aufgabe der Ontologie. (Being and Time, 27)

Immediately preceding this statement is the reassurance that we are asking for an answer to the question "What is 'Being'?" It is, we are told, a matter of the question of being itself and not a question of the meaning of being (*Being and Time*, 26–27); though he does not seem to understand the radical nature of the question of being, and not the question of just the meaning of being, when he adds parenthetically to a remark about the "theme of our investigation," that it is "(the being of entities, or the meaning of being)." The evidence suggests that being and its meaning are one and the same.

That this is only an initial protestation can be seen by following the theme running through *Being and Time* that being and its intelligibility coincide. In §2 Heidegger measures being "itself" according to its intelligibility when he notes that

meaning of Being [*der Sinn von Sein*] and the full scope of the understanding of Being have in general been clarified. Only then can one also analyse primordially what belongs to the concept of a science *of Being as such*. . . . " The next paragraph of *Being and Time* adds immediately: "The answer to the question of the meaning of Being has yet to be given [*steht . . . aus*]." And then Division One of *Being and Time* closes with a final problem, one in which hope and despair at achieving the philosophic vocation are equally—and all-too-painfully—apparent, the problem of bringing Dasein "into view [*in den Blick*] as a whole."

In his "Letter on Humanism," Heidegger notes that the third division of the first part was held back "because thinking failed in the adequate saying of this turning [*Kehre*]. . . . This turning is not a change of standpoint from *Being and Time*, but in it the thinking that was sought first arrives at the location of that dimension out of which *Being and Time* is experienced, that is to say, experienced from the fundamental experi-

in the question which we are to work out, *what is asked about* is Being—that which determines entities as entities, that on the basis of which [*woraufhin*] entities are already understood. (*Being and Time*, 6)

The suggestion is that being is the meaning of entities: being *is that* the entity *is* intelligible in its being. Not simply that it appears, but that it appears to be intelligible to us.

On page 17 Heidegger notes that this analysis of Dasein is not only incomplete, but also provisional since it "merely brings out the Being of this entity, without Interpreting its meaning."

Here the suggestion is that being is deficient with respect to its meaning. An entity that has not become thoroughly intelligible as to its being, that does not coincide with the intelligibility of its being, that has stubbornly refused to reduce itself to its intelligibility, eludes being in the precise sense that it cannot be interrogated as to its being—but being is the object *simpliciter* of interrogation. Such an entity has no ontological status. The only relationship that it has with its being is that it deprives itself of every relationship to it; it is allergic to it. It disavows its own presence. It is in the strictest sense meaningless: an entity that has refused all relationship to its being repudiates the very possibility of meaning, and so has

---

ence of the oblivion of Being" (208). Some pages later he offers another *caveat*: "It is everywhere supposed that the attempt in *Being and Time* ended in a blind alley [*sei in eine Sackgasse geraten*]." *Geraten* has the sense of finding oneself having ended up in something unintentionally. *Sackgasse* is a blind alley, or, more literally, a dead-end, a cyst-alley, a sac-alley. *Geraten in eine Sackgasse* is, then, a very precise way of saying what philosophy is, that it is the aporematic art of finding oneself once again having ended up at a dead-end. Besides the term ἀπορία, ancient Greek has a number of terms to express this notion of *geraten*: the term ἀποτυγχάνω means 'to fail in hitting, to miss, to lose' and, when used absolutely, 'to miss the truth, be wrong'; the term ἁμαρτία also means 'to miss the mark.' In the *Odyssey* Homer says (7.292) μύθων ἡμάρτανε, which we might render as "failed of good telling." Aristotle, who says being is a homonym only "accidentally

determined the meaning of meaning to be in principle meaningless.

And if this entity be that entity in and through which is achieved the coincidence of being with its intelligibility, what then? A new possibility emerges that was hitherto hidden in the hermeneutic circle, to which Heidegger obliquely attests when, in defending the circularity by which being enters into its intelligibility, he notes that "in the circle is hidden a positive possibility of the most primordial kind of knowing" (*Being and Time*, 153).

This possibility is inherent in being; and for this reason being is thoroughly mediated by the possibility of eclipsing its own intelligibility. So being is mediated by the lack of coincidence between itself and its intelligibility.

And this possibility is the possibility of the entity expelling itself from its relationship to its being, disqualifying it, invalidating it. As such, this possibility is also the possibility of being being the reunion of the entity with what denatures it, deprecates it, undoes it as entity. With this possibility the entity is dissipated, undone, dissolute, derelict, skidding into the sheer indetermination of beings slip-sliding away from their disclosure. With this possibility beings as a whole are abandoned from being, being from its interpellation, and its interpellation from itself. The entity falls into self-estrangement, where it collapses in upon itself, from an infinitely discreet implosion.

[ἀπὸ τύχης]," uses forms of ἁμαρτία many times in the *Nicomachean Ethics* (cf. 1126a1, 1118b1, the long discussion of the different kinds of injuries to another at 1135b8ff., and 1104b33). This term is in sharp contrast to the opening line " . . . hence it has been well said that the good is that at which all things aim [ἐφίεται]," as well as the closing remark of the second paragraph, "Will not then a knowledge of this supreme good be also of great practical importance for the conduct of life? Will it not better enable us to attain what is fitting, like archers having a target to aim at [ἄν τυγχάνοιμεν τοῦ δέοντος;]?" (1094a22ff.). Curiously, language in general seems to have a positive correlate to this notion of finding oneself astray and waywarding. So Greek has ἁρμόζω and μάρπτω, as well as τυγχάνω; German has '*zufällig*', meaning 'fortuitous', 'falling into things in the right way'; while English has 'serendipity', 'fortuitous', 'gratuitous', etc.

[134] THE CUNNING OF BEING

This implosion destroys the possibility of any question about the meaning of the entity. And with this implosion being retires itself as the anonymous muffling rustling of an unstable and indeterminate 'there is', the being that is there when there is nothing. Language becomes the indifferent nominalization of the world where things are set adrift by their names.

With the possibility that Dasein has become allergic to rendering itself intelligible the amphiboly of being turns into the antinomy of being, that the entity abjures its being and being is the aversion to the entity. In this event ontology collapses in upon itself, leaving only an indiscernible black hole node of nonmeaning. Ordinarily, to understand the being of an entity presupposes a prior encounter with that entity, while to understand the entity presupposes a precursory comprehension of its being. This is the ordinary structure of the hermeneutic experience. But if the entity is the refusal of any relationship to its being, then to understand the entity requires an abjuration of its being, and to understand the being of an entity requires understanding that the entity is the voidance of all questions as to its being, the undermining of any possible articulation of its meaning. Everything is radically separated from its intelligibility, including being. Everything is the failure to coincide with its intelligibility. Everything, including being, is moot, mute, meaningless.

All of these positive correlates suggest that we hit upon the right way unintentionally, that we find that it just so happens that we are on the way where things turn out right, that things just sort of fall into place without requiring our deliberation. It would seem obvious why there are more terms expressing one's not knowing one's way about than there are terms expressing the opposite notion of deliberately deciding to be on track: given that the way of being that we are is to make it up as we go along, we only can raise the philosophic issue of why things do not seem to fit properly. Being wanderers and wayfarers, waywarding all the way, we view ourselves as on an errand, the errand of faring along the way of errancy, the way of straying from the way.

Heidegger continues: "Let us not comment any further upon that opinion [*Meinung*]. The thinking that hazards [*versuch (sic)*] a few steps in *Being and Time* has even today not advanced beyond

The amphiboly signifies, then, that being can never be pure and simple, but can only be a mediated being, a being mediated, a being itself its own mediation, mediated by itself. Being encloses itself within saying as a something other that goes beyond saying. This is the precise sense in which being is its own mediation: in saying being gives itself to itself by incising within itself the excising of its recitation.

And it is in its failure to name being pure and simple, in an immediate relationship to the immediacy of being, that language achieves self-consciousness. With this emergence language identifies itself with a suspicion barely voiced, namely, that it is the exceeding of being and the deficiency of language to capture this exceeding that indicates a yonder tucked into language, a linguistic yonder, a nameless faceless something *other* lodging deep inside language like little black hole eddies of the antipredicative.

Yet this suspicion dispels itself as soon as it arises, for it forces language to search within itself for a purer but also more unobtrusive language, capable of calling into question—in order to disappear in it—the very Other of all language, this Other, which, however, is nothing more than a language which also has the essential task of searching within itself for its Other in order to disappear in it. As soon as we suspect language is inadequate, we recognize this inadequacy as the essence of all saying, so that it runs the risk of never being adequately inadequate. Every saying testifies to the fact that language does not lack enough of its lack, that language is itself this lack of language *and* the lack of this

---

that publication. But perhaps in the meantime it has in one respect come farther into its own matter [*Sache*]. However, as long as philosophy merely busies itself with continually obstructing the possibility of admittance into the matter for thinking, i.e., into the truth of Being, it stands safely beyond any danger of shattering [*zerbrechen*] against the hardness of that matter. Thus 'to philosophize' about being shattered [*über das Scheitern*] is separated by a chasm from a thinking that is shattered. If such thinking were to go fortunately [*glücken dürfen*] for a man no misfortune would befall him [*geschähe kein Unglück*]. He would receive the only gift [*Geschenk*] that can come to thinking from Being" (222–23).

lack. The lacking of language is language completing itself. With the emergence of self-consciousness language consists of identifying itself as the limits to itself. Within language, language and the limits of language coincide.

In this guise we see that philosophy has always been exclusively concerned with its final and most extreme possibility—for this dialectic of saying is precisely this. And with this dialectic—that the saying of being exposes being as being mediated by itself—the amphiboly of being completes the world with an essential ambiguity. Why is there ambiguity in the world? Ambiguity is its own answer. We cannot answer it except by rediscovering in it the ambiguity of our answer, and an ambiguous answer is a question about ambiguity. It is as though philosophy were a hidden trap forcing ambiguity to reveal its own traps. The trap, however, is too well-hidden. It is as though in demarcating the amphiboly of being, the essential ambiguity to word-world relations, philosophy were attempting to keep it—in a place where it fulfills itself without threatening the presumed transparency and entrenched stability of discourse to entrap it wholly within its own hidden trap. Philosophy has always struggled at its outer limits to ferret out the vague and volatile indeterminacy to which amphibolous being retreats and retracts, a slippery-slope instability which causes all meaning to slip-slide down into ambiguous indeterminacy. The meaning of being shows itself to be the meaning of meaning, that, while determining meaning, it also surrounds that determination with ambiguous indeterminacy, placing us precipitously teeter-tottering on the brink of a thinksink. And this encompassing indeterminacy is the presence of meaning that is constantly shifting and sliding the entity around its sense.

All we can say about this essential ambiguity to the world is that it designates the fact that language cannot contain the truth about itself. And the truth of language? It is ambiguous: on the one hand it refers to things, names them, restores them to their identity, gives them to us; on the other hand its only interest in the thing is in the meaning of the thing, which is given by denying its existence, by affirming it only in its absence. In a word, language gives us what appears, but only in the absence of its appearing. Language is that nothing lies behind the entity save the disappearing of its appearing. The disappearing, hidden in what appears, of its appearing we designate by being; but we also designate by being the thing that appears. And in the case of Dasein, this ambiguity is especially bewitching inasmuch as Dasein is such that what appears is that there is appearing, such that in and through this appearing it itself appears. The appearing of Dasein consists in the relationship between what appears *as* Dasein and the appearing of Dasein, a relationship that is its own appearing. *Dasein is the site for the identifying of the appearing thing and the thing appearing.* To put it in a word, the appearing of Dasein *is* Dasein; the appearing of Dasein is the *Da* of appearing.

Dasein identifies the appearing thing and the thing appearing in and through the "articulation of meaning." This "articulation of meaning" gives the thing a definite character by bringing it forth to show itself. And the disclosure of the thing as what it is and as that it is what it is is its meaning:

> But that which is understood, taken strictly, is not the meaning but the entity, or alternatively Being. Meaning is that wherein the intelligibility [*Verständlichkeit*] of something maintains itself. That which can be Articulated in a disclosure by which we understand, we call "meaning." . . . *Meaning is the "upon-which" of a projection in terms of which something becomes intelligible as something; it gets its structure from a fore-having, a fore-sight, and a fore-conception.* (*Being and Time*, 157)

To address something *as* something is to address it with a view to its being what it is and that it is as it is, i.e., with a view to what Heidegger calls its Being. This implies that the basic element of the "articulation of meaning" is, on the one hand, the *as* structure (the addressing of something *as* something) but, on the other hand, the difference between being and entities. Both of these attest to the basic amphiboly of being, inasmuch as an entity can be taken only as being the entity that it is, and being is seen to be that the entity is the entity that it is. And both of these volatilize the metaphysical vocation of rendering the ground of beings intelligible.

In an epigram to a series of lectures he gave in the spring of 1928, published under the title *The Metaphysical Foundations of Logic*, Heidegger gives a definition of what it means to do philosophy:

To philosophize means to exist from ground.[13]

And it is precisely the meaning of ground in *Being and Time*, which Heidegger attempts to elicit according to the *as* structure of being and to its difference from entities, that volatilizes the metaphysical venture, for in *Being and Time* the intelligibility of the ground revolves around the hermeneutic circle until it collapses into the auto-apotropaia of the *Ab-grund*, a perpetual turning the gaze away from the ground by turning the *Ab-grund* away from its own groundlessness. And this collapse of metaphysical grounding arises from the inability to hold fast to the distinction between the ontic and the ontological when analyzing the "*Da*" in and through which this distinction emerges.

V

The unpretentious thing evades thought most stubbornly. Or could it be that this self-refusal of the mere thing, this self-contained independence, belongs precisely to the nature of the thing?
    Martin Heidegger, "The Origin of the Work of Art"

Death is the side of life which is not turned towards us nor illuminated by us.
    Rainer Maria Rilke, Letter to Hulewiecz

---

13. Martin Heidegger, *The Metaphysical Foundations of Logic*, 324.

> For, nearing death, one perceives death no longer, and stares ahead—
> perhaps with large brute gaze.
>
> Rainer Maria Rilke, *Duino Elegies, VIII*

> Everything looks as if it were genuinely understood, genuinely taken hold of, genuinely spoken, though at bottom it is not; or else it does not look so, yet at bottom it is. Ambiguity not only affects the way we avail ourselves of what is accessible for use and enjoyment, and the way we manage it; ambiguity has already established itself in the understanding as a potentiality-for-Being, and in the way Dasein projects itself and presents itself with possibilities.
>
> Martin Heidegger, *Being and Time*

But what is the sense of "ground" here? In the lecture series proper Heidegger notes:

> Philosophy, it has always been known, should not be derived from somewhere else, but it must ground itself.[14]

And this ground from which the philosopher exists is that *primary* something for the sake of which one exists. And, furthermore, the ground of an entity is that for the sake of which the entity is that it is what it is. Later Heidegger will abandon metaphysics entirely when he comes to see that the entity is just for the sake of itself, and that is all that can be said about it: it is that it may be. But here that for the sake of which an entity is as it is is that Dasein encounters entities for its own sake. In this way the ground of an entity turns round Dasein throwing over entities the project of being thrown open into the world. Being for its own sake, and in being for its own sake the throwing over the entity its being thrown open in the world, Dasein is freedom for grounds, freedom toward ground, freedom to ground. This freedom, Heidegger instructs us, is the "*ground of ground.*"[15]

So if we are, as metaphysicians, destined to inquire as to how

---

14. Ibid., 212.
15. Ibid., 214.

ground belongs essentially to being, we must first clarify how, although thrown into a world it never made, Dasein makes the world just as it is by throwing open entities into the world, by throwing entities into the open. This is to ask after how Dasein understands its own ground, this "for the sake of itself" that is at the same time that for the sake of which the entity is as it is.

Dasein lays the ground for itself, but it can never take power over this ground. Yet insofar as existence involves a constituting of itself, Dasein must take over being its own ground. It never exists "*before* its ground, but only *from* it and *as this ground*" (*Being and Time*, 284). "In itself, being a ground *is* a nullity of itself," inasmuch as Dasein is thrown into the world in order to take up this thrownness as its *own* project, its *own* accomplishment. In taking over its thrownness as its own accomplishment Dasein is *released* from its ground, *not through* itself but *to* itself, so as to be "*as this ground.*" "Dasein is not itself the ground of its being, inasmuch as this ground first arises from its projection; rather, being its own self, it is the *being* of its ground" (285).Ced Dasein is the understanding of its ground; it is *that* it is its ground made intelligible to itself.

Here we find that the ground of Dasein is that upon which Dasein projects itself: Dasein throws itself forth and throws itself off upon its ground. The ground of existence, then, is its intelligibility, because intelligibility maintains itself in meaning and meaning is "*the 'upon-which' of a projection in terms of which something becomes intelligible as something*" (*Being and Time*, 151).

Since Dasein is not itself the ground of its being but rather takes itself over as the being of its ground, its being consists entirely in "being the ground of a nullity [*Nichtigkeit*] (and this being the ground is itself null)" (*Being and Time*, 285). Again, the ground of Dasein is that with which and through which the world becomes intelligible, for "a 'ground' becomes accessible only as meaning, even if it is the abyss of meaninglessness [*der Abgrund der Sinnlosigkeit*]" (152).

So the meaning of Dasein, that wherein its intelligibility maintains itself, is that it is at basis a nullity, groundless. But note that this is already contained in the notion of existence as standing outside itself. Dasein exists for the sake of accomplishing its own grounding. As existing in this way, Dasein stands outside itself in a thrusting into its ground. But insofar as it is the being of this ground, Dasein is again outside itself, this time outside itself as its own grounding. So in attempting to accomplish itself as its own grounding, Dasein casts itself off away from its ground, averts itself from it, repudiates it. This is a circular happening, for standing outside itself for the sake of standing within and in (the) place of its ground is to be thrust away from its ground—for it necessarily will always be doubly outside it—and back to standing outside itself in order to accomplish itself as its own grounding. The circularity of this happening is the precise sense in which we say Dasein is groundless: its ground is the self-refusal of ground while it itself is the repudiation of ground; its abandonment is its abandonment into "the abyss of meaninglessness," which is now seen to be the condition for its possibility.

Dasein is always circling its ground but never able to catch itself up into it, and the circle this orbit inscribes is the groundlessness of Dasein. But Dasein is *the* metaphysical entity. Heidegger tells us,

> There is some way in which Dasein understands itself in its Being, and that to some degree it does so explicitly. It is peculiar to this entity that with and through its Being, this Being is disclosed to it. *Understanding of Being is itself a definite characteristic of Dasein's Being.* Dasein is ontically distinctive in that it *is* ontological. (*Being and Time*, 12)

He notes a little further on:

> But the roots of the existential analytic, on its part, are ultimately *existentiell*, that is, *ontical*. (*Being and Time*, 13)

And opening Division Two he recapitulates this idea:

> In ontological Interpretation an entity is to be laid bare with regard to its own state of Being; such an Interpretation obliges us first to give a phenomenal characterization of the entity we have taken as our theme. (*Being and Time*, 232)

Dasein provides the ontico-ontological condition for the possibility of any and all ontologies, inasmuch as it is that entity that can interrogate the ontical as to its ontological status, as well as take the ontological conditions for the possibility of the ontic as themselves ontical. Moreover, the ontological, that is, the giving of grounds, cannot give itself the grounds for being the giving of grounds, but rather must be accounted for by the ontic. It is only by affirming our indwelling in the entitative order that the nonentitative experience can be opened up. But in this affirmation is affirmed that behind the entitative there is nothing but the disappearing of its appearing. I would like to suggest that the proper way to understand the polemic between the ontic and the ontological that runs through *Being and Time* is that Dasein has an ontological relationship to the ontic and an ontic relationship to the ontological only because with fundamental ontology ontology in general is possible only as the self-repudiation of the ontical, and ontics is the resistance to an acknowledgment of the ontology that was supposed to have made it possible in the first place. Let us see an instance of this.

The text of *Being and Time* constantly testifies to this exchange between the ontic and the ontological. From the beginning it cleaves itself into a remarkable ambiguity. On the same page (42), we find:

The essence of Dasein lies in its existence.

The being of any such entity is *in each case mine*.

The *mineness* of Dasein means that Dasein takes its ontic status as ontologically significant. *Existence* inverts this relationship: the ontological can only be ontological if it emerges into the ontic dimension of existence. If we recall the aforecited closing passage of page 436, the suggestion is—insofar as Heidegger raises the question of ontical foundations for ontology only at the closing of the published portion of *Being and Time*—if we recall that passage, then the suggestion is that laying the ontological ground for ontology necessarily founders in the face of the neglect of the ontic. The "mineness" of Dasein tears the ontological groundworking asunder, for as soon as Heidegger says that Dasein is the entity that is *in each case mine*, he is necessarily led to the question of "who" Dasein is; but this is a question that can be asked only of a particular individual entity, and not of the conditions for the possibility of that entity being who it is, conditions that are, of course, ontological. So the question of "who" Dasein is is a question that recoils from ontology back upon the ontic realm of particular beings, individuals the sole "ontic" content of which consists in identifying themselves as themselves, as particular concrete "whos."

This ontological abandonment of the ontic is dramatically portrayed in Heidegger's intent to "capture a whole Dasein." This requires owning up to the fact that no matter what one does to lead a fulfilling and meaningful life, a thriving flourishing life that contains philosophic sensitivities, it is all in vain, for the final possibility of existence—death—is the absolute loss of all meaning and meaningfulness. To live the philosophically exacting life is to realize that the philosophic life deprives itself of all significance and value. But notwithstanding that, it is only by virtue of the fact that death is implicated in the constitution of Dasein that existence can be meaningful. The philosopher discovers that meaning upon "learning how to die." What makes me disappear from the world cannot find its guarantee there; and thus, in a way, having no guarantee, it is not certain. No one is really certain of his own mortality. Yet meaningfulness is obtained by searching for death's possibility; by trying to come face to face with one's own mortality. It is not enough for me to know that I am mortal; I have to somehow become mortal, mortal twice over, sovereignly mortal, born again into my mortality. That is the peculiarly human vocation; we are infinitely mortal. In owning up to my own mortality—if I can ever in fact do that and not rather forestall on such owning up—in owning up to my own mortality I make death double itself: there is my death which circulates among my possibilities, which is determined as the freedom to die and the capacity to take mortal risks; and there is the other death, the death which makes of me my other, the death which I cannot grasp, which is not linked to *me* by any relation of any sort. This other death is that which never comes and toward which I cannot direct myself.

Owning up to my mortality is my feeble and frustrated attempt, my futile attempt, to eliminate death, to strip it of what is outstanding about it. But what is outstanding in my death is its absolute futurity: my death is an unforeseeable future that can never arrive, that can never become a past, that never could have been, and so that which never will be for me. Death never comes until after its arrival. Death itself is my perpetual flight before my death; it signifies my radical inability to be honest about my mortality, it is what is dishonest about my own mortality. It is what makes of us mortals immortals who live pretending that *they* have the key to the back door. Death is the deep of dissimulation. It is what life is: we the living push back and back upon death and against it, but it is silent in its absolute rebuttal: we can never get at it; we can never get to it.

Heidegger defines my-death as "the possibility of my own impossibility." So it is a question of facing up to this impossibility. But as soon as my-death is confronted as the possibility of my own impossibility it is transfigured into the impossibility of all possibility, including, most notably, the possibility of dying, and so the possibility of dying into this impossibility. Death removes all possibility, makes of possibility the impossible. Nonetheless, confronting "mortality's dishonor" makes possible *for the first time* all possibility, makes possibility possible. To face one's death is to open onto that region where death no longer appears as possible, but as the empty deep of the impossible, and out of this deep life becomes possible *again*, becomes possible for the first time, as that which is wholly unto itself, there being nothing else, and so as pure gratuity, sheer fortuity. Death proves that getting born is the issue, not death. My death is my most extreme power, my most proper possibility; but it is also the death which never comes to me, with which there is no relation possible. Indeed, I elude my death when I think I master it through "anticipatory resoluteness." Death is that which happens to no one, the uncertainty and indeterminacy of that which never happens at all. It is its own disintegration, vacant and radical auto-debilitation. Rather: one comes into one's dying, where, finally, one is free from both life and death, free finally *for* life.

To die is to shatter the world; it is the loss of the person, and, insofar as appearing involves something for the sake of which there is appearing, to die is the annihilation of being. And so to die is also the loss of death, and therefore the loss of the significance this my-death bestows on my life, the absolute loss of the meaningfulness that mortality confers upon existence. When I die I cease being mortal, I am no longer capable of dying, and my impending death horrifies me because I see it as it is: no longer death, but the impossibility of dying. I do not die; rather I die always other than myself. Moreover, one never dies simply of an illness, say, an illness from which one never recovers; one dies of one's death.

On the other hand, however, the activity of dying prevents my death from ever taking over. I am too caught up in the activity of dying to ever be dead. My dying separates me from my death by an impossible and untraversable gap in time; for no matter how close I am to death, I still have a little more time left before I am dead. My death is that which is always outstanding in my dying. It is that which dying forestalls. My dying proves that I will never be dead, for dying is something I can in principle never complete. Rather, death is the movement of dying always more, of dying immeasurably more. Dying is a task without term. Dying is not to die but to let go into the dying. Dying is to transform the fact of death, to expose myself to what of myself can never be exposed, to become the intimacy of such self-exposure-non-exposure, an intimacy with death where death no longer can be faced, where *my* death, death which is proper *only* to me, *uniquely mine*, becomes anonymous. In dying *I* do not die, I have fallen from the power to die. In dying *they* die; they do not cease and they do not finish dying. In dying death is that which cannot be accomplished by dying, that which the accomplishment of dying can never realize.

Here we see the almost contradictory nature of death and dying. Dying is an ontic affair, it concerns the "who" that is dying. As such it prevents the ultimate ontological event—my death— from ever arriving, from ever being possible. And the activity of dying and *only* the activity of dying can preclude the possibility of death from arriving; for the possibility of death is inscribed in the essence of every other activity. Yet the act of dying is the condition for the possibility of death; so dying is the condition for the possibility of that which it renders in advance impossible. And death, that final possibility, renders all possibility, including that possibility—dying—that is the condition for its possibility, impossible. Death delivers me over to the impossibility of dying. That is to say, *death is the condition for the possibility of its own impossibility as well as the impossible condition for its own possibility*.

Given that with the resolute anticipation of my death being gets cosmologicized and the ontological dimension of the world is opened up, we can conclude here that the ontical is the condition for the possibility of that ontology which it has in advance rendered impossible; and ontology is that possibility that renders impossible all ontic considerations, including the ontic need to develop ontology.

The groundless quality of existence is what makes this dialectic of death possible. For only for a being that is at bottom the reflection of an infinite abyss can death be a possibility. But in that case dying would be the aggressive, desperate, and disdainful denial of this groundlessness. It would be the activity of providing its own grounding in the face of this groundlessness it has refused to accept. So dying is not the being of the ground of existence, but the being of its groundlessness: groundlessness in the aversion to itself.

Thus it is apparent that Dasein is always circling its fabled ground, but never able to catch itself up with it, and the circle this orbit inscribes in being is the groundlessness of existence.

Dasein misunderstands itself in its groundlessness. To understand, to recall the litany, is for Dasein to "project" itself "*towards a potentiality-for-being for the sake of which any Dasein exists*" (*Being and Time*, 336). The suggestion is that that for the sake of which Dasein exists is to identify its groundlessness with the circular attempt to ground itself.

The key word here is 'project', "*Entwurf.*" Of course, 'project' takes as its clue a phrase from the *Critique of Pure Reason*, "the reason discovers only what her own projects educe" (Bxiii). The projects in this case are the structures which anticipate what will be discerned in the object. 'Project' then is a precursory ontological comprehension, a structure that ontologically precedes Dasein's comportment to entities. This project is a prepossession, an anticipatory seizure of the being of those entities to be encountered. To project means, then, to seize by anticipation the ontological structure of a being still to be encountered; to bring to pass the seizure of this ontological structure in the happening of its encounter, so that that whereupon this project projects is the meaning of that which is encountered, that it appears as intelligible.

Project, as we know, is circular. Kant noted this when he noted that such is the primordial integrity of human experience that he is able to prove "the highest principle of all synthetic judgments" ("the conditions of the *possibility of experience in general* are likewise conditions of the *possibility of an object of experience*" [A158 = B197]) by showing that the principles of pure understanding (the educing projects of reason) are made possible by that which they themselves make possible—the nature of experience. The circularity of such proofs arises from the essential circularity of experience. Kant says of each principle of pure understanding that

> it has the peculiar character that it makes possible the very experience which is its own ground of proof, and that in this experience it must always be presupposed. (A737 = B765)

In like vein Heidegger notes that

> if we are inquiring about the meaning of Being, our investigation does not then become a "deep" one, nor does it puzzle out what stands behind Being. *It asks about Being itself in so far as Being enters into the intelligibility of Dasein.* The meaning of Being can never be contrasted with entities, or with Being as the 'ground' which gives entities support; for a 'ground' becomes accessible only as meaning, even if it is itself the abyss of meaninglessness. (*Being and Time*, 152; my emphasis)

It is this "abyss of meaninglessness" that we need to focus our attention upon.

Also:

> Entities 'have' meaning only because, as Being which has been disclosed beforehand, they become intelligible in the projection of that Being—that is to say, in terms of the "upon-which" of that projection. The primary projection of the understanding of Being 'gives' the meaning. The question about the meaning of the Being of an entity takes as its theme the "upon-which" of that understanding of Being which underlies all being of entities. (*Being and Time*, 324–25)

We can see now that the ground of the being of Dasein is not that which is projected upon, but lies in projecting, which is always a projecting itself around and around in its circularity. And if we take these last two citations together, then the suggestion is that that upon which the "primary projection of the understanding of Being" projects (itself) is the meaning of being, yet this meaning itself emerges from out of an "abyss of meaninglessness."

Being is only insofar as it enters into intelligibility. But something becomes intelligible only insofar as it is projected upon its meaning. And as we know, the intelligibility of something lies in its ground, that is to say, its meaning. So the suggestion now is that not only can being come to pass only insofar as it is grounded in its intelligibility, it is nothing but this grounding in its intelligibility. That is to say, being comes to pass as the grounding of itself in an identification with its intelligibility.

Here Heidegger fulfills *and* exhausts the venture of metaphysics: to seek a coincidence of being with its intelligibility. Being *is*, we find, only insofar as it is intelligible. Thus it is that Heidegger announces the most extreme possibility of metaphysics:

> Being (not entities) is something which 'there is' ['*es gibt*'] only in so far as truth is. And truth *is* only in so far and as long as Dasein is. (*Being and Time*, 230)

> Only as long as Dasein *is* (that is, only as long as an understanding of Being is ontically possible), 'is there' Being. (*Being and Time*, 212)

If I may be pardoned a tarrying with the language here, it is possible to set up a series of identities in which being drops out. These identities are:

Since Dasein is the freedom for grounds, groundless, and the being of its ground, the ground of Dasein is not just a groundless freedom, but is the free and ultimately groundless projecting of ground. Projecting, then, is the groundless grounding of ground. And this is itself a groundless encircling around itself; for only a groundless encircling around itself could accomplish the groundless grounding of ground. The grounds for projecting grounds are lacking insofar as they are themselves fully invested in the projecting of grounds. Or rather, they are given in and through the projecting of grounds precisely *as* the projecting of grounds: that grounds can be given for anything is itself the ground for giving grounds. But look what happens in this case. The intelligibility of being, that is, the giving of grounds, is simply this self-encircling groundlessness. This implies that being *itself* is excluded from this self-encircling groundlessness; for the sole content of this groundlessness that is the encircling of itself is just this quality, this engagement, of encircling around and around itself. That is to say, nothing can enter into this self-encircling, for it is simply the abrogation of any content.

But if we reverse our starting point and begin with being, then we get a similar series of identities in which being is included as what is only excluded.

If being comes to pass in being projected upon its intelligibility as its ground, then it is projecting that attains primacy. But this projecting is the circular movement of grounding itself. As the incessant endeavor to ground itself grounding itself, so to speak, to see itself seeing itself as that which does the seeing, projecting circles itself, and this encircling itself is precisely the lack of any appeal to a ground. So projecting is—again—seen to be a self-encircling groundlessness excluding all content. Hence projecting is the groundless grounding of itself in its own groundlessness. This circular groundlessness evaporates all being and all entities. Everything disappears from it as from something like the opposite of a black hole. Being is simply this free-floating disappearing act of the one and all.

All there is is meaning circling round and round itself in order to see that it is really being. But if all there is is meaning in its self-encircling groundlessness, in endlessly encircling itself, then all there is is that there is meaning means nothing.

This is the end of philosophy.

The Hermeneutic Circle
As Auto-Critique

The principle of the ground—the ground of the principle. Let us stop for a moment, supposing that we are permitted to do so: the principle of the ground—the ground of the principle. Here something turns around in itself. Here something curls itself up in itself without, however, closing itself, but rather unlocking itself at the same time. Here is a ring, something like a snake. Something catches itself with its own tail. Here there is a beginning, which is already completion.

Martin Heidegger, *Der Satz vom Grund*

Whenever thought is caught in a circle, this is because it has touched upon something original, its point of departure beyond which it cannot move except to return. . . . The writer, then, is one who writes in order to be able to die, and he is one whose power to write comes from an anticipated relation with death. The contradiction subsists, but is seen in a different light. Just as the poet only exists once the poem faces him, only after the poem, as it were—although it is necessary that first there be a poet in order for there to be a poem—so one senses that if Kafka goes toward the power of dying through the work which he writes, the work itself is by implication an experience of death which he apparently has to have been through already in order to reach the work and, through the work, death. But one can also sense that the movement which, in the work, is the approach to death, death's space and its use, is not exactly the same movement which would lead the writer to the *possibility* of dying. One can even suppose that the particularly strange relations between artist and work, which make the work depend on him who is only possible within the work—one can even suppose that such an anomaly stems from the experience which overpowers the forms of time, but stems more profoundly still from the ambiguity of that experience, from its double aspect which Kafka expresses with too much simplicity in the sentences we ascribe to him: *Write to be able to die—Die to be able to write.* These words close us into their circular demand; they oblige us to start from what we want to find, to seek nothing but the point of departure, and thus to make this point something we approach only by quitting it. But they also authorize this hope: the hope, where the interminable emerges, of grasping the term, of bringing it forth.

Maurice Blanchot, *L'Espace litteraire*

There is a beginning. There is not yet beginning to be a beginning. There is not yet beginning to be a not yet beginning to be a beginning. There is being. There is nonbeing. There is not yet beginning to be a not yet beginning to be nonbeing. Suddenly there is nonbeing. But I do not know, when it comes to nonbeing, which is really being and which is nonbeing. Now I have just said something. But I don't know whether what I have said has really said something or whether it hasn't said something.

Chuang Tzu

But we have all along been prepared for experiencing being as what circulates in the circuitry of meaning encircling itself. For *Being and Time* is the classic statement of being circulating within the circular structure of its meaning; this work expounds and espouses the hermeneutic circle as the dynamics of inquiry into the meaning of being, such as where Heidegger speaks explicitly of "the circular Being of Dasein" (*Being and Time*, 315, 363). *Being and Time* is itself circular in its procedure; it is the *circular* exposition (*Auslegung*) of the circularity of being and meaning, that is, of the meaning of being. This exposition consists in the circular "retrieval" (*Widerholung*), from out of the future, of possibilities that have all along been available to us, into which we have always already been inserted.

However, given, as I have suggested, that the tendency toward philosophizing is itself a function or index of the everydayness of anonymity, idle talk, and curiosity in which Dasein falls away from its proper ontological understanding of itself, waylaying itself in dispersion, evasion, and errancy, this exposition must always be a forceful setting free (*Frei-legung*) of the matter to be understood which counteracts Dasein's own tendency to fall away from encountering itself into dispersal and self-evasion.

> The laying free of Dasein's primordial Being must rather be *wrested* [*abgerungen*] from Dasein by following the *countertendency* [*im Gegenzug*] from that taken by the falling onticoontological tendency of interpretation. (*Being and Time*, 311)

The work of hermeneutics is to recover the meaning of being, being that tends to withdraw, to recede and retract itself, to cover itself over with errancy and dissimulation, to remove itself as what gives itself, to promote its own oblivion. Hermeneutics is a violent act, a *Destruktion* (*Being and Time*, §6).

Being and Time is a theory of the hermeneutic circularity of meaning; but it is itself circular—for strategic, programmatic, and methodological reasons, reasons, we would assume, that are themselves circular in nature. Of these reasons Heidegger points out:

> Philosophy will never seek to deny its 'presuppositions', but neither may it simply admit them. It conceives them, and it unfolds with more and more penetration both the presuppositions themselves and that for which they are presuppositions. (*Being and Time*, 310)

It is a matter of making explicit what we are always already familiar with, but only in a preconceptual way. "What is decisive is not to get out of the circle but to come into it in the right way" (*Being and Time*, 153).

> Where are ontological projects to get the evidence that their 'findings' are phenomenally appropriate? Ontological Interpretation projects the entity presented to it upon the Being which is that entity's own, so as to conceptualize it with regard to its structure. Where are the signposts to direct the projection, so that Being will be reached at all? (*Being and Time*, 312)

Heidegger's answer to this ensemble of *aporiai* is that we all along understand ourselves in terms of our being, an understanding that is both preontological and covered over by our own tendency toward dispersion and self-evasion. The question arises from and returns to this understanding.

However, this is not a matter of elaborating a deductive system. Here there is no formal, deductive movement from premise to conclusion but rather a retrieval (*Widerholung*) of our "precursory comprehension" that makes what is comprehended explicitly in and of itself.

> One can never carry on researches into the source and the possibility of the 'idea' of Being in general simply by means of the 'abstractions' of formal logic—that is, without any secure horizon for question and answer. One must seek a *way* of casting light on the fundamental question of ontology, and this is the way one must *go*. Whether this is the *only* way or even the right one at all, can be decided only *after one has gone along it*. (*Being and Time*, 437)

Far from securing a presuppositionless view of being, the issue is to see how we are always already understanding the phenomenon according to implicit "forestructures."

> We have indeed already shown, in analysing the structure of understanding in general, that what gets censured inappropriately as a 'circle', belongs to the essence and to the distinctive character of understanding as such. In spite of this, if the problematic of fundamental ontology is to have its hermeneutical Situation clarified, our investigation must now come back to this 'circular argument'. When it is objected that the existential Interpretation is 'circular', it is said that we have 'presupposed' the idea of existence and of Being in general, and that Dasein gets Interpreted 'accordingly', so that the idea of Being may be obtained from it. But what does 'presupposition' signify? In positing the idea of existence, do

we also posit some proposition from which we deduce further propositions about the Being of Dasein, in accordance with formal rules of consistency? Or does this pre-supposing have the character of an understanding projection, in such a manner indeed that the Interpretation by which such an understanding gets developed, will let that which is to be interpreted *put itself into words for the very first time, so that it may decide of its own accord whether, as the entity which it is, it has that state of Being for which it has been disclosed in the projection with regard to its formal aspects?* . . . We cannot ever 'avoid' a 'circular' proof in the existential analytic, because such an analytic does not do *any* proving *at all* by the rules of the 'logic of consistency'. (*Being and Time*, 314–15)

This remark refers us to an earlier insight into how science proceeds:

In a scientific proof, we may not presuppose what it is our task to provide grounds for. But if interpretation must in any case already operate in that which is understood, and if it must draw its nurture from this, how is it to bring any scientific results to maturity without moving in a circle, especially if, moreover, the understanding which is presupposed still operates within our most common information about man and the world? (*Being and Time*, 152)

So circular is the hermeneutic situation that, if we play the *ingenue*, if we feign obtuseness or even if we raise the critical eyebrow, if we protest at all in the face of this circularity, we have misunderstood the nature of understanding:

But if we see this circle as a vicious one and look out for ways of avoiding it, even if we just 'sense' it as an inevitable imperfection, then the act of understanding has been misunderstood from the ground up [*vom aus Grund*]. (*Being and Time*, 153)

This hermeneutic inquiry Heidegger inaugurates is violent; it has been forced to move against the tendency of Dasein to evade the issue of its being, to cover up this issue with idle talk and curiosity. As the counterthrust to the pull of fallenness, the hermeneutic inquiry has cast forth a sketch of that which tends to withdraw, of that which tends to lapse into sedimentation, violently drawing out that which tends to have all along been evaded in order to wrest this being free in its being. Here lies the danger, for what is to protect this inquiry from being arbitrary, from being simply forced? How do we know that this being, Dasein, has come to speak from itself, in accordance with its being?

> Where does this Interpretation get its clue, if not from an idea of existence in general which has been 'presupposed'? How have the steps in the analysis of inauthentic everydayness been regulated, if not by the concept of existence which we have posited? And if we say that Dasein 'falls', and that therefore the authenticity of its potentiality-for-Being must be wrested from Dasein in spite of this tendency of its Being, from what point of view is this spoken? Is not everything already illumined by the light of the 'presupposed' idea of existence, even if rather dimly? Where does this idea get its justification? (*Being and Time*, 313)

The answer is: we *are* the beings to be investigated; even though we have fallen into a misunderstanding of ourselves, we have already understood our being. If the exposition of the meaning of the being of Dasein shows itself to be circular, this is because understanding is itself circular:

> The 'circle' in understanding belongs to the structure of meaning, and the latter phenomenon is rooted in the existential constitution of Dasein—that is, in the understanding which interprets. An entity for which . . . its Being is itself an issue has, ontologically, a circular structure. (*Being and Time*, 153)

The hermeneutic circularity of the understanding is, then, the very condition under which understanding is possible; to "avoid" this circle would be to undermine understanding, to subvert it, to render it its own impasse, to make of it the loss of passage to and through itself.

> When one talks of the 'circle' in understanding, one expresses a failure to recognize two things: (1) that understanding as such makes up a basic kind of Dasein's Being, and (2) that this Being is constituted as care. To deny the circle, to make a secret of it, or even to want to overcome it, means finally to reinforce this failure. We must rather endeavour to leap into the 'circle', primordially and wholly, so that even at the start of the analysis of Dasein we make sure that we have a full view of Dasein's circular Being. (*Being and Time*, 315)

The hermeneutic circle, then, is simultaneously the method of investigation, the way of being of us who undertake the investigation, and the being of the being being investigated.

Now, *Being and Time* is the canonical or classical work of hermeneutics, laying out the framework for what, for the sake of argument, I would like to call "postmodern" philosophy. That this claim will not meet with much dispute is a testimony to how readily *Being and Time* has been accepted and absorbed into the contemporary philosophic scene. But here, exactly, is where we should become suspicious, for the wholesale acceptance of this work shows that its own assertions may simply get passed along emptied of their original force. The very strength of *Being and Time*, its explosive and destructive force of thought, its insight into the fallen character of language and of inauthenticity in general, can turn into its weakness: it can become *Gerede*, a matter of idle talk and curiosity, common coin, routine stuff.

> Whenever a phenomenological concept is drawn from primordial sources, there is a possibility that it may degenerate if

communicated in the form of an assertion. It gets understood in an empty way and is thus passed on, losing its indigenous character, and becoming a free-floating thesis. Even in the concrete work of phenomenology itself there lurks the possibility that what has been primordially 'within our grasp' may become hardened so that we can no longer grasp it. And the difficulty of this kind of research lies in making it self-critical in a positive sense. (*Being and Time*, 36)

All this is to say, then, that if Dasein essentially falls away from a proper understanding of itself, if Dasein essentially *misunderstands* itself, then what assurance do we have that we, the readers, have not essentially misunderstood the circular happening of meaning that is proper to Dasein's understanding? What assurance do we have that "the act of understanding" has *not* been misunderstood "from the ground up"? As we know, Heidegger himself asks, at the end of *Being and Time*, "whether this is the *only* way or even the right one at all" (437). Moreover, as we saw in the preceding chapter, Heidegger's closing comment that the existential analytic "remains only *one way* which we may take," leads him to ask, "can one provide *ontological* grounds for ontology, or does it also require an *ontical* foundation? And *which* entity must take over the function of providing this foundation" (436). With this question, as we have seen, we enter into a slippaging of sense, a skewering of sense, that leads us to the bottom dropping out of being.

For me, it is a question of "retrieving" an understanding of understanding, of demonstrating the appropriateness of this understanding, to have not misunderstood Heidegger's assertions about the fallen character of understanding, about how we cannot but misunderstand ourselves. But then I could only misunderstand how we misunderstand ourselves. So for me, it is a question of understanding the meaning of the "hermeneutical situation." For me, it is a matter of entering into the hermeneutic circle until the matter of thinking becomes the matter for thinking and the matter for thinking becomes simply the matter of thinking, until T. S. Eliot is heard aright:

> We shall not cease from exploration
> And the end of our exploring
> Will be to arrive where we started
> And to know the place for the first time.[1]

But most importantly—again, *for me*—is to understand properly how the dynamics of understanding—the hermeneutic circle—can be misunderstood "from the ground up," to expose and elucidate the essential possibility of misunderstanding and thereby perhaps to open up the possibility of *another* way.

Now, most of us are grateful to *Being and Time* for conducting us into the hermeneutic experience, an experience to which it gives theoretical and procedural testimony. Most of us feel, for having ventured into this experience, that we can negotiate the conjugations, declensions, and inflections of the properly philosophic dimension to life. That is to say, we can now "encounter authentic existence."

Nonetheless, the hermeneutic experience must come under some kind of suspicion if we are to gain assurance that the *particular* way that Heidegger took in his existential analytic of Dasein is appropriate and proper. And if it is but *one* way, then perhaps we need to ask if that particular way closes off on other ways. Perhaps we need to ask what would another way be. After all, Heidegger closes his existential analytic with the cautionary note that "the conflict [*Streit*] as to the Interpretation of Being cannot be allayed, *because it has not yet been enkindled*" (437). It seems to me that it is precisely in the possibility of misunderstanding the dynamics of the understanding "from the ground up" that this conflict would even arise. It is a question, then, of whether the understanding can even be misunderstood; that is to say, it is a question of whether we can understand how we have all along misunderstood ourselves. To open up this conflict, to engage in the contestation of being, I should like to try to understand how the understanding

---

1. T. S. Eliot, "Little Gidding," in *Collected Poems, 1909–1962*, 222.

could be misunderstood—and then how we can understand *this*.

Now, as we know, what is the properly hermeneutic dimension of experience is precisely this circular structure of returning to our point of departure, of retrieving what is important in it, of exponentiating it, yet still preserving its untheorizability. That is to say, the departure is simply the exponentiation of that from which it departs. And it is precisely because of this exponentiating, this making the implicit explicit, that this circularity is nothing vicious. Yet—again—there is the possibility of misunderstanding the nature of this circularity. But if misunderstanding is possible, then it is necessarily a structural feature of the hermeneutic circle; inscribed into the dynamism of the understanding is it misunderstanding itself. So if we are to make explicit what is implicit in the hermeneutic circle, we would need to exponentiate this misunderstanding, for it and only it seems to be what has not yet been explicated, what alone remains unthematizable and untheorizable about understanding, about what gets understood and how it gets understood. The suggestion is that the hermeneutic circle is engaged by making the assumption of errancy, of misdirection, of being misled and waylaid, askewed and askanced. But this is not to correct such errancy; rather it is to retrieve it and preserve it as the mysteriousness of understanding, its *Unumgänglichkeit*.

Textually we find testimony to this errancy, this faulting of the understanding, this straying astray in and by fallibility, this vagrancy and aimlessness. *Being and Time* opens, after a brief untitled and unnumbered section admonishing us that "it is fitting that we should raise anew *the question of the meaning of Being*," with the bold statement, "This question has today been forgotten" (2). It is a question of "wresting" the phenomena from their lapsing into the obliviation of everyday self-evidentiality.

> Now what must be taken into account if the formal conception of the phenomenon is to be deformalized into the phenomenological one . . . ? Manifestly, it is something that does *not* show itself at first and for the most part, something

that is *concealed*, in contrast to what at first and for the most part does show itself. But at the same time it is something that essentially belongs to what at first and for the most part shows itself, indeed in such a way that it constitutes its meaning and ground. (*Being and Time*, 35)

Here Heidegger adds, "And precisely because phenomena are at first and for the most part *not* given is phenomenology needed" (36), where "the phenomenological concept of phenomenon . . . means the Being of being—its meaning, modifications, and derivatives [*Der phänomenologische Begriff von Phänomen meint als das Sichseigende das Sein des Seienden, seinen Sinn, seine Modifikationen und Derivate*]" (35). The suggestion is, no doubt, that "Being" gives itself only in and through its modifications and derivatives; being is, as we have seen, an amphibolous figuration of itself, the enambiguating of itself. Heidegger names this auto-amphibolizing of being the *oblivion* of being, the *oblivion* of the ontological difference. The modifications and derivatives in and by which being gives itself are precisely what manifests itself "at first and for the most part." The giving of itself of being covers up and covers over this giving, giving rather, not the giving of itself, but beings, particular beings as what is there without any 'there is', without there being any 'there is'. For this reason the phenomenological act of retrieval promotes its own degeneration (cf. 36). This is not merely a matter of the phenomenological investigation falling back into the dispersiveness, evasiveness, and auto-obstructiveness of its object, everydayness, from which it always must be forcibly extricating itself. Much more decisive is the fact that the discourse stands in contradiction with what the discourse is about—the validity of its description is undermined by what it describes. Everydayness subverts the attempt to understand it. That is to say, everydayness, the "at first and for the most part," is what must be interpreted phenomenologically, yet renders impossible its being interpreted phenomenologically. *Being and Time* is an allegory of the figure of everydayness which relapses into the figure it deconstructs. Accordingly, *Being and Time* is structured like an aporia: it persists in performing what it has shown to be impossible to do. The law of this text, *Being and Time*, is too devious to allow for a simple relationship between its discourse and its object. The text can be considered as the theoretical description of everydayness but also as the disintegration of this same everydayness as soon as it is described. However, everydayness reabsorbs its theoretical description, thereby invalidating it.

However, it is still too soon to enter into this paradoxical relationship of the discourse of *Being and Time* with its object. Yet things are beginning to look a little suspicious—we seem to be doing what we say is in principle impossible to do. We still need to open this problem up some more.

It is a question of determining the way proper to encountering "Being and the structures of Being in the mode of phenomenon" (*Being and Time*, 37), a way that would let the phenomenon of being show itself *on its own terms*. But, "insofar as Being means the Being of beings, beings themselves turn out to be what is *interrogated* in the question of Being" (6). And, of course, as we know, Dasein is the exemplary being:

> Thus to work out the question of Being means to make a being—he who questions—perspicuous in his Being. Asking this question, as a mode of *being* of a being, is itself essentially determined by what is asked about in it—Being. (*Being and Time*, 7)

And:

> If the interpretation of the meaning of Being is to become a task, Dasein is not only the primary being to be interrogated; in addition to this it is the being that always already in its Being is related to *what is sought* in this question. But then the question of being is nothing else than the radicalization of an essential tendency of Being that belongs to Dasein itself, namely, of the preontological understanding of Being. (*Being and Time*, 14–15)

As we know, it is precisely this preontological understanding of being that *Being and Time* sets out to explicate. Yet such an understanding obstructs all attempts at rendering it ontologically explicit:

> The ontic-ontological priority of Dasein is therefore the reason why the specific constitution of the Being of Dasein—understood in the sense of the 'categorial' structure that belongs to it—remains hidden from it. (*Being and Time*, 16)

So it is expressly this ontological obstructiveness of understanding that needs to be clarified. But then, by virtue of this obstructiveness, such an analysis could never be more than "preparatory," "preliminary" (17), since, it would seem, the analysis would itself fall prey to this ontological obstructiveness, it would become the obstruction to itself. As Heidegger notes:

> The manner of access and interpretation must instead be chosen in such a way that this being can show itself to itself on its own terms [*daß dieses Seiende sich an ihm selbst von ihm selbst her zeigen kann*]. And furthermore, this manner should show that being as it is *at first and for the most part*—in its average *everydayness*. . . . By looking at the fundamental constitution of the everydayness of Dasein we shall bring out in a preparatory way the Being of this being. (*Being and Time*, 16–17)

Understanding is the obstruction to understanding itself; and Being is, for Heidegger, from the beginning of *Being and Time* on, what gets misunderstood. Again, we are thrown back to the need to misunderstand the hermeneutic circle. Moreover, because of the self-obstructing of understanding and the self-retracting of the giving of itself of being, this need to misunderstand the hermeneutic circle gives rise to the need to understand if it is even possible *not* to misunderstand it. Does misunderstanding the hermeneutic circle in principle entail understanding that it has been misunderstood? Does this entail understanding it authentically? Can *this* be understood? The way of Dasein is the way of errancy, of leading itself astray away from itself. Again, this way of errancy needs to be clarified—if, in fact, that is possible, for how could an analysis of errancy not be itself errant if the way of understanding *is* the way of errancy?

Let us see if we can get clear on this point, namely, not so much that our way is the way of errancy, but rather our ability to understand *that*. In "On the Essence of Truth," Heidegger starts to address this issue, even while he fails to realize how his discourse itself must participate in errancy, thereby voiding and invalidating itself.

> However, because truth is in essence freedom, historical man can, in letting beings be, also *not* let beings be the beings which they are and as they are. Then beings are covered up and distorted. Semblance comes to power. In it the dis-essence [*Unwesen*] of truth comes to the fore. However, because ek-sistent freedom as the essence of truth is not a property of man; because on the contrary man ek-sists and so becomes capable of history only as the property of freedom; the dis-essence of truth cannot first arise subsequently from mere human incapacity and negligence. Rather, untruth must derive from the essence of truth. Only because truth and untruth are, *in essence, not* irrelevant to one another but rather belong together is it possible for a true proposition to enter into pointed opposition to the corresponding untrue proposition. The question concerning the essence of truth thus first reaches the original domain of what is at issue when, on the basis of a prior glimpse of the full essence of truth, it has included a consideration of untruth in its unveiling of that essence. Discussion of the dis-essence of truth is not the subsequent filling up of a gap but rather the decisive step toward the adequate posing of the *question* concerning the essence of truth. Yet how are we to comprehend the dis-

essence in the essence of truth? ("On the Essence of Truth," 130)

Heidegger then points out that, because we are open to the manifestness of particular things, the "as a whole" or "in totality" (*im Ganzen*) of being appears incalculable and incomprehensible:

> Although it ceaselessly brings everything into definite accord, still it remains indefinite, indeterminable; it then coincides for the most part with what is fleeting and most unconsidered. However, what brings into accord is not nothing but rather a concealing of beings as a whole. Precisely because letting be always lets beings be in a particular comportment which relates to them and thus discloses them, it conceals being as a whole. . . . In the ek-sistent freedom of Da-sein a concealing of being as a whole comes to pass [*ereignet sich*]. ("On the Essence of Truth," 132)

Then he argues that the concealment of beings as a whole—"untruth proper"—is the condition for the possibility of letting-be. As such, however, it is concealed. That is, the concealing of an anterior concealment of being as a whole is what lets letting-be be. The concealing of what is concealed as well as the concealment of *this* is the fundament of Dasein. In this light Heidegger notes: "In letting beings as a whole be, which discloses and at the same time conceals, it happens that concealing appears as what is first of all concealed" ("On the Essence of Truth," 133). But this presents a conundrum: If concealment is from the first concealed, how can we even suspect that there is something like concealment? Is not the concealing of concealment just a tangled-up way of disclosing that nothing is concealed? Consider:

> As letting beings be, freedom is intrinsically the resolutely open bearing that does not close up in itself. All comportment is grounded in this bearing and receives from it directedness

toward beings and disclosure of them. Nevertheless, this bearing toward concealing conceals itself in the process, letting a forgottenness of the mystery take precedence and disappearing in it. ("On the Essence of Truth," 133–34)

It is in our everyday concerns that we find that nothing is concealed. But, as we know, when *in extremis*, such as anxiety in the face of our own mortality, we are overwhelmed with the mysteriousness of this nothing that is concealed, we exist aching and hollowed out by the anonymous muffling rustling of this mysteriousness, lost within the astonishing fact that there is nothing behind or besides appearing but its disappearing, nothing concealed but the concealment of beings as a whole, which, then, is what is there when there is nothing.

For the listener, who listens in the snow,
And, nothing himself, beholds nothing
That is not there, and the nothing that is.[2]

It is a question of sighting what there is when there is nothing. In order to begin to get this within our sights, withinsight, consider a rather pedestrian phenomenon of concealment, forgetting. Forgetting is, as Heidegger, in *Being and Time*, says in passing, a "positive" mode of being. Elsewhere he argues that forgetting is a "specific mode of retention. . . . This is not nothing; a very definite type of comportment of the self toward the bygone [*Vergangenheit*] is exhibited in it—a mode in which I close myself off from the bygone, in which it is veiled over for me" (*Basic Problems of Phenomenology*, 260). This forgetting is not the absence and failure to appear of a recollection, so that in the place of a recollection there would be nothing. It is, rather, a peculiar positively ecstatic mode of temporality (290).

Heidegger is saying that what is forgotten in forgetting some-

---

2. Wallace Stevens, "The Snow Man," in *The Collected Poems of Wallace Stevens*, 10.

thing is not what has been but rather one's own having-been-ness (*Gewesenheit*). Forgetting something disengages one from one's own particular having-been-ness, closing off that from which it disengages. Forgetting, in closing off on a particular bygone, closes itself off for itself. Thus if it is true that I have forgotten to do my assignment, then I have also forgotten that I forgot to do my assignment. But this latter forgetting is not a second-order forgetting, a forgetting of forgetting. The peculiarity of forgetting is that there can be no meta-forgetting. Rather, the characteristic of forgetting is that it forgets itself. In the same way that we can realize *this* Heidegger is arguing that concealment conceals itself, concealment conceals that it is a concealing. Thus Heidegger notes:

> But the forgotten mystery of Dasein is not eliminated by the forgottenness; rather, the forgottenness bestows on the apparent disappearance of what is forgotten a peculiar present [*Gegenwart*]. ("On the Essence of Truth," 134)

There are two issues here: the possibility of attuning to beings *as a whole* (*im Ganzen*); and the possibility of uncovering concealment, given that it conceals itself. These two issues are, of course, the same. Heidegger parlays the first from the beginning, from the introduction to *Being and Time*:

> Dasein is a being that does not simply occur among other beings. Rather it is ontically distinguished by the fact that in its Being this being is concerned *about* its very Being. (*Being and Time*, 12)

"Dasein," he insists, "*is* in such a way that, by being, it understands something like Being" (*Being and Time*, 17).

It is precisely Heidegger's resoluteness in facing the issue of attuning to beings as a whole that has proved decisive. In virtually all his lectures before the famous "*Kehre*" he begins with this claim. One has only to read the opening pages of *Vom Wesen des Grundes, An Introduction to Metaphysics*, or "Was ist Metaphysik?"

to have this point made forcefully enough. For instance, in the opening few pages of "Was ist Metaphysik?" Heidegger points out:

> Man—one being among others—"pursues science." In this "pursuit" nothing less transpires than the irruption by one being called "man" into the whole of beings, indeed in such a way that in and through this irruption beings break open and show what they are and how they are. The irruption that breaks open in its way helps beings above all to themselves. ("What Is Metaphysics?" 97)

But this is not a matter of comprehending the totality of beings; philosophy is not a matter of giving a comprehensive account of the all. Rather, it is a matter of noting that in taking our bearings toward this or that particular being we are already beyond particular beings as such—we are "transcendence."

> As surely as we can never comprehend the ensemble of beings in themselves we certainly do find ourselves stationed in the midst of beings that are revealed somehow as a whole. In the end an essential distinction prevails between comprehending the ensemble of beings in themselves and finding oneself in the midst of beings as a whole. The former is impossible in principle. The latter happens all the time in our existence. It does seem as though we cling to this or that particular being, precisely in our everyday preoccupations, as though we were completely abandoned to this or that region of being. No matter how fragmented our everyday existence may appear to be, however, it always deals with beings in a unity of the "whole," if only in a shadowy way. ("What Is Metaphysics?" 101)

Heidegger reiterates this idea in "On the Essence of Truth":

> The openedness of beings as a whole [*Die Offenbarkeit des Seienden im Ganzen*] does not coincide with the sum of all

immediately familiar beings. On the contrary: where beings are not very familiar to man and are scarcely and only roughly known by science, the openedness of beings as a whole can prevail [*walten*] more essentially. (131)

This irruption by existence into the midst of beings that lets beings be the beings that they are Heidegger calls "attunement," "*Stimmung*." But the primary significance of attunement is that we disperse the "as a whole" by taking our bearings toward this or that particular being, by our being preoccupied with what immediately concerns us. And it is because of our preoccupation that we become oblivious to the fact that we have taken up a position with respect to beings as a whole. As Heidegger says:

> Every mode of open comportment [*Verhalten*] flourishes in letting beings be and in each case is a comportment to this or that particular being. As engagement in the disclosure of beings as a whole as such, freedom [= "ek-sistent disclosive letting beings be"] has already attuned all comportment to beings as a whole. ("On the Essence of Truth," 130–31)

However, because we have always already fallen into preoccupation with particular beings, this and that being *in particular*, this "as a whole" recedes as what is incalculable and incomprehensible, for it cannot be understood on the basis of or in terms of the particular beings with respect to which we have taken our bearings. In this way the "as a whole" remains indefinite, indeterminate, *concealed*. Thus Heidegger has it that

> precisely because letting be always lets beings be in a particular comportment which relates to them and thus discloses them, it conceals beings as a whole. Letting-be is intrinsically at the same time concealing. In the ek-sistent freedom of Dasein a concealing of beings as a whole comes to pass [*ereignet sich*]. ("On the Essence of Truth," 132)

This seems to me to be a kind of transcendental deduction, for nowhere, in accordance with no mood (*Stimmung*), do we encounter this concealment of beings as a whole. Thus it is that Heidegger quickly points out that concealment is anterior to letting-be in the sense that letting-be is itself the concealing of this concealment. This is the mystery.

> In letting beings as a whole be, which discloses and at the same time conceals, it happens [*geschieht es*] that concealing appears [*erscheint*] as what is first concealed. ("On the Essence of Truth," 133)

Because of the fact that the concealment of beings as a whole is itself obliviated in our attunement being attuned to beings in particular, we are the way of errancy (*Irre*).

> The concealing of the concealed being as a whole holds sway [*waltet*] in the disclosure of particular beings [*jeweiligen Seienden*], which, as forgottenness of concealment, becomes errancy. ("On the Essence of Truth," 136)

Again, there is a dialectic here between *what* is asserted and *that* it is asserted: if our way is the way of errancy, of, that is, the obliviating of the fact that we have always already taken up a position in the midst of beings as a whole with respect to beings as a whole, how can we recuperate from out of this oblivion that beings as a whole have gotten obliviated? What leads us to suspect such obliviating? But more to the point, what authorizes Heidegger to assert that the concealing of beings as a whole is concealed? Has he opened up anew beings as a whole? Has he in fact recovered this originary vision that, even for him, must have fallen away into oblivion? Must not his analysis of the way of errancy itself be errant? And if it is, in the name of what does it claim to have overcome its own tendency to waylaying waywardness?

We still cannot, as far as I am concerned, see the problem. And Heidegger certainly addresses it, even while he is himself oblivious to the tension between what is asserted and that it is asserted. Consequently, in closing "On the Essence of Truth" he does in fact remark upon the possibility of owning up to our waylaying waywarding. But he does not provide any basis for his claim—with the singular exception of the address itself.

> By leading him astray, errancy dominates man through and through. But as leading astray, errancy at the same time contributes to a possibility that man is capable of drawing up from his ek-sistence—the possibility that, by experiencing errancy itself and by not mistaking the mystery of Da-sein, he *not* let himself be led astray. ("On the Essence of Truth," 136)

This address, "On the Essence of Truth," is premierly this glance askance into the mystery from out of the experience of its *own* errancy. It is a question, the question of "what being as such is as a whole" (137).

This, it seems to me, is the basis for the parenthetical and editorial remarks in *Being and Time* about misunderstanding the hermeneutic project "from the ground up," "*vom Grund aus*," that is, from out of its ground. I hope it is clear that it is necessary not only to understand how the hermeneutic circle can be misunderstood "from the ground up," but also to clarify if in fact that project can be understood at all, given that the text asserts something that denies the very possibility of making such an assertion. The problem—to repeat—is that it seems both impossible to misunderstand the hermeneutic circle (given that it is the principle of understanding proper), yet unavoidable (given that understanding is "at first and for the most part" the obstruction to understanding understanding). It is not enough to say simply that we risk falling prey to the evasiveness and obstructiveness of everydayness, thereby losing the insightfulness and originarity of the hermeneutic project.

More pointedly, it is a serious matter as to whether we have ever really recuperated our understanding from this evasiveness and obstructiveness. This question would seem to be in principle impossible to answer. What is required is that before we even begin to understand the hermeneutic circle properly, we need to begin to understand how the hermeneutic circle can be misunderstood; but before that we need a strategy that will enable us to understand this misunderstanding, but, paradoxically, without thereby eliminating it—we need to cultivate a strategy of deliberately setting out to misunderstand the hermeneutic circle that would let us understand this misunderstanding. For such a strategy of misunderstanding will itself be the understanding proper to understanding understanding. But this, of course, can neither be said nor shown.

The impossibilities are starting to multiply, starting to multiply exponentially. To arrest this exponentiation of impossibility let me begin again.

Again, when Heidegger closes the published portion of *Being and Time* with the *apologia* that "whether this is the *only* way or even the right one at all, can be decided only *after one has gone along it*," he is claiming that there is no literal proof demonstrating the validity of his enterprise, that there can be no attempt to justify its legitimacy, that at best there is an indicial 'see how it is' and the occasional programmatic admonishment that we should not be scandalized by the audacity involved in thinking in terms of and according to the hermeneutic circle.

But this is no accident, for the greatness of *Being and Time* lies in demonstrating procedurally, thematically, and theoretically how fundamental the circle is. No accident, again, because this demonstration is precisely a demonstration of the self-adjudicating legitimacy of the hermeneutic circle. The hermeneutic circle, we best suspect, is self-verifying, self-validating.

But there still remains the possibility—essential and necessary—of misunderstanding the hermeneutic circle. And if so, then it would be necessary to expound, tentatively anyway, some sort of critique of the hermeneutic project. But, here again, we are cautioned that even to attempt to critically appraise the hermeneutic circle is to have misunderstood what it is about. Here we cannot understand how we misunderstand; we misunderstand entirely if we in fact attempt to understand how we can misunderstand what is involved in the hermeneutic circle. How can the formal principle of understanding be at all misunderstood? It would seem that we misunderstand the hermeneutic circle if we think that it can be misunderstood; yet it is not clear that we can really understand it—the issue of the possibility of misunderstanding the hermeneutic circle hollows it out and perhaps breaches it.

At this juncture there emerges, it would seem, an unvoiced uneasiness, that things are not quite that settled. It is this possibility of misunderstanding that provokes one to attend to the propriety of the order and object of our discourse. But here there is hesitancy, here it seems our discourse disappears into itself, collapsing under its own vacuity; here it seems our discourse eliminates itself, degenerating into, not a tighter circle, but an impasse, an impassability that eliminates its object. For surely the hermeneutic circle designates precisely that way of thinking that implicates and precipitates its own critique. For does not thinking about the hermeneutic circle necessitate that thinking has already been thinking hermeneutically? For how can the hermeneutic circle be thought without its being thought hermeneutically? By all rights, the hermeneutic circle is precisely that way of thinking that should participate in its own critique. Yet for this reason this critique is never forthcoming; understanding the formal structure of understanding is just an instance or instantiation of that formal structure, so that every attempt to demonstrate the legitimacy of the hermeneutic circle is just itself an instance of hermeneutic circularity. It would seem that the hermeneutic circle not only forestalls—in advance and in principle—any objection to its legitimacy, a legitimacy that then would be self-adjudicating, but it so entirely subsumes every attempt to demonstrate its validity that every such demonstration becomes a further indication that there is nothing needing to be demonstrated.

Here there is loss of passage, for such is the nature of the hermeneutic circle that it absorbs any critique of itself, subsuming it as another index of its self-adjudicating legitimacy, deflating it as a critique, resolving it into that which both presupposes the hermeneutic circle and is presupposed by it.

Hence the uneasiness, for any attempt to exhibit the structure of the hermeneutic circle must be a description of it that, in exhibiting it, exposes itself as subject to it, conditioned and determined in advance by that which it describes. It must expose the hermeneutic circle as a relationship of which it is itself a term. Yet let us not forget the possibility that we are all along misunderstanding the problem.

But these are just suspicions, suspicions formulated with a certain kind of arrogance, a torquing of the matter at hand. Yet it is only along the lines suggested by these suspicions that anything like a constructive dialogue between the hermeneut and the hermeneutic heretic can take place: there is no 'see how it is' to which one can appeal. So in light of these doubts as to the validity of a critique of the hermeneutic circle let us interrogate it. On this score Heidegger cautions us:

> What is decisive is not to get out of the circle but to come into it in the right way. (*Being and Time*, 153)

As signposts directing us to our entrance examination into the hermeneutic circle, let us recall three famous passages from *Sein und Zeit*. I would like to note, if only to style myself the hermeneut, that these passages are chosen from the rigor of the interrogation itself; but without cheapening the insight that locates in these three passages something pivotal about the hermeneutic circle, I merely offer them after the fashion of a heuristics.

The first passage is from the famous section entitled "The Kind of Being which Truth Possesses and the Presupposition of Truth." It reads:

> It is not we who presuppose 'truth'; but it is *'truth'* that makes it at all possible ontologically for us to be able to *be* such that we 'presuppose' anything at all. Truth is what first *makes*

possible anything like presupposing. (*Being and Time*, 227–28)

The second is Heidegger's famous definition of time:

> The character of "having been" arises from the future, and in such a way that the future which "has been" (or better, which "is in the process of having been") releases from itself the Present. This phenomenon has the unity of a future which makes present in the process of having been; we designate it as "*temporality*." (*Being and Time*, 326)

The third is about the structure of forgetting. It reads:

> This forgetting is not nothing, nor is it just a failure to remember; it is rather a 'positive' ecstatical mode of one's having been—a mode with a character of its own. (*Being and Time*, 339)

A forgetting, then, has a special and "positive" temporal character; and this can only be that in forgetting forgetting forgets itself, that what is forgotten in every forgetting is the forgetting of what is forgotten. And truth, we have read, is the presupposition for any and every presupposition. Every presupposition presupposes that it is truth that has made it possible; and since every thought is possible only because of its presuppositions, is made possible by them, truth makes possible the thought that strains to attain to the truth. And truth makes possible the thought that strains to attain to it as an inbreaking of the future making present the truth in the process of showing it has always already been.

The hermeneutic circle is bound up with these statements. And these three passages will be our means of breaking into the hermeneutic circle. So given that it is undecidable whether I am here misunderstanding the hermeneutic circle properly, in a way appropriate to it, perhaps I need to promote myself more actively as the ingenue that I am, that we all are, and pretend to begin with a definition of the hermeneutic circle. But this task is what presses us into uneasiness: and again, we fail to find a voice adequate enough to say whence this uneasiness. Nonetheless, to define the hermeneutic circle is to break into it; and now I have hinted at what breaking into it is about: forgetfulness as a positive mode of temporality, as a positive modalization of time; that to think the truth about something is to presuppose that the truth that thinking strains to attain to is the inbreaking from what has not yet been attained of this truth, so that this truth is seen to have already been. But, in point of fact, anything can effect entrance into the hermeneutic experience. Nonetheless, forgetfulness *et al.* define the very process of breaking into the circle: only in forgetting what is at issue—viz., the essential possibility of misunderstanding what is at issue—in this attempt to interrogate the hermeneutic circle do we break into it.

The problems incumbent upon interrogating the hermeneutic circle, considered as the formal principle of understanding, are not entirely unique. In his self-criticism, *Der Satz vom Grund*, Heidegger begins with this same problem of elucidating the "formal" character of the principle of understanding, the enigmatic circle such an attempt throws us into. He begins with an attempt to hear authentically the claim the "Principle of Ground" (the Principle of Sufficient Reason: *Nihil est sine ratione*; nothing is without reason) makes upon us, as it was formulated by Leibniz. He comments on its self-evidence, despite, he adds, that it took some two thousand years to formulate. And despite the fact that the Principle of Ground seems so transparent to us that we are already finished with it as soon as we hear it, it is nonetheless the most "enigmatic' (*rätselvollste*) of all propositions (*Der Satz vom Grund*, 16).

The "enigmatic" character that Heidegger sees in the Principle of Ground has to do with its "formal" character as a "principle" (*Grundsatz*). This "first principle" throws us into a perplexing circle: inasmuch as it is a "principle," it is the ground (*Grund*) of other propositions, of every proposition (*Sätze*), "*Der Satz vom Grund ist ein Grundsatz*" (21); thus, in order to elucidate the Principle of Ground we need to know what a "principle" is, but in order to know what a "principle" (*Grundsatz*) is, we need to know what "ground" or "fundamental" means, yet where are we to find what "ground" means except in the Principle of Ground? According to Christian Wolff, a principle is "that which contains within itself the reason [*rationis*] for another." A "principle" thus contains the "reason" for what follows from the principle (*Der Satz vom Grund*, 30–31).

Furthermore, as Heidegger points out, the Principle of Ground is itself a proposition. So are we to say that it falls under its own scope and that it must itself have a ground? But if there is a ground for the Principle of Ground, then we may also ask what is the ground for the ground for the Principle of Ground, thus generating an infinite regress. But if we deny that the Principle of Ground has itself a ground, then we are left with the disconcerting result that the very assertion which claims that there is nothing without reason is itself without reason. Either way, we fall into the groundless (*Der Satz vom Grund*, 27–28).

But of course the circular structure of the hermeneutic circle prevents an infinite regress just as surely as it eliminates in principle recourse to an originary principle of principles. Or as Heidegger argues, "In the question of the meaning of Being there is no 'circular reasoning' but rather a remarkable 'relatedness backward and forward' [*Rück- oder Vorbezogenheit*] which what we are asking about (Being) bears to the inquiry itself as a mode of Being" (*Being and Time*, 8). Yet does not the term 'hermeneutic circle' designate the formal principle of understanding? And if so, is there anything problematic about understanding it? Is its formal character transparent? Or does it participate in some way in our attempt to understand it, thereby distorting any understanding of it? Can the measure of understanding be itself measured?

This problem is reminiscent of the great introduction to the *Phenomenology of Spirit*. In accordance with the insight promoted by this introduction we can develop the following argument.

It is a question of securing the way proper to an examination of what the hermeneutic circle represents, namely, the formal principle of understanding. But here it seems that, independent of immediate concession to the self-evident transparency of the hermeneutic circle, a concession against which the examination must forcibly proceed, it is a matter of elucidating the criterion ensuring the appropriateness of our inquiry. But at this point we must become cautious, perhaps even skeptical. For would not such a criterion, if we could establish it, be simply the means by which we can come to understand the principle of understanding? But if this criterion were a means, then by employing it in our examination of the hermeneutic circle, it would bring about the opposite of its own end. That is to say, employing a criterion would deflect us from what we are trying to understand, and so would itself need to be understood. But, then, the adequacy of the criterion would have to be examined with respect to the hermeneutic circle. In this way the means by which we could come to elucidate the hermeneutic circle would necessarily eliminate itself precisely by obstructing us from understanding the hermeneutic circle. Moreover, even to raise the issue of the means by which we can evaluate the hermeneutic circle would be to turn back away from the hermeneutic circle, back to the problem of the means.

Yet all these aporiai are rendered vacuous upon the realization that we are all along attempting to understand the hermeneutic circle by thinking *in terms of and according to it*. It is, after all, the formal principle of understanding anything at all. It is itself the means to understanding it. However, that the hermeneutic circle has become somehow problematic, that it has become questionable, indicates a certain troubling errancy in its dynamic, namely, that we think it is necessary to disengage thinking from its hermeneutic circularity in order to reintegrate the hermeneutic circle back into our thinking. What makes the hermeneutic circle problematic is *not* that we must first enter into it, but rather that we, circulating already within and therefore from within the circularity of this circle, must bring forth and open out our relation to this circularity, bringing it before itself. The presentation of the hermeneutic circle would, then, be the incessant running to and fro in an "in-between," an *inter-esse*, that prevails in our relation to it. We ourselves are the "remarkable relatedness backward and forward" to the hermeneutic circle.

It would seem that the examination of the hermeneutic circle, its presentation, would be superfluous. And it is with this realization that the presentation could properly begin. Or rather, we would realize that the presentation had begun before we undertook to begin it. And this realization would bring it to an end, for it is nothing else but the realization that it will never get to begin.

Nonetheless, it still is not clear that we have established a proper relation to the hermeneutic circle, for the manner in which its presentation is related to it, or is even the same as it, remains obscure. Once again, the examination of the hermeneutic circle is what is in question. On the one hand, our examination must subscribe to the standard of the hermeneutic circle in order to begin; on the other hand, this standard can be realized only in undertaking the examination. Or again, on the one hand, our examination of the hermeneutic circle must be an instance of it; on the other hand, the hermeneutic circle could only be elaborated as the result of our examination.

Now, the examination seeks to establish a relation to the hermeneutic circle that would elucidate it. In this way the examination presupposes that the hermeneutic circle is not dependent on it, that it exists independently of the examination. But for this reason the examination of the hermeneutic circle, in order to assert its adequation to its object, must become at the same time an examination of itself. The examination is not only an examination of the hermeneutic circle but also an examination of the means of examining the hermeneutic circle. Yet as soon as the examination examines itself, it realizes that the hermeneutic circle is itself the relationship of this examination to it and a term of this relationship; the hermeneutic circle engages itself as its own examination. But this is to say that the hermeneutic circle provides itself as its own criterion. Consequently, the attempt to elucidate the hermeneutic circle is simply an instance of it. To this extent such an attempt proceeds as the eliminating of itself.

Thus it is that the examination of the hermeneutic circle proceeds both by preceding itself and by being always already ahead of itself: it precedes itself insofar as the hermeneutic circle is itself its own measure as well as the means to understanding it, so that the examination proceeds by realizing that it is already at an end; yet insofar as it realizes that, in forcing to examine its means, the examination is already an instance of the hermeneutic circularity it is to examine, it will never have been able to begin; it will never begin to begin.

An examination of the hermeneutic circle, consequently, can contribute nothing except the insight into its own superfluity. And this insight into its own superfluous character is not itself an achievement, but rather designates, negatively, that such an examination consists solely in eliminating itself. Accordingly, this insight is impossible, for the self-eliminating character of the examination is itself eliminated.

Nevertheless, that an examination into the hermeneutic circle is superfluous does not divest the hermeneutic circle of its questionability. It still must be entered into "in the right way" (*Being and Time*, 153), even though entering into it means that we have already entered into it yet have yet to begin to enter into it.

In spite of these aporiai, and alerted by whatever dangers they may invite, indeed, deliberately attempting to fall prey to such dangers, let me give an ad hoc definition of the hermeneutic circle, a definition that would require a running commentary on the problem of its validation, a commentary that could exist only as an indirect discourse on its own validity, its own possibility.

The meaning of being can be understood only in terms of human being, for human being is that being for which the meaning of being is at issue, but human being can only be understood in terms of the meaning of being in general. So to ask the question of the meaning of being requires beforehand that we answer the question of the meaning of human being. But the meaning of human being is that it is that being for which the meaning of being is at issue. Therefore we can know what human being is only if we have prior understanding of the meaning of being in general.

It would appear that human being is exceptional and exclusive and exists as the ascendancy over all other being, for it is only for human being that the meaning of being is at issue. But since human being is that for which the meaning of being is at issue, a being encountered by human being can be understood only in terms of the meaning of being. Yet insofar as the meaning of being becomes what is at issue only on the basis of and in terms of the encountering of beings, the meaning of being can be understood only in terms of the encountering of beings. Being and the entity each relates to itself on behalf of the other and to the other on behalf of itself. This is what, to force the issue, the hermeneutic circle signifies. But it signifies this only on the condition that the meaning of the relationship between being and entities is at issue, that this relationship is meaningful. So the hermeneutic circle is not so much the unique relationship between being and the entity as it is that the difference between being and entity is meaningful, i.e., that being has a sense irreducible to the meaning of the entity—but also irreducible to the meaning of the concept or word 'being.'

The hermeneutic circle signifies that the entity is encounterable because its being has a sense in which it is meaningful independent of the encountering of the entity itself yet without being reducible to the meaning of the word or concept 'being.' But this sense is possible only because the entity is encounterable as the entity that it is. Being has its own meaning because the entity is encounterable as an entity; yet the entity is encounterable as an entity only because something like the meaning of being has already been understood.

The hermeneutic circle ultimately signifies, then, not that being is discoverable in terms of and on the basis of beings and beings are discoverable only in terms of and on the basis of a precursory comprehension of the meaning of being, but rather it signifies the unique relationship that obtains between being and meaning.

Let me try to be more precise. What do we mean by 'being' and 'meaning'? 'Meaning,' Heidegger tells us in *Being and Time*, is "that wherein the intelligibility of something maintains itself"

(*Being and Time*, 151). The German word for "intelligibility" here is *Verständlichkeit*. Hans-Georg Gadamer says in *Truth and Method* that "language is the *Verständlichkeit of being*"—language is the intelligibility of being. And Heidegger says in *Being and Time* a little further down that "the meaning of Being can never be contrasted with entities, or with Being as the 'ground' which gives entities support; for a 'ground' becomes accessible only as meaning, even if it is itself the abyss of meaninglessness" (152).

Being is in some sense inseparable yet distinct from its meaning. But again, what do we mean by *being*, by *Sein*? By 'being' we mean the *encounterability* of the entity or the entity *in its encounterability*, that it manifests itself as an entity. But by *meaning* we mean that the entity is intelligible in its being encountered: the meaning of an entity is that in reference to which (*das Woraufhin*) the significance of its being arises, that upon which its intelligibility or understandability depends. But this is to say simply that by meaning we mean that the entity can be encountered as an entity. Meaning is the encountering of the entity as the entity that it is, that is to say, the encountering of the entity in the intelligibility of its being encountered as the entity that it is.

Being and the meaning of being are not easily distinguished, but they must be distinguished if there is to be a difference between them. Furthermore, it would appear at this stage that they can only be distinguished by means of and in terms of the hermeneutic circle; the hermeneutic circle *effects* the relationship of meaning to being and of being to meaning.

So we inquire into the concept of the hermeneutic circle, into the hermeneutic circle as a concept, that is, into the unique relationship effected between being and meaning. And here we hesitate: there seems to be a seemingly innocuous and scarcely conspicuous play between "the concept of the hermeneutic circle" and "the hermeneutic circle." But as to this difference between the concept of the hermeneutic circle and that of which this concept is a concept—because of the circularity to this circle, each is absorbed into the other: the hermeneutic circle, in the course of its exhibition, deteriorates into the concept of itself; while the concept of the hermeneutic circle, in the course of its analysis, expands into that of which it is the concept. But as I have already noted, as long as the discussion of the hermeneutic circle attempts a dialogue between the hermeneut and the heretic, we inevitably come up against certain traps, pitfalls, and swindles, certain forcings and torquings, certain hidden trapdoors and unexpected false starts, certain sinkholes, certain thinksinks. And this is one of them, for it would seem that the distinction between the hermeneutic circle and its concept is not just misleading but specious. To speak of the concept of the hermeneutic circle is to attempt to examine it, to elucidate it as it is for itself. It is to engage in a presentation (*Darstellung*) or exposition (*Auslegung*) of the hermeneutic circle. But as I have tried to show, any presentation of the hermeneutic circle is superfluous, for it eliminates itself precisely in and by its getting elaborated.

So perhaps it is too misleading to attempt to differentiate between the hermeneutic circle and the concept of the hermeneutic circle, for the hermeneutic circle is a concept, a philosophic concept. It signifies the formal principle of understanding, that is, of the unique relationship obtaining between being and meaning. But as a concept, it needs to be subjected to a critique. That is to say, it itself needs to be understood, grasped in its essentiality. But, again, the understanding that understands the hermeneutic circle is an instance embodying it, since the hermeneutic circle is the formal principle of understanding.

So if the hermeneutic circle is the formal principle of understanding, it could only be understood hermeneutically; if the hermeneutic circle were the formal principle of understanding, any attempt to understand it in a nonhermeneutic way, in a way that would be otherwise than in terms of and according to it, would be a complete misunderstanding of it; it would deprive itself of what it is trying to understand, for such an understanding would not be able to enter into the circularity of the hermeneutic circle. For here it would be the case that the relationship between being and meaning is articulated in a way that is at variance with what the hermeneutic circle says constitutes this relationship; the relationship signified by the hermeneutic circle could not be understood. In this case it would be unintelligible, or at best proclaimed to be a particularly slick version of a vicious circle and therefore rejected as unintelligible.

So we need to attempt to understand the hermeneutic circle hermeneutically. We need to attempt to understand the relationship between the being and the meaning of all that is understood. But since what we are to understand in this is the relationship, we are inquiring into the relationship between the being and meaning of the relationship between being and meaning.

What, then, is the relationship that obtains between the *being* of the relationship between being and meaning and the *meaning* of that relationship? It is precisely here where thinking breaks away from phenomenology. It is precisely here that Heidegger begins to depart from an analysis of being to an analysis of the meaning of being, its truth. In *Being and Time* the being to be understood is "projected" first and in a preliminary way upon its "Being" and then in a second and determinative way upon the "meaning" of that Being. Meaning is not the object of understanding, *what* is understood by the understanding—for that is being—but rather that upon which the understandability of the being depends, that around which it is "maintained" (*sich halten*). It is only upon determining the meaning of the being of a being that we understand ontologically that being. "To lay bare the 'upon-which' [*das Woraufhin*] of a projection amounts to disclosing that which makes possible what has been projected" (*Being and Time*, 324).

Thus to inquire into that unique relationship obtaining between being and meaning that is designated by the term 'hermeneutic circle', we are already beyond being.

> We confront the task not only by going forth and back from a being to its being but, if we are inquiring into the condition of possibility of the understanding of being as such, *of inquir-*

ing even beyond being as upon which being itself, as being, is projected. (Basic Problems, 282)

Thus it is that the later Heidegger abandons his search to elucidate the meaning of being in favor of the attempt to show that there is being, *"es gibt Sein,"* being which is irreducible to its meaning, keeping itself back from meaning anything, being which is itself, by not being a being, being what is different from beings by virtue of which the entitative as such gets nominated. Now, as we know, this attempt is the project of realizing its own destitution in the face of what it seeks; it is the project of the essential philosophic failure, for it is "the attempt to think Being without regard to its being grounded in terms of beings."[3] Yet all there is are beings, beings in particular, beings as a whole, beings as such. Accordingly, in this same lecture, delivered January 31, 1962, Heidegger notes:

To think Being itself explicitly requires disregarding Being to the extent that it is only grounded and interpreted in terms of beings and for beings as their ground. ("Time and Being," 6)

To think "Being" explicitly is to disregard Being, to be already beyond it.

What is peculiar to Being is not anything having the character of Being. When we explicitly think about Being, the matter itself [*Sache*] leads us in a certain sense away from Being. ("Time and Being," 10)

Nonetheless, for us to be led away from being we need to be led to think being. But the attempt to think being leads us to think *that there is* being; yet this is to think how being is there, how it becomes the issue—and this is to be led away from being itself to the issue of being being at issue, i.e., to the meaning of being.

---

3. Martin Heidegger, "Time and Being," in *On Time and Being*, 2.

But this directs us to determine the hermeneutic circle, that unique relation giving being and meaning as determinative of each other.

So it is a question of determining the relationship obtaining between the *being* of the relationship between being and meaning and the *meaning* of that relationship. Again we are already driven beyond being to the "giving" of the relationship between being and meaning. This 'giving' is the hermeneutic circle; the being of the hermeneutic circle and its meaning are just the hermeneutic circle *simpliciter*, yet there is neither a being *simpliciter* nor a meaning *simpliciter* but just the relation obtaining between them, the relation effecting them. That is to say, the *being* of the hermeneutic circle is precisely this relationship obtaining between being and meaning that effects them; yet the *meaning* of the hermeneutic circle is also this relationship. To think the hermeneutic circle is to think that there is being by virtue of there being meaning yet there is meaning by virtue of there being being; and in there being being and there being meaning there is this *being there*, and this *being there* is what the hermeneutic circle effects. On the basis of there being the being there of being and there being the being there of meaning, with each being there by virtue of the other being there, the late Heidegger feels compelled to dispense with the very notion of the hermeneutic circle and develop instead a more originary hermeneutic *relation*.

Japanese: In short, you would abandon your earlier view?

Inquirer: Quite—and in this respect, that talk of a circle always remains superficial.

Japanese: How would you present the hermeneutic circle today?

Inquirer: I would avoid a presentation [*Darstellung*] as resolutely as I would avoid speaking *about* language.[4]

Apparently the hermeneutic circle obstructs any attempt to understand it from a standpoint transcendent to it, for it is precisely *the* standpoint from which and back to which standpoints are developed; the hermeneutic circle in principle reduces any attempt at transcendence as a violence that exists only to be refused. The hermeneutic circle does not deflect access to itself from such a standpoint, but rather reduces such a perspective to a moment immanent to it, to an instance embodying it. The attempt to understand the hermeneutic circle critically generates something like the opposite of an infinite regress: each attempt to understand the last level that the understanding has obtained of the hermeneutic circle collapses into that previous level, is absorbed into it as an instance of it. Here we have the greatest delight for the philosophic juggler, a great metaphysical conundrum: that the attempt to understand the nature of the hermeneutic circle always ends up as an instance of that which we are trying to understand.

If the hermeneutic circle defines the formal structure of philosophic questions, then here we gain insight into the nature of these questions. Kierkegaard writes of this phenomenon in the "Diapsalmata" of *Either/Or I*:

> My philosophy is at least easy to understand, for I have only one principle, and I do not proceed from that. It is necessary to distinguish between the successive dialectic in either/or, and the eternal dialectic here set forth. Thus, when I say I do not proceed from my principle, this must not be understood in opposition to a proceeding forth from it, but is rather

---

4. Martin Heidegger, "A Dialogue on Language," in *On the Way to Language*, 51.

a negative expression for the principle itself, through which it is apprehended in equal opposition to a proceeding or a non-proceeding from it. (*Either/Or* 1:38)

In a similar vein, here, with our inquiry into the hermeneutic circle, every proceeding forth from the principle of the hermeneutic circle generates an inversely recursive series of instantiations of this principle, where every proceeding forth simply proceeds to establish that that from which it proceeds forth is the principle of which it is an instantiation. In this way it would be in principle impossible to start: each attempt to proceed forth, etc., has already been collapsed to an immanent instance of that from which the proceeding forth is to have proceeded forth. Alternatively, every attempt to proceed forth from this principle of hermeneutic circularity would have to establish its validity. But if that is the case, then every attempt to proceed forth from this principle would have to have already established itself as *the principle of proceeding forth*, and so as the principle from which it is now necessary to proceed. In this case, again, it would be in principle impossible to start.

In this way I want to say that the hermeneutic circle is a self-instantiating concept: any attempt to explain it or its validity to the heretic simply issues in an instance of it. Which the heretic could not understand. So not only is the hermeneutic circle a self-instantiating concept, it is also, as we have seen, a self-eliminating one. The unfolding of this principle is its self-enfolding, its enfolding itself up into itself; yet its self-enfolding is its unfolding. If we make the claim (as anyone who has thought about it would) that the hermeneutic circle embodies the very principle by means of and according to which philosophy accomplishes its ordained tasks, then we have the peculiar situation that the hermeneutic circle signifies that it is impossible *not* to proceed in terms of and according to it just as surely as it *is* impossible to proceed in terms of and according to it.

At this juncture we can say that our analysis of the hermeneutic circle affirms the impossibility of a statement about it that is transcendent to it while nevertheless realizing this impossibility by the very statement of this impossibility. And with this insight (that itself is impossible to state yet necessarily needing to be stated) neither the hermeneut nor the heretic can be assured of seeing or saying anything but impossibility.

Again, either understanding is circular in the hermeneutic sense, in which case the hermeneutic circle is the condition for the possibility of any understanding of it; or else it is not, in which case the hermeneutic circle signifies the condition for the impossibility of understanding itself. The hermeneutic circle is either self-validating—because it is self-instantiating, or else it disqualifies every attempt to understand it. We shall see that the self-validation of the hermeneutic circle and the self-disqualification of every critique of it are one and the same.

So we want to analyze the concept of the hermeneutic circle, and this can only be done hermeneutically. But this means that in order to analyze the concept of the hermeneutic circle we must already be thinking in terms of and according to it. But such is the circular way of our thinking that to be thinking in terms of and according to the hermeneutic circle and yet to know what this means presupposes that we have already thought through, thought about, thought along around, it. By the hermeneutic circle, therefore, we mean that way of thinking that, to begin to think about, requires that the thinker already think along the way proper to it, but to think along the way proper to it requires an antecedent thinking about.

But what do we mean by 'concept' here? Does not the hermeneutic circle simply designate a way of thinking; in particular, that way in and by which certain fundamental phenomena can be thought? Is not this circle simply the inner logic for that way of thinking in and by which grounds are given? If that is the case, does not this appellation, "the hermeneutic circle," signify the way in and by which the giving of grounds gets conceptualized?

But then, what would we understand by that concept—the concept of the hermeneutic circle—that is, the conceptualization of this way of conceptualizing? Surely this concept can only designate that way of conceptualizing that is appropriate to the giving of grounds. But the way of conceptualizing that is appropriate to the giving of grounds is precisely the giving of grounds.

Tentatively, then, we can see that the hermeneutic circle is that formal principle which proves to be its own instantiation. The hermeneutic circle is a concept that cannot be thought except insofar as it has recoiled back upon thought, determining thinking to think according to the manner it prescribes. Yet as soon as thinking learns to think hermeneutically, the concept of the hermeneutic circle eliminates itself as a concept, for it becomes now the principle of conceptuality in general. Every attempt to understand it as a concept eliminates it as a concept by becoming an instance of it. This principle is now that by means of which and according to which we think. As such, it is a way of thinking, not an object for thought.

If this is not clear, it will become so: the hermeneutic circle is the self-eliminating enabling and enacting of itself. The suggestion is that it is both necessary and impossible to think the hermeneutic circle: necessary, because it is the provenance and therefore the true matter for real thinking; impossible insofar as it eliminates itself in favor of an instance of which it is the formal principle, yet as soon as we attempt to think this instance, it itself is eliminated in favor of another instance of which it now is the formal principle.

It would appear then that the formal analysis of the hermeneutic circle is simply another instance of it, another verification of its validity. But the formal analysis verifies it in such a way that the hermeneutic circle qua a formal concept for a unique way of thinking gets obliviated in favor of a particular instance of that unique way of thinking. So since every attempt at critiquing it must necessarily move along the way that is prescribed by it, the hermeneutic circle absorbs every critique of itself as another instantiation of it, as further verification of its validity. Yet insofar as every critique is just further instantiation of the hermeneutic circle, every critique of it occludes that of which it is to be the critique. So the critique of this formal principle, insofar as it operates by means of and according to this principle yet occludes this principle as the formal principle of which it is an instance, forgets this formal principle and therefore forgets itself as being a critique of this formal principle. The self-validating nature of the hermeneutic circle and the self-disqualifying nature of any critique of it are one and the same thing.

But this is what we would expect: the attempt to think the hermeneutic circle transforms thinking into the encircling of thinking and what is thought around each other, so that each is the orbiting around itself of the other. If by thinking we mean the enabling and enacting of meaning and if by being we mean something like the enabling and enacting of beings, then the hermeneutic circle signifies that being is the orbiting around itself of meaning and meaning is the orbiting around itself of being. If the hermeneutic circle transforms thinking into the encircling of thinking and what is thought around each other with each the orbiting around itself of the other, then the relation of thinking to being enjoys a new configuration: meaning becomes the encircling of being around meaning and being becomes the encircling of meaning around being.

But in this light the hermeneutic circle is a self-encrypting thought, for once the thinker is drawn into its orbit in an attempt to think of it, he or she is thereafter commanded by it to think by means of and according to it, and so cannot think otherwise than in the manner it has already determined. Not just a self-encircling thought, the hermeneutic circle is also a self-enclosing, a self-encrypting thought, closing itself up in upon itself with no more exit or entry, enshrouding itself within itself, tucking itself away in an inner pocket of itself.

So to think what is involved in thinking the hermeneutic circle is simply to recognize that we already thought about it but have forgotten what it was we had thought and have even forgotten that we had already thought it. Since this thought itself will have been forgotten, after which we will come to recognize that we have forgotten it, this thought is itself the avowed forgetting of itself.

It is the thought that thinks the undoing of its own possibility, since it is a thought that can only be thought as the forgetting of what was thought and so the forgetting of what was to be thought and so the forgetting of what it itself was to have thought. To think this thought is simply to accede to the forgottenness of this thought, that it can only be thought as what has always already and thus henceforth been forgotten, that is to say, forgotten in such a way that we have forgotten that it has always already and thus henceforth been forgotten. A thought, then, the condition for the possibility of which is the obliteration of the possibility of being thought. The hermeneutic circle produces itself as the unthought of itself. The only thing that can be thought of the hermeneutic circle is that it leaves itself unthought, that it itself is the unthought in every thought of it.

But with equal force we can say that since the thought of the hermeneutic circle is self-obliviating, it is its own repetition—in the threefold sense of: (1) retrieving the unthought of itself; (2) the fetching back of itself and taking itself up again as what is to be thought; and (3) the re-petitioning of itself, the entreaty to make itself appear again out of its own self-obliviating. In this light, the thought of the hermeneutic circle is that it is the repeating of itself. It is an absolutely formal principle: since it is the unthought of itself, what is retrieved in thinking this thought is the unthought of itself—but this is just itself. It simply retrieves the retrieving of itself. Yet inasmuch as it is simply the leaving of itself unthought, it retrieves nothing but that it is its own retrieval from itself as the unthought of itself.

But of course, none of this can readily be believed, for I have just now retrieved this thought from out of its own self-obliviating. Or have I? Is it not the case that I have simply retrieved *that* this thought is its own retrieval from out of its self-obliviating? And have I not done this because I have, in advance of forgetting this thought, thought that it can only be thought as the forgetting of itself? Again, the circle: to retrieve this thought is to retrieve nothing more than that this thought is its own retrieval, so that this thought can only be retrieved by having been retrieved in advance; but that it has always already been retrieved in advance of the thought that retrieves it presupposes the thought that is actually retrieving it. And inversely: to forget this thought—the hermeneutic circle—is to think in advance of forgetting it that it can only be thought as the forgetting of itself; but to be thought as the forgetting of itself requires that it already has been thought, but then forgotten.

We can now begin to discern the temporal structure of the hermeneutic circle, that is to say, the temporal structure of understanding. Since it is the repeating of itself, the hermeneutic circle formally signifies that it will be repeated in the future, so what will be repeated is that it will be repeated in a further future. Yet it is also the forgetting of itself. As both the thought that thinks only that it itself has already been thought but then forgotten and yet as the thought that thinks only that it itself will be thought again with a view to thinking what has been left still unthought about itself, as, that is, the thought that thinks only that it has yet to think itself, the hermeneutic circle radically infinitizes time; it is the radical infinitization of time. Consider:

Thinking that it itself had already been thought but then forgotten, this thought really thinks that when it had been thought before, it had even then only been the thought that it had before that been thought but then forgotten, and so on, without a first time of ever being thought, without a time before which it had yet to be thought. In relation to its history the hermeneutic circle is a way of opening up the infinitization of the past: not only can there not be a first time, a time before which it had yet to be thought, but there must be a past more remote than all past, a past before the ability to retain the past first emerged, a past before there was a past and so a nonrecuperable past. The present presents itself as what is still unthought about the past, and the past presents itself as what is still unthought about a more remote and even nonrecuperable past.

Yet insofar as the hermeneutic circle is the retrieving of itself as what has yet to be thought about itself, it is the recognition that it will be taken up again in the future as what has yet to be thought about itself. But this recognition entails the recognition that when it will be taken up again in the future it will be only the thought that thinks that it will be taken up again at an even later date as what has still to be thought about itself. The thought that thinks that it has yet to be taken up and thought through is the thought that thinks that when it will be taken up again as what has yet to be thought about itself, even then it will simply be the thought that it has yet to be taken up, that what is still unthought about itself is its sole content. In this way the hermeneutic circle is the thought the sole content of which is that there are infinite possibilities yet to be thought about itself.

Thus the hermeneutic circle expresses that the present exists as the relationship to the inbreaking of infinite possibility; it is the inbreaking of infinite possibility. But we have seen that the present is what has yet to be thought about the past and so is what is still outstanding about the past. So the inbreaking of the infinite possibility of this thought that has yet to be thought is what has yet to be thought of the past. The hermeneutic circle signifies formally that the future, as the inbreaking of infinite possibility, determines how the past confronts us in the present, it signifies that the future brings to bear on the present what has yet to be thought of the past.

There is something infinite in this thought; and yet something radically finite. Infinite and finite in the same way, in this way, that nothing really gets thought—rather, the horizon for the understanding of the meaning of being gets opened up, but in such a way that this horizon is itself horizonless, is itself the horizonlessness to the question of the meaning of being.

What is horizonless about the question of the meaning of being is the issuing issuing forth in the issue of the hermeneutic circle. This issue is what is at issue in thinking the relation of being to meaning. What is at issue is not being nor is it meaning. What is at issue is also neither being in its relation to meaning nor meaning in its relation to being. What is at issue when the hermeneutic circle becomes the issue is just this issuing forth of the hermeneutic relation. This issuing forth brings being and meaning into their own by virtue of issuing each to the other, by virtue of letting each be what is at issue for the other, by virtue of issuing each as the issue of the other, that there is being by virtue of there being meaning and there is meaning by virtue of there being being.

But this issuing issuing forth being and meaning, issuing forth being and meaning in each being what is at issue for the other, in each being the issue of the other, in each issuing the other as what is at issue for itself, as it own issue, this issuing forth does not issue itself, is not its own issue. Rather, the issuing that issues forth into what is at issue, precisely because it issues forth the issue of what is at issue, cannot itself be at issue. It is nothing; it is nothing that is there, and it is nothing that is not there. To make of it an issue is simply to realize that it keeps itself from becoming what is at issue, so that the issue is that it cannot be at issue. But this is itself what is at issue for philosophy. Philosophy is ultimately without issue.

So as what is at issue, the hermeneutic circle closes in upon itself and keeps itself from being the issue, forestalling the arising of an issue and foreclosing on taking issue with it. What is ultimately at issue, then, is that the hermeneutic circle is the resistance to its presentation—and this resistance *is* its presentation. But only by deliberately and strategically seeking to misunderstand the hermeneutic circle "from the ground up" can *this* be realized. Yet this realization is possible only on the condition that it is seen to be impossible: as the resistance to its presentation the hermeneutic circle is at the same time the resistance to realizing that it is the resistance to its presentation—the exposition of the hermeneutic circle is nothing but a running commentary on its own intrinsic impossibility.

Philosophy casts itself off and throws itself away. It is the objection to itself; it is the abjection of itself. It is *abjection*.

The snake, instead of biting its tail, sheds its skin, having developed, for the skin fitting too tight, an allergy to it as fatal as our allergy to its bite, and slips away back into the underbrush, in order to accustom itself to a skin that, being not yet a skin, fits the snake for being the snake itself, a skin that is not yet skintight but more like a belt that is so befitting to the belly that the belly is forgotten. Left behind is a translucent hollowed-out semblance of itself.

Postface

I have published a lot, but there is someone in me, I still can't identify him, who still hopes never to have done it. And he believes that in everything that I have let pass, depart, a very effective mechanism comes to annihilate the exposition. I write while concealing every possible divulging of the very thing which appears to be published.
Jacques Derrida, La Carte postale

It is probable, indeed, that the philosophical activity has no other boundaries than those of its own dissatisfaction with any results it can achieve.
Gabriel Marcel, Mystère de l'être

It is the common presupposition of all philosophizing that philosophy as such does not possess a language that is adequate to the task assigned it.
Hans-Georg Gadamer, "Philosophie und Poesie"

The question of our discussion concerns the nature of philosophy. If this question arises from a need and is not to remain only a hypothetical question for the purpose of making conversation, then philosophy as philosophy must have become worthy of question. Obviously we can indicate this only if we have already taken a look into philosophy. In order to do this we must know beforehand what philosophy is. Thus, in a strange manner, we are being chased around in a circle. Philosophy itself seems to be this circle. Assuming that we might not be able to escape immediately out of the ring of this circle, we still are permitted to look at the circle. In which direction should our glance turn?
Martin Heidegger, Was ist das—die Philosophie?

I would have liked to have been able to do philosophy. I have always wanted to be able to do philosophy. But I do not know that I can say why I have always wanted to be able to do philosophy. I do not know if I can say what it would be like to be able to do philosophy. It is as if a long time ago I had received a messenger sent by the king. That the king had sent the messenger to me I understood to be of singular importance. It made me feel like I was one of the elect. However, it is as if I recall now that back then not only could I not understand anything that the messenger was telling me but the messenger himself was telling me that I could understand nothing of what he had to tell me; it was as if the message the messenger was to have given me was that I would be unable to understand a single thing he was to say, and that was the message. But it is as if I was even unable to understand that, that that was the message, so much so that I can no longer be certain that there was really a messenger at all.

I would have liked to have been able to do philosophy. I have always wanted to be able to do philosophy. I have always found what little of it I could fathom to be interesting. I have always found philosophy interesting precisely because it makes the claim that it is more than merely interesting. Yet I cannot say what this higher claim is. If I were to try to say what it is, I would be able to do so only in the interest of evaluating it. But then, I suspect, I would have missed the point. To find something interesting precludes being in earnest about it; yet the interesting is the turning point or threshold by which earnestness comes around to stake its claim. The interesting delimits itself by coming to itself from out of its limit of earnestness. Thus it is ministerial to earnestness yet retracts and retreats from venturing into earnestness. My interest in philosophy consists in my inability to take it as anything more than the interesting, knowing full well that what makes it interesting is precisely its commanding me to earnestness, a commanding I can regard only with a soft sadness, the way a lost love comes to retire quietly from remembrance.

It seems to me that philosophy engages us in the incommensurability between recognizing the need to give a comprehensive account of the whole and realizing the impossibility of fulfilling this need. Philosophy is this struggle of itself with itself, for itself, the struggle to accept one's humanity in this struggle between such false hope and such excessive despair. Nothing is more easily ignored than this struggle, unless such false hope and excessive despair are the effects of such ignorance. Philosophy consists in accepting the challenge of this struggle, to accept one's humanity. This struggle plays itself out as a sportive, festive, perhaps even contentious game, where the stakes are the winning of "the earnestness of existence," the winning of actuality, by means of finding this game the most bewitching game there is. Nevertheless it is still a game, a contest waged for the sake of eliciting what is most interesting. In this sense philosophy is the "noblest possible game" (*Laws* 803c8); yet since it is merely a game, it is a laughable matter. Precisely because philosophy holds forth the promise of winning "the earnestness of existence," yet, in being the most interesting, waylays us within the interesting, it holds back on its promise. I want to say that if philosophy bewitches us into cleverness and chicanery and contentiousness and contestations, then it promotes a certain kind of waywardness, a kind of fatuity; it is a comedy of erring, as if we were spoiling for the grief we endure in not doing it right—and finding relief in this grief.

It seems to me that this dialectic between being merely interesting and being earnestness itself has always troubled the philosopher; the philosopher has always occupied an unnatural place in the world, and for this reason the philosopher is always reflecting on the significance of the philosophic activity, bewitched and befuddled by its claim to seriousness while indulging in its sportive and contentious facetiousness. In the Platonic dialogues this is made evident, so much so that it might even seem that Plato wrote, not philosophy proper, but puns, puns that, for our not being able to hear them, make fun of us. Consider: the young Socrates in the *Parmenides* (which is not a dialogue proper but a story narrated by Cephalus, who tells how it was repeated to him by Antiphon, who had heard it from Pythodorus, who was present as a listener when Parmenides conversed with Socrates, when he was young and

Plato, who in fact made up this story, was not yet born), worrying about the consequences of the doctrine of forms, that it must be the same for all things, runs away from this stance, "fearing that I shall fall into a sea of babble [εἴς τινα βυθὸν φλυαρίας] and be destroyed" (*Parmenides* 130d3–9).

Moreover, it is striking that in the Platonic corpus, Socrates is accused of "babbling" by three men who, each in a different way, take life seriously: Thrasymachus, Callicles, and Alcibiades. In the *Republic* Thrasymachus, a teacher of political rhetoric, begins his attack on Socrates by accusing him of babbling (τίς, ἔφη, ὑμᾶς πάλαι φλυαρία ἔχει . . . *Republic* 1.336b8–c1). Callicles, who is preparing to run for political office, also prefaces his accusation of Socrates with the abusive charge: "Look how this man does not stop babbling" (οὑτοσὶ ἀνὴρ οὐ παύσεται φλυαρῶν; *Gorgias* 498b7). The context here is that of the definition of terms. Callicles asks whether Socrates is not ashamed at his age to be "chasing after" words (i.e., playing with them: ὀνόματα θηρεύων; 489b7). This accusation is a direct consequence of Callicles' denunciation of philosophy as something that is appropriate for children but, when practiced by adults, is destructive (484c4ff.). "It is noble to participate in philosophy for the sake of education and not shameful to philosophize if one is a youth" (485a4–5). At Socrates' age, it is laughable, "and I am affected by those who philosophize exactly as I am by those who speak indistinctly and play like children" (485a6–b2). Mature philosophers are babblers and lispers, "laughable, unmanly, and deserving to be smacked" (485c1–2). And of course, in the *Symposium*, Alcibiades exposes Socrates' ostensibly erotic interest in beautiful youths as ironical, as nonerotic. And lest we forget, Plato, who, after all, is the author of these dialogues, understands the *seriousness* of these charges; if we are entitled to assume that philosophy is the noblest possible game, it is nonetheless a game that the serious-minded do not take seriously—it is the game of pretending to take seriously what is not entirely worthy of seriousness, and in this way showing, precisely, what is serious about life, about having been born. This is the philosopher's artifice—the philosopher's cunning, the philosopher's conning.

Also, in the *Philebus* Protarchus notes, in commenting on the need in philosophy of responding to everyday human affairs, that "the knowledge which is only superhuman . . . is ridiculous [γελοίαν] in man"; yet truth is divine; its pursuit carries us away from τὰ τῶν ἀνθρώπων πράγματα, our "human concerns," even though Socrates, in "chasing after" words, is merely struggling against their tendency away from the real τὰ τῶν ἀνθρώπων πράγματα. Finally, it is appropriate here to recall the discursus in the *Theaetetus* where Socrates compares the philosopher with the lawyer (172c2–176a1): Jestingly, Socrates says that just as the Thracian maid jeered at Thales for falling into a well, "the same jest [σκῶμμα] applies to all who pass their lives in philosophy" (*Theaetetus* 174a5–b1). Such a person is a "laughing-stock" (γέλωτα), "his awkwardness is terrible, making him seem a fool" (καὶ ἡ ἀσχημοσύνη δεινή, δόξαν ἀβελτερίας παρεχομένη— ἀσχημοσύνη = 'deformity, indecency'; ἀβελτερίας is the privative of the comparative of ἀγαθός, good, hence it means the opposite of better, thus meaning 'good-for-nothing, silly, fatuous'); he appears "ridiculous" (γελοῖος), and in general, "is derided by the common herd, partly because he seems to be contemptuous, partly because he is ignorant of common things and is always in perplexity" (174c4–6, 175b5–7). If the philosopher is laughable, then, as Socrates is demonstrating in this discursus, the philosopher himself initiates the laughter against himself, he delights in his not knowing his way about, in being an ἰδιώτης, an anexpert, an *idiot savant*.

So, again, I would have liked to have been able to do philosophy. I have always wanted to be able to do philosophy. But, again, if I try to say why I have always wanted to do philosophy, I am rendered speechless, or at the very least incoherent. It is as if I am constantly trying to recuperate an insight that I think I had a long time ago, but so long ago that I can no longer even be certain that I even had the insight. Yet I cannot stop thinking that a long time ago I had an insight, an insight that would redeem all, if only I could remember what it was. It is as if I am constantly on the verge of remembering this insight that would have saved all had I only kept it in mind. Now, however, not only can I not remember the insight, I can no longer even remember if in fact I did have such an insight.

I would have liked to have been able to do philosophy. I have always wanted to be able to do philosophy. Yet I cannot even say why it is that I have always wanted to be able to do philosophy, for this would require that I do philosophy; but in having always wanted to be able to do philosophy I have always wanted to know what it means to do philosophy. However, I cannot know what it means to do philosophy without having already been doing it. So it would seem that not only have I always wanted to be able to do philosophy, but I have also always wanted to have already been doing it. But to want to have had already been doing philosophy is not the same as to be already doing it. In fact, it seems to me that the desire to have already been doing philosophy carries within itself knowledge of the impossibility of ever having already been doing philosophy, and so the impossibility of ever beginning to do philosophy. Rather than eliminating itself by obtaining its object, my desire to have already been doing philosophy eliminates the possibility of ever beginning to do philosophy; it is itself the knowledge that I can never attain to having already been doing philosophy. In desiring to be able to do philosophy I would seem to eliminate the possibility of ever being able to do philosophy.

I would have liked to have been able to do philosophy. I have always wanted to have been able to do philosophy. I want that I will eventually be able to do philosophy. But again, it seems to me that to desire to be able to start doing philosophy forestalls ever having actually begun to do philosophy, as surely as desiring to be able to do philosophy forecloses on ever having already been doing philosophy.

But of course, I cannot understand any of this. For the desire to have already been doing philosophy is itself not only not doing philosophy but the acknowledgment of the impossibility of ever being able to start doing philosophy. But this last notion can only be understood by those who can do philosophy. But it is precisely these latter that, by doing philosophy, could never raise the issue of wanting to be able to start doing philosophy.

And of course, I cannot understand anything of what I have just now said, for to understand any of it I would need to be doing philosophy. This I would like to be able to do. But if I even understand this, that philosophy is what I would like to be able to start doing, I am doing philosophy. But if I am already doing philosophy, I cannot understand any of *this*; the issue of always wanting to have been able to do philosophy could not arise, for I would always already be doing philosophy. It would seem that I could have written *this* only because I am not able to do philosophy, but want to be able to start doing philosophy. But to understand *this* is to do philosophy. But to understand that I am already doing philosophy is to recognize that I cannot understand any of this talk about having always wanted to have been able to do philosophy. But to recognize that I cannot understand any of this talk is to be unable to do philosophy. But such recognition is itself the doing of philosophy. And the *but*s start multiplying exponentially, culminating neither in a terminal "*but*" nor an " . . . and so on," but rather in the interminable reiteration of this chain-reaction of *but*s.

Obviously, I am confused. Obviously, I get confused fairly easily. In being confused, in getting confused easily, I never know if I am saying anything or not. It feels like I am saying something of infinite meaning, but which, for that very reason, is the absolute vaporization of meaning, leaving only a simple and immediate vacuity.

But then, to be in a state of confusion is exciting; it seems to be itself the promise of liberatory insight. Thus it is that I wrote these exercises, not knowing if they say anything of philosophic interest or not. They seem to me to be philosophy in the same way wood is wood for a wood sculptor, a medium for transacting something that is other than just wood, the material register for an ideality that exists just to the extent that this material register is self-removing, that it is a self-secluding hollow subjected to the intention to open up to view precisely this self-secluding.

Thus it is that I wrote these exercises as an attempt to say if it is even possible to do philosophy. They strike me as being the product of a maddening foolhardy form of folly, a testimony to a proudful and secret arrogance, a conceit, the vain jesterings and gesturings, pranksterings and posturings of a penniless fop denied admittance to the royal ball. It is as if I live my life trying to make of it a refutation of life, as if only a life that refutes life could justify life. It is as if I live my life trying to verify the unspeakable suspicion that life is, on its own terms, not quite worth the effort, a suspicion unspeakable because everything can confirm and verify it, yet nonetheless nothing can confirm or verify it. It seems to me that one would do philosophy in an attempt to validate life. But, then, to even suspect that life ought to be validated implies a suspicion that life would be meaningless, or at least wanting, without some such validation. The attempt to validate life, consequently, must turn back upon itself, searching for what could count as a refutation of life, some sort of proof that life cannot really be worth the effort. Of course, to demand such a proof is sheer degeneracy, yet surely only a life that has faced its own refutation could justify life, for only such a life can no longer indulge in the luxury of pretending to be a mere pretending.

But, then, such a validation of life is a principle transcendent to life, for it is founded on the moment of the refutation of life, which is not only a moment in life that presumes it is founded on what is other than life but is also a moment that presumes an ascendancy over life. If, as Nietzsche says, the "value of life cannot be estimated," nevertheless the value of life cannot *but* be estimated. It seems we live only insofar as our life is itself the estimation of the value of life. But if life cannot be lived without itself being the estimation of the value of life, whence comes this most uncanny of guests, the suspicion that life might just be in deficit to itself, itself its own shadow, pure στέρησις, depriving itself of what it promises precisely by promising it?

I don't think we are astonished enough by the fact that we

can even raise the question of the value of life. How is it even possible that existence can turn against itself, can turn into a dissatisfaction with itself, that it can become the interruption of what should have been the incessant satisfaction with itself? How is it possible that there could even arise the suspicion that life is lacking, that it is a pathology of itself, that it is a deprivation of precisely that which would render life inherently and indisputably valuable, infinitely valuable? It would seem that life frustrates itself, contrary to its intentions. When Socrates insists, in the *Phaedo*, that his young companions think about the opposite of life, why are we not scandalized, how do we so easily, so lightheartedly, so cavalierly consider for ourselves the opposite of life, *as if there were even anything at all other than life*?

If life can become the question of its own value, then it would seem that life has the form of something like a catastrophe, that is, that it develops into the radical discontinuity and incommensurability of the interiority of life with its world. Existence would seem to be affected—from without, from a beyond that is always arriving but that never arrives—by an overthrowing which abruptly alters it in its interiority, in its relating to itself, which disturbs and disrupts this relating-to-itself and obliges it to violate its own self-relation. The moment that the question of the value of life arises, life becomes an essential singularity, as the mathematicians understand this term: life becomes, not an object for itself, but the *ab-ject*, the turning away from itself, breaking with itself, the rupture and rending of itself, life as the laceration of life. This is to say, does not existence presuppose its own fracturing when negotiating its value? Does not the insistence on estimating the value of life make of life the intrigue of its own subversion, a subversion always threatening its *coup* yet for this reason incorporated into existence as its own agency, its proper protocol? In becoming questionable, is this not the shattering and unsettling of life, its inscription into a wound that can never heal, a fracturing flash of brokenness escaping from a hollow of vertigo? Why, to put the question as bluntly as possible, do we punish ourselves for suffering our finitude, our humanity? Why do we punish ourselves for our inability to accept life as life its own self? This is the scandal in which philosophy finds itself embroiled.

But here let us retreat. The desire motivating the question of the value of life is the desire to achieve total satisfaction. But by the very act of opening up to question the value of life this desire betrays the impossibility of its own satisfaction and in so doing puts into effect the impossibility of achieving satisfaction in general, and thus puts into effect the anticipation of impossibility, the desiring of the impossible, the desire become need for a limitless loss from and upon which there is no return, an "expenditure without reserve" (Bataille), pure uselessness, a savage unchecked squandering for no reason and to no purpose. In the absolute *surprise* of this moment, philosophic desire proper commences. At this moment the value *of* life becomes the value life has *for* life. This is a simple tautology, empty and immediate: I live that I may live. Here all reason falls away, being beside the point. Here all purpose disappears, for the purpose of such a life consists simply in living it in a purposeless way. This life fulfills the purpose of life precisely because it no longer needs to have a purpose except to live. Here the *purposelessness* of the philosophic activity becomes painfully obvious. Here life is come upon as what it is: pure gratuity to which there can be only immediate and trusting accession and of which there can be only grateful acceptance. Life is lagniappe for not not being. And here the rendering of the rending becomes the meandering of its mending.

If I were able to do philosophy, no doubt I would write exclusively about the unnatural relation to everyday life that philosophy initiates, enables, and empowers. For, were I able to do philosophy, I fear that it would seem to me that the philosophic insight into how to live the well-lived life would be itself the cause and proof of the impossibility of living the well-lived life—rather than the evidence that I would in fact be living the well-lived life. Now, in my inability to carry out this philosophic insight into living the well-lived life, it seems to me that philosophy makes of *life* the cause and proof of its own impossibility. Yet, there it is, I have always wanted to be able to do philosophy. This makes me wonder whether philosophy is a curative, a restorative, the ultimate therapy that makes of life the living of what is blessed, or whether philosophy is not rather simply a disease that presumes to be its own cure. Life does seem, for those I know who take the philosophic path through life, to be riddled with black hole nodes of monstrous irreality. Yet it is precisely for this reason that these people are able to win philosophic insight into life. Such people are here to win life back from its exile and truancy in philosophy, in its smokescreens and mirrors of *arcanae*, back into us. In such winning the god comes to dwell again. Ἐνθουσιασμός.

Postscript

You mean to see we have been hadding a sound night's sleep? You may so. It is just, it is just about to, it is just about to rolywholyover. Svapnasvap. Of all the stranger things that ever not even in the hundrund and badst pagcans of unthowsent and wonst nice or in eddas and oddes bokes of tomb, dyke and hollow to be have happened! The untireties of livesliving being the one substance of a streamsbecoming. Totalled in toldteld and teldtold in tittletell tattle. Why? Because, graced be Gad and all giddy gadgets, in whose words were the beginnings, there are two signs to turn to, the yest and the ist, the wright side and the wronged side, feeling aslip and wauking up, so an, so farth. Why? On the sourdsite we have the Moskiosk Djinpalast with its twin adjacencies, the bathouse and the bazaar, allahallahallah, and on the sponthesite it is the alcovan and the rosegarden, boony noughty, all purapuvthry. Why? One's apurr apuss a story about brid and breakfedes and parricombating and coushcouch but others is of tholes and oubworn buyings, dolings and chafferings in heat, contest and enmity. Why? Every talk has his stay, vidnis Shavarsanjivana, and all-a-dreams perhapsing under lucksloop at last are through. Why? It is a sot of a swigswag, systomy dystomy, which everabody you ever anywhere at all doze. Why? Such me.

And howpsadrowsay.

Lok! A shaft of shivery in the act, anilancinant. Cold's sleuth! Vayuns! Where did thots come from? It is infinitesimally fevers, resty fever, risy fever, a coranto of aria, sleeper awakening, in the smalls of one's back presentiment, gip, and again, geip, a flash from a future of maybe mahamayability through the windr of a wondr in a wildr is a weltr as a wirbl of a warbl is a world. (*Finnegans Wake*, 597)

Now, then, where were we?

Bibliography

Agacinski, Sylviane. *Aparté: conceptions et morts de Søren Kierkegaard*. Paris: Flammarion, 1977.

Aristotle. *De Anima*. Translated by W. S. Hett. Cambridge: Harvard University Press, Loeb Classical Library, 1975.

———. *The "Art" of Rhetoric*. Translated by John Henry Freese. Cambridge: Harvard University Press, Loeb Classical Library, 1975.

———. *The Categories*. Translated by Harold P. Cooke. Cambridge: Harvard University Press, Loeb Classical Library, 1967.

———. *Eudemian Ethics*. In *The Athenian Constitution. The Eudemian Ethics. On Virtues and Vices*. Translated by Harris Rackham. Cambridge: Harvard University Press, Loeb Classical Library, 1952.

———. *On Interpretation*. Translated by Harold P. Cooke. Cambridge: Harvard University Press, Loeb Classical Library, 1967.

———. *Magna Moralia*. Translated by G. Cyril Armstrong. Cambridge: Harvard University Press, Loeb Classical Library, 1969.

———. *The Metaphysics*. Translated by Hugh Tredennick. Cambridge: Harvard University Press, Loeb Classical Library, 1969.

———. *The Nicomachean Ethics*. Translated by Harris Rackham. Cambridge: Harvard University Press, Loeb Classical Library, 1975.

———. *De Partibus Animalium*. Translated by A. L. Peck. Cambridge: Harvard University Press, Loeb Classical Library, 1937.

———. *The Physics*. Translated by Philip H. Wicksteed. Cambridge: Harvard University Press, Loeb Classical Library, 1970.

———. *The Poetics*. Translated by W. Hamilton Fyfe. Cambridge: Harvard University Press, Loeb Classical Library, 1973.

———. *Posterior Analytics*. Translated by Hugh Tredennick. Cambridge: Harvard University Press, Loeb Classical Library, 1976.

———. *On Sophistical Refutations*. Translated by E. S. Forster. Cambridge: Harvard University Press, Loeb Classical Library, 1965.

———. *Topica*. Translated by Hugh Tredennick. Cambridge: Harvard University Press, Loeb Classical Library, 1976.

Aubenque, Pierre. *Le Problème de l'être chez Aristote: essai sur la problématique aristotélicienne*. Paris: Presses Universitaires de France, 1966.

Blanchot, Maurice. *L'Espace litteraire*. Translated by Ann Smock, under the title *The Space of Literature*. Lincoln: University of Nebraska Press, 1982.

Brentano, Franz. *Von der Mannigfachen Bedeutung des Seienden nach Aristoteles*. Darmastadt: Wissenschaftliche Buchgesellschaft, 1960. Translated by Rolf George, under the title *On the Several Senses of Being in Aristotle*. Berkeley: University of California Press, 1975.

Chuang Tzu. *The Complete Works of Chuang Tzu*. Translated by Burton Watson. New York: Columbia University Press, 1968.

de Man, Paul. *Allegories of Reading*. New Haven: Yale University Press, 1979.

———. *Blindness and Insight*. 2d ed. rev. Minneapolis: University of Minnesota Press, 1983.

———. "The Rhetoric of Temporality." In *Blindness and Insight*, 2d ed. rev. Minneapolis: University of Minnesota Press, 1983.

Derrida, Jacques. *La Carte postale*. Translated by Alan Bass under the title *Post Card; From Socrates to Freud and Beyond*. Chicago: University of Chicago Press, 1987.

———. *La Dissémination*. Paris: Editions du Seuil, 1972.

———. *Memoires for Paul de Man*. Translated by Cecile Lindsay, Jonathan Culler, and Eduardo Cadava. New York: Columbia University Press, 1986.

———. *Of Grammatology*. Translated by Gayatri Chakravorty Spivak. Baltimore: Johns Hopkins University Press, 1976.

———. "Tympan." In *Margins of Philosophy*, translated by Alan Bass. Chicago: University of Chicago Press, 1982.

———. "White Mythology: Metaphor in the Text of Philosophy." *New Literary History*, vol. 6, no. 1 (Autumn 1974). Also in *Margins of Philosophy*, translated by Alan Bass. Chicago: University of Chicago Press, 1982.

Eliot, T. S. *Collected Poems, 1909–1962*. London: Faber & Faber, 1963.

Gadamer, Hans-Georg. "Philosophie und Poesie." In *The Relevance of the Beautiful and Other Essays*, translated by Nicholas Walker. Cambridge: Cambridge University Press, 1986.

Hartman, Geoffrey. *Saving the Text: Literature / Derrida / Philosophy*. Baltimore: Johns Hopkins University Press, 1982.

Hegel, G. W. F. *The Difference between the Fichtean and Schellingian Systems of Philosophy*. Translated by Jere Paul Surber. Atascadero, Calif.: Ridgeview Publishing Co., 1978.

———. *Hegel's Science of Logic*. Translated by A. V. Miller. London: George Allen & Unwin, Ltd., 1969.

Heidegger, Martin. "The Anaximander Fragment." In *Early Greek Thinking*, translated by David Farrell Krell and Frank A. Capuzzi. New York: Harper and Row, 1975.

———. *The Basic Problems of Phenomenology*. Translated by Albert Hofstadter. Bloomington: Indiana University Press, 1985.

———. *Basic Writings*. Edited by David Farrell Krell. New York: Harper and Row, 1977.

———. *Being and Time*. Translated by John Macquarrie and Edward Robinson. New York: Harper and Row, 1962.

———. "A Dialogue on Language." In *On the Way to Language*, translated by Peter D. Hertz. New York: Harper and Row, 1971.

———. "The End of Philosophy and the Task of Thinking." In *On Time and Being*, translated by Joan Stambaugh. New York: Harper and Row, 1972.

———. *The Essence of Reasons / Vom Wesen des Grundes*. Bilingual edition. Translated by Terrence Malick. Evanston, Ill.: Northwestern University Press, 1969.

———. "On the Essence of Truth." In *Basic Writings*, edited by David Farrell Krell. New York: Harper and Row, 1977. Also in *Existence and Being*, edited by Werner Brock. Chicago: Henry Regnery, 1949.

———. *Existence and Being*. Edited by Werner Brock. Chicago: Henry Regnery, 1949.

———. *Identity and Difference*. Translated by Joan Stambaugh. New York: Harper and Row, 1969.

———. *Kant and the Problem of Metaphysics*. Translated by James S. Churchill. Bloomington: Indiana University Press, 1962.

———. "Letter on Humanism." Translated by Frank Capuzzi and J. Glenn Gray. In *Basic Writings*, edited by David Farrell Krell. New York: Harper and Row, 1977.

———. *The Metaphysical Foundations of Logic*. Translated by Michael Heim. Bloomington: Indiana University Press, 1984.

———. *On Time and Being*. Translated by Joan Stambaugh. New York: Harper and Row, 1972.

———. "The Onto-theo-logical Constitution of Metaphysics." In *Identity and Difference*, translated by Joan Stambaugh. New York: Harper and Row, 1969.

———. "The Origin of the Work of Art." In *Basic Writings*, edited by David Farrell Krell. New York: Harper and Row, 1977.

———. *The Question of Being*. Translated by William Kluback and Jean T. Wilde. New Haven: College and University Press, 1958.

———. "The Question concerning Technology." Translated by William Lovitt. In *Basic Writings*, edited by David Farrell Krell. New York: Harper and Row, 1977.

———. *Der Satz vom Grund*. Tübingen: Neske, 1971.

———. *Sein und Zeit*. Tübingen: Max Niemeyer Verlag, 1977.

———. "Time and Being." In *On Time and Being*, translated by Joan Stambaugh. New York: Harper and Row, 1972.

———. *Was ist das—die Philosophie? / What Is Philosophy?* Bilingual edition. Translated by William Kluback and Jean T. Wilde. New Haven: College and University Press, n.d.

———. "What Is Metaphysics?" In *Basic Writings*, edited by David Farrell Krell. New York: Harper and Row, 1977. Also in *Existence and Being*, edited by Werner Brock. Chicago: Henry Regnery, 1949.

———. *Wegmarken*. Frankfurt am Main: Vittorio Klostermann Verlag, 1967.

Jaeger, Werner. *Aristoteles: Grundlegung einer Geschichte seiner Entwicklung*. Berlin: Wiedmann, 1923.

James, William. *The Varieties of Religious Experience*. New York: Modern Library, 1936.

Joyce, James. *Finnegans Wake*. New York: Viking Press, 1976.

Kant, Immanuel. *Critique of Pure Reason*. Translated by Norman Kemp Smith. New York: St. Martin's Press, 1965.

———. *Werke*. Edited by Ernst Cassirer. Vols. 8, 9. New York: De Gruyter, 1977.

Kierkegaard, Søren. *Either/Or*. Vol. 1. Translated by David F. Swenson and Lillian Marvin Swenson. Princeton: Princeton University Press, 1971.

———. *Of the Difference between a Genius and an Apostle*. In *The Present Age*, translated by Alexander Dru. New York: Harper Torchbooks, 1962.

Levinas, Emmanuel. *Otherwise than Being, or Beyond Essence*. Translated by Alphonso Lingis. The Hague: Martinus Nijhoff, 1981.

Marcel, Gabriel. *Mystère de l'être*. Translated by G. S. Fraser in two volumes under the title *The Mystery of Being*. New York: University Press of America, 1978.

Merleau-Ponty, Maurice. *In Praise of Philosophy*. Translated by John

Wild and James M. Edie. Evanston, Ill.: Northwestern University Press, 1963.

Natorp, Paul. "Thema und Disposition der aristotelischen Metaphysik." *Philosophische Monatshefte* 24 (1887): 37–65, 540–74.

Owens, Joseph. *The Doctrine of Being in the Aristotelian "Metaphysics."* Toronto: Pontifical Institute of Mediaeval Studies, 1951.

Patzig, Günther. "Theologie und Ontologie in der 'Metaphysik' des Aristoteles." *Kant-Studien* 52 (1961): 185–205.

Ricoeur, Paul. *The Rule of Metaphor*. Translated by Robert Czerny. Toronto: University of Toronto Press, 1979.

Rilke, Rainer Maria. *Duino Elegies, VIII*. Translated by Stephen Spender and J. B. Leishman. New York: W. W. Norton & Co., 1967.

Ross, W. D. *Aristotle's Metaphysics I*. Oxford: Clarendon Press, 1912.

Stevens, Wallace. *The Collected Poems of Wallace Stevens*. New York: Alfred A. Knopf, 1977.

———. "The Snow Man." In *The Collected Poems of Wallace Stevens*. New York: Alfred A. Knopf, 1977.

Wittgenstein, Ludwig. *Philosophical Investigations*. Translated by G.E.M. Anscombe. New York: Macmillan, 1968.

Index Locorum

ARISTOTLE

Categories

5	2a11	85
12	14b7	17

De Interpretatione

3	16b20–26	61
5	17a14	14
13	22b22–25	21
	23a18–20	21

Posterior Analytics

1.2	71b26–29	18
1.24	86a4–10	27
2.1	89b24–25	54
2.2	90a32–34	55
2.7	92b4–14	52
	92b12–14	51–54
	92b15	55
	92b38–39	55
2.8	93a17–21	55
2.19	100b13	19

Sophistical Refutations

1	165a9	41
1	165a10ff.	41
1	165a12	43, 114

Physics

1.8	191b29	14
2.2	194b14–15	15

De Anima

3.5	430a20–21	21
3.5	430a21ff.	20
3.8	432a1–2	49
	432a2	50

De Partibus Animalium

1.5	645b26	71n
4.10	687b2–5	50

Metaphysics

1.2	982a7	83
	982b8	84
	982b12–13	31
	983a5–11	15
	983a13	31
1.3	984b9	32
1.5	986b31	32
1.9	991a19–21	73
	992b19–26	79–80
2.1	993b23–26	48
3.1	995a26	32
	995a28	32
	995a31	36
	995a34	32
3.2	997a34–998a19	58
3.3	998b10	59
	998b14–999a23	58, 59
	998b19	59
	998b21	83
	998b23ff.	78n
3.4	999a24–25	58
	999a26–28	58

Metaphysics (continued)

	999b32	59
	1001a6	59
3.5	1001b29	59
	1002b24	59
	1002a28	59
4.1	1003a21	13, 82, 83
	1003a23	83
	1003a24	13
	1003a31	13
	1003a33	44
4.2	1003a33–b3	74
	1003a33–b6	48, 71
	1003b5–10	75n
	1003b12–15	49
	1003b14	75, 84–85
	1003b16–18	75
	1003b16	49
4.3	1005a21–b1	84
	1005a27	83
	1005b11–20	39
	1005b15	84
	1005b32–34	39
4.4	1006a34–b13	41
	1006b7	45
	1007a27	44
5.5	1015a32–33	67
5.6	1016b31–1017a3	70–71
5.7	1017a24	43, 114
5.11	1018b19 ff.	17
	1019a1 ff.	17
	1019a12	17
6.1	1026a10–12	13
	1026a10–13	16
	1026a17–18	13
	1026a21	13
	1026a23–32	16, 22
	1026a30	23
6.4	1028a5	43, 114
7.1	1028a10	43, 114
	1028b2	73

Metaphysics (continued)

	1028b3–4	18
7.3	1029b7	18, 33
7.4	1030a32–b4	74
7.15	1039b27–29	65
	1039b34	66
	1040a2–3	65
10.2	1053b16	84
	1053b20	84
11.1	1059b33 ff.	78n
11.5	1061b34–36	39
	1062a14 ff.	42
12.5	1071a37	67
12.6	1071b3–9	67
	1071b20–28	67
12.7	1072a25–26	67
	1072b12 ff.	20
12.9	1074b25 ff.	22
14.6	1093b19	71n

Nicomachean Ethics

1.2	1094a22 ff.	134n
1.6	1096a28	50
	1096a30	14, 51
	1096b26–30	72
1.7	1098b7	31
2.3	1104b33	134n
3.10	1118b1	134n
4.5	1126a1	134n
5.8	1135b8 ff.	132n
7.2	1146b7	32
10.8	1177b26 ff.	20

Eudemian Ethics

1.8	12.17b33–34	50
	1218a1	51

Rhetoric

3.2	1404b37–1405a1	42, 70

GENERAL INDEX

Alexander of Aphrodisias, 25, 50
Andronikos of Rhodes, 12
ἅπαν, 53–54, 62–63
Aporia: as related to being qua being, 32–39, 97; intelligibility of, 33; paradox of, 38; understanding of, 37; subjectivity of, 34–36
Attunement: primary significance, 171

Being: amphiboly exposed, 122; amphibolic sense of, 121; as mediated being, 136; as temporalizing, 112; attempted resolution of the amphiboly of, 129–30; beginning and ending of, 102; beingness of, 108; circularity of, 154; concealment of, 167–68; disclosure of, 110; forestructures of, 156–57; ground of, 140–41; intelligibility of, 118, 131–35, 149–50, 184; irreducibility of, 62–64; meaning of, 131–32, 137, 183–84, 186; naming of, 131; negativity of, 115–17; not a genus, 24–25; not a substance, 84; ontic ground of, 109; ontical foundation of, 123; ontological ground of, 109; paronymy of, 85; possibility of discourse on, 82–85; qua being, 25–28; relation to knowledge, 19; said paronymously, 71–72; science of being qua being, 26–28, 47; transcendental dimension of, 63, 64
Being and Time: as circular exposition, 154

Concealment: of being, 172
Contradiction: law of, 38–39
Critique of Pure Reason, 43, 60, 148

Dasein: ground of, 141–42, 149; meaning of, 141–42; understanding of itself, 160
Death, 143–47
Demonstration: as showing itself, 62
Derrida, Jacques, 40, 68, 76, 77n, 78; end of metaphysics, 4–5
Descartes, René, 34
Diffractiveness: principle of, 93
Dying, 146–47

Ego: self-forgetting, 94–95; transcendental, 96
Eliot, T. S., 160–61
Errancy, 166, 172
Essence: knowledge of, 51; relation to being, 44, 52
Everydayness: inauthentic being, 126, 163
Existence: demonstration of, 53; groundlessness of, 148; knowledge of, 51; simpliciter, 56; versus essence, 53

Existential predication, 60–62

Focal meaning, 70n
Forgetfulness: science of, 76
Forgetting, 168–69, 177
Freud, Sigmund, 8

God: necessity of existence, 67
Good, the: idea of, 50, 51
Gorgias, 204

Heidegger, Martin: end of metaphysics, 4; end of philosophy, 105; on Aristotle's first philosophy, 11–12
Hermeneutic circle: ad hoc definition of, 182; formal analysis of, 191–92; possibility of transcendence, 189; self-instantiation of, 190; self-obliteration of, 194; temporal structure of, 195
Hermeneutic experience: ordinary structure, 135
Homonymy: principle of, 40
Husserl, Edmund: on reflection, 8

Intelligibility: limits of, 33

Jaeger, Werner, 39

Kant, Immanuel, 23, 29, 148; on Aristotle's categories, 78; on existential predication, 60–62
Kierkegaard, Søren: on reflection, 8; on the structure of philosophical questions, 189; on the vitality of metaphysics, 105; on the problems of metaphysics, 6
Knowledge: possibility of, 58–59

Language: Aristotle's theory of, 39–40, 42–44; presupposes ontology for Aristotle, 43–44, 47; purpose of, 68; relation to ontology, 9–10; truth of, 137–38
Laws, 203

Meaning: as disclosure, 138
Megarics, 44
Metaphysics: ambiguity of, 110–12; beginning, 31; end of, 3–5, 106–7; essential ambiguity of, 108; function of, 107–8; general versus particular, 47–49, 66; ground of, 108–9; legitimacy of, 28–29; limits of, 76–77; metaphysics of, 29–30; possibility of, 29; prescientific character of, 79–80
Middle voice: use of, 81

Names: types of, 68–69
Necessity: of being, 66–67
Nietzsche, Friedrich: the exhaustion of metaphysics, 105; problems of metaphysics, 6
Nous: νοῦς, 19–20, 21–22, 33, 49, 50

ὄν, 107–8
Odyssey, 133n
Ontic: versus ontological, 142–44
Ontology: as authentic understanding, 127; fundamental, 123; possibility of, 128–29, 130, 143; relation to language, 9–10; versus theology, 13–15, 23–24
Originarity: sense of, 88–89, 90–91, 94

Other: of language, 10, 136
οὐσία, 52–53

Parmenides, 22, 203–4
Parmenides, 62
Paronymy: definition of, 82; of the copula, 74; paradox of, 97–98; possibility of the science of, 77–79; presupposes itself, 97; principle of, 91–93, 95; science of, 75–78, 80–81, 86–87, 89–94, 96–98
Particularity: disclosedness of, 63–64; in general, 57–58
Particularizing: as giving itself, 65–66; impossibility of the science of, 64; of the particular, 59
Patzig, Günther, 76
Performative writing: amphibolic, 101–51; apophantic, 3–99; hermeneutic, 153–98
Phaedo, 209
Phenomenology of Spirit, 179
Philebus, 205
Philosophical reflection: on philosophical description, 8; on philosophical legitimacy, 8; possibility of, 8–9
Philosophy: as a game, 203; as description, 7; as inauthenticity, 126; as logic, 7–11; as objection to itself, 197; as poetry, 7–11; beginning, 19, 32; beginning of, 102–3; divisions and classifications of, 13; end of, 104, 150–51; first, 12–19, 22–23, 24, 28, 49; first, knowledge of 17–18; first, principles of, 17; first, priority of, 16–17; ground of, 140; on what it is, 7
Plato, 22, 52, 73, 111, 203–5
Principle of identity, 43
πρὸς ἕν, 80–82, 84–87
Pynchon, Thomas, 106

Republic, 204
Resolute anticipation: of death, 147
Ross, W. D., 52

Science: delimitations of, 83; possibility of, 19, 27, 58–59; proceeding of, 157
Signification, 39–40, 42–43, 45, 69; plurality of, 46
Something versus nothing, 57
Subjectivity, 93
Substance: relation to being, 24, 49, 52, 85
Symposium, 204

Theaetetus 2, 59, 205
Time: definition of, 177
τὸ ὄν, 110–12
Transcendence: ambiguity of, 108
Truth, 176–77

Understanding: as circular, 158–59; fallen character of, 160; formal principle of, 178, 180, 185; formal structure of, 175; of aporia, 37; preontological, 165
Universals: possibility of knowing, 26–27

Wisdom, 22
Wittgenstein, Ludwig: the end of metaphysics, 4

DATE DUE

HIGHSMITH # 45220